WHEN THE FLAG DROPS

WHEN THE FLAG DROPS

JACK BRABHAM

WITH **ELIZABETH HAYWARD**

Coward, McCann & Geoghegan, Inc.
New York

First American Edition 1972

Copyright © 1971 by Jack Brabham

SBN: 698-10502-8

Library of Congress Catalog Card Number: 72-87578

Printed in the United States of America

For Betty and the boys

FOREWORD

In writing this foreword, there are two things in which I find difficulty in believing: firstly Jack Brabham has finally retired from motor racing after being the father figure and inspiration to us all; and secondly that he has actually written a book.

Jack has always been known as the 'Quiet Australian', but it would appear that once again the wily old fox has foxed us, for in this book we learn more about Jack Brabham than we ever did in all his years of motor racing! I rate Jack Brabham as one of the great racing drivers of our time; others may have received more acclaim, but few more success. Three times World Champion, the last time in a car bearing his own name—the first, and probably the last, time this has ever occurred. He was one of the very few complete racing drivers the world has known. He has in his career beaten every one of the acknowledged stars of the day and was doing so right up to the time of his retirement.

When the Flag Drops has completed the picture of a very successful racing driver who has been a credit to motor racing and an ambassador for his country.

Graham Hill

Contents

Chapter		Page
1	One Door Closes	11
2	An Australian Youth	22
3	My First Attempts at Motor Racing	38
4	The Raw Recruit	58
5	The Race to the Top	70
6	Still Climbing	86
7	I Discover I Need Wings	98
8	Achievement	120
9	Improvement	142
10	Green Cars in Gasoline Alley	152
11	Brabham and Tauranac	166
12	New Life Begins at Forty	177
13	The Changing Face of Grand Prix Racing	186
14	The Dangerous Side of the Game	199
15	The Twenty-Third Year	209
16	Back to My Grass Roots	229

CHAPTER I

One Door Closes

I don't think it matters exactly *what* you do in this life—the important thing is that you should *enjoy* what you are doing. Motor racing, for me, was something that started purely as a hobby, an interest, a sport. When I started making a living out of it, it became all the things I enjoyed rolled into one. And it was very difficult for me to realise that one day I wouldn't be motor racing any more. My life was so deeply involved in it; it took up almost every minute of my time for twenty-three years, not only the driving itself, but being interested in the building of the cars and the modifications we made to improve them. That was all I used to think about, all I used to do, and all I really enjoyed doing.

Now I have retired from race driving, officially this time, having juggled with the idea for years, and sometimes I sit down and wonder why on earth I took such a step! I even tried to word the press release on my retirement so that it suggested I had given up Grand Prix racing only, which might then have left the opportunity open to do something else—Transam or Rallycross or Indianapolis-type racing.

It was so difficult to turn round suddenly after all those years and say: 'I have finished with motor racing completely.' But the advent of the banquet which Ford gave in my honour, and the Brands Hatch meeting that they named 'Homage to Jack Brabham', plus all the other presentations, speeches and so on that have taken place since the Mexican Grand Prix in October 1970, have made it virtually impossible for me to step into *any* sort of racing car again. I must admit it would take very little encouragement to get me back into one . . . ! But this is why I must try to stay away from it a bit and try to fill my life with other interests.

The day at Brands Hatch was the most difficult thing for me to go through with. There was too much attention being directed at me personally, and I am not used to that sort of thing. I would rather stand behind somebody than stand out in front of them. I have been like that all my life. It is not exactly shyness—I just don't like the limelight directed straight at me. I have never been in motor racing for that reason.

Right from the very first day I drove a racing car, what other people thought, or whether they were watching me, has never been of any importance to me. I was just interested in driving, and if there had been no people there at all it wouldn't have affected the way I drove in any way. It was just something I had to come to terms with, really, the fact that people had to come and watch. Maybe that is one of the reasons I haven't been too popular with the Press —I haven't got on badly with them, but I know I haven't bothered to go out of my way for them as I should have done. My 'Chatty Jack' reputation is a valid piece of criticism, and only now am I becoming fully appreciative of the Press, particularly those people concerned in specialised motor racing coverage. Considering my reluctance to talk to anyone, they have treated me very well, especially over the Brands Hatch farewell meeting on November 29th 1970.

That really was an ordeal. It was a very wet day, and I didn't think many people would come along and get soaked just to wave goodbye to me. I was genuinely overcome by the number of those who did, and how they really seemed to care about me and were going to miss me. I found the first part of the day quite easy; a television interview, a bit of lunch, a wander round the Paddock—it was all quite normal, and pleasant. Even getting into my own Formula 1 car, still wearing its British Grand Prix numbers, for the billed seven demonstration laps, didn't bother me too much. My mechanics were working as usual, and there were photographers all over the place, but I wasn't suffering at all at that time.

It was only during the last two laps that I began to realise

12

One Door Closes

. . . that was when it hit me. This was *really* the end. I couldn't concentrate. It was terrible. It really was.

I knew that after I'd finished those few laps I would have to stop and talk to people, and receive gifts and make a speech. I would have been much happier if I could have stepped out of the car and gone straight home. I don't want to give the wrong impression. I was very appreciative of the whole thing. I just found it very difficult to carry through. The weather improved and the sun came out while I was driving, so that when I went up onto the balcony and received a fanfare from trumpeters and saw the people waving and clapping in the grandstand, I thought 'I can't go through with this. I can't give up racing.' There was the traditional chorus of motor horns from the cars parked on South Bank, a lot of my best friends were gathered below looking up; my wife, Betty, my son, Geoffrey, the Brabham designer, Ron Tauranac were all up there with me, and people were making the most flattering speeches I've ever heard—all for *me*. I think my feelings show in the photographs taken that day.

Anyway, that part of the ordeal being over, my old boss John Cooper lightened the atmosphere by doing one of his traditional head-over-heels victory rolls on the track—all in the puddles, and something like ten years since he did the last one. It made John happy, if uncomfortable, and the crowd loved it.

Then I had to drop the starting flag for a race consisting entirely of Brabham cars. And I came as near as dammit to being flattened! They have a kind of trolley thing at Brands that they push out onto the track for the starter, and when I saw where they'd put it I said: 'There's no way you're going to get me to stand as far out as that—it's just plain dangerous.' So they reluctantly pulled it back a foot or two, and I raised the flag, brought it down smartly—no messing about—and the next thing I knew a Brabham BT28 and a BT15 were trying to climb up my legs! One of them had not been able to start, it was shunted by two other cars, and they were all coming straight for me. I tell you, it's safer driving than standing out there with a flag. I reckon if I

13

hadn't insisted on pulling that trolley back a bit I'd have been well and truly retired!

The rest of the day was a blur of rain and spray, and the faces of old friends appearing as if out of the past. I think the startline shunt, although it shook me up a bit, was good for me, because it made me throw off the depression I had felt during my own laps of the familiar circuit. And I knew that the next night we would be attending the Ford banquet given in my honour where I would see even more old friends — and adversaries — so we left Brands for the last time with something to look forward to.

I think that dinner at the Savoy on the Monday night, November 30th, was the climax of my retirement. I'd even say it was the climax of my whole career. Ford, stimulated as so often by the enthusiasm of Walter Hayes, Vice-President, Ford of Europe, invited people from all over the world, and hardly had one refusal. I think it was more successful than even Ford had hoped, and it was only unfortunate, they said, that the invitation list couldn't have been longer. I was very, very impressed with the whole thing, mostly because so many people had made the effort to come from abroad. Even those who didn't come sent telegrams, including Enzo Ferrari — that must be something pretty unusual; Ferrari himself sending a cable to a man who has never driven for him! There was a good one from Innes Ireland, too — how did it go now? 'Having had the gate shut on me so often by Jack Brabham, I am only sorry I can't be there to see the gate finally shut on *him*', and more in Innes's best witty style. Walter read these out after dinner and then went on to make a marvellous speech, as he always does, then handed over to Graham Hill, who had us all rocking with laughter within a few seconds. These things made it easier for me to get up and talk. And I talked as I have never talked before!

It wasn't the wine, and I hadn't planned a speech properly. I just made a few notes of people to mention, but when I stood up and saw all those people, some of whom I hadn't seen for years, I began to think of the old days and of all the things that had happened when I was with them. They tell me I didn't stop for nearly fifty minutes; and I could have gone on into the night. But I heard a bit of nattering at the back and I knew it was time to stop. Ford's filmed the whole thing and recorded some of my speech, but the only part I remember clearly is what I said after I'd waited for the initial applause to stop: 'The first thing I have to say after all that is that I have changed my mind—I don't want to retire.' That made people clap all the more, and honestly, if I could have left it at that I'd have been delighted. But I knew I had to go through with the whole farewell bit, so I went on. 'The opportunity of having everybody here tonight is something I am going to remember for the rest of my life. I'd like to thank Fords, and particularly Walter, who came up with the idea. I'm sure he didn't know what he was in for when he began it. Looking around me I think the best thing I can do is stage a comeback for South Africa.' This remark had everyone clapping and cheering again, so I had to climb down in a hurry because my wife was beginning to look daggers at me.

'This evening has been a wonderful opportunity for me to bring together some of my friends who have helped me in the past. As you know, with the party here tonight and with Brands yesterday, I can't really say that I am going to change my mind. I have to go on with it. Betty is here to make sure I do, anyway. Twenty-three years of motor racing and we're still married; that must be a record on its own—and she's talking to me now, as well!

'My father is here too, thanks to Ford. That really is something. In the early days Pop was my greatest fan. My mother wasn't quite on my side, but at least Pop was. He wasn't mixed up in racing at all himself, but when I got in he was right behind me, and I'm grateful for that. He helped me pay for my very first proper racing car, which was a Cooper Bristol. I can always remember this car being parked behind a window, and I guarantee my nose imprint is still on the glass. I looked, and drooled over this car for six months before we had enough money to buy it. And, of course, Pop is to blame for teaching me to drive in the first place!

'I am really pleased that so many drivers have come here tonight; in spite of all the things Graham has said, one of the best things in motor racing is the companionship between the drivers. The spirit is terrific, it is a really clean sport and everyone is on friendly terms. I think that is what I have enjoyed so much about motor racing—we can ràce together as competitors and yet be the best of friends.'

This is true, but I had never actually put it into words before. Perhaps it is because we are facing the same dangers or because we just have to trust each other on the track; maybe it is because we have the same burning interest, or the same love of the sport. Whatever it is, we are very conscious of our reliance on each other, even when we are having a proper dice out on the track. I could never hope to find such true friends, such give and take in other sports, I'm sure. And when one of our number is killed, it is almost like an amputation for the rest of us. We never forget those we have lost, and we are *not at all* unaffected, as people sometimes think, when they see us go straight back onto the track after an accident or a fatality. It is, perhaps, our way of getting back at the forces which took the life of a friend.

But I was talking about the Ford dinner. I know I went on to mention a few of the people who had helped me over the years, like Dean Delamont, John Cooper, Phil Irving of Repco, Ron Tauranac, Alan Brown, Rob Walker, Roy Salvadori, Reg Tanner and Geoff Murdoch of Esso, Leonard Lee of Coventry Climax, 'Jabby' Crombac, the French/Swiss journalist without whom most of us would have been in difficulties abroad more than once, Leo Mehl of Goodyear . . . the list could be almost endless. I remember ending by saying that I just wished Bruce McLaren, Piers Courage and Jochen Rindt could have been with us too—that would have made my own happiness, and the evening in general, complete.

Then we all left the dining-room and went upstairs to a room where we could mix and talk. It was a wonderful night, and I'll always be grateful to Ford for it.

Before I go on I must make it clear that I didn't give up motor racing because I don't like it any more, nor because I felt that my driving was going off, nor because I lost interest in it. I didn't retire for any of these reasons, and the spate of accidents during 1970 had nothing whatever to do with it either. If I had had no family and other responsibilities I would just have continued racing until I was tired of it. This was the most difficult thing I'd had to do in all my life, announcing my formal retirement and my move back to Australia. And even then, if I had been able to talk to Betty on the Friday evening while we were in Mexico, I think I would have tried to persuade her that I wanted to go on for another year.

But I had already done that once—well, more than once, really. The first time I thought seriously about giving up was in 1965. Dan Gurney was driving for us, I missed a couple of races and Denny Hulme drove a couple instead of me. I resigned myself to the fact that I was going to give up racing at the end of that year.

I don't quite know why. I suppose it was the first time that I realised that trying to do all the things I wanted to do *and* motor race was very difficult. I wasn't being fair either to my motor racing, or my business associations or to my family. They were all suffering.

My big problem at that time was the difficulty of obtaining and maintaining the Coventry Climax engines we were using. There were too many cars using the same unit, rather the same situation as now applies to the Cosworth Ford V8, and it was becoming increasingly difficult to keep the engine situation up to standard. I thought if we could get Dan to go on driving for us in 1966 I would retire and spend more time on the preparation of the cars and see that they were right for Dan. Then Dan decided to go off on his own and build his Eagles, so I thought 'Now Dan has gone I might as well drive myself!'

The other thing that encouraged me to go on was the prospect of a new power unit. It was quite early in 1965 when I got the brainwave to do something with Repco, which is an Australian company. We had Phil Irving come over here from Repco, and I was spending every minute of the day on motor racing, and then staying up night after night until 2 or 3 in the morning designing the engine with Phil. The whole thing was really getting on top of me and I got to the stage where I didn't think it was all worth the amount of time I was putting into it.

Then, towards the end of the year when I could see that the engine was beginning to look as though it was what we wanted and things seemed to be moving along all right, I got really interested in the Repco engine project, and everything else took second place. So when Dan decided to go it alone, I felt that I *did* want to drive the following year, 1966, because I could see the fruit of all that work coming. And in 1966 we had a pretty good season—I won both the Drivers' and the Constructors' Championships! So it had all been worthwhile.

I didn't seriously consider giving up motor racing again until the end of 1969. By then I had more or less told the family and a few other people that I would be giving up at the end of 1969, and I had virtually convinced myself that that was what I wanted. The thing that changed the picture there was that we were trying to get Jochen Rindt to come back and drive for us. We were in the middle of negotiations at the Canadian Grand Prix at Mosport, with Jochen and Goodyear, and it looked like being finalised. Jochen, we knew, felt that he would like to drive for us, and everything seemed to be going well until Colin Chapman heard about it. And Colin was able to put his hand on a lot more money than we were. So that was it. Money made all the difference.

When the decision was made I just felt deflated. We had intended to do a big deal around Jochen for 1970, and when it all fell flat Ron and I were pretty depressed. I had already told Betty that I was going to retire at the end of 1969 and there were still three more races to run. We had had a rather bad year with the engine, and people had begun to write me off as a driver. Well, I just didn't feel that my driving ability *had* gone off. We were in a position to come to some arrangement with Ford at the end of the year, the new car, the monocoque, looked particularly good, and with all these things combined we felt perhaps we had a good chance of winning again in 1970.

I rang Betty from Mosport, so that she couldn't do much about it from that distance anyway, and told her I wanted to

18

drive for another year. It was a long talk—probably cost
nearly as much as Jochen's driving fee—and I *promised* that
1970 would definitely be my last year, no messing about.
That would be it. Of course, I had to carry out that promise.
And after the Ford banquet and the meeting at Brands
Hatch I would really have looked an idiot if I had popped up
at Kyalami. . . .

My last Grand Prix was the Mexican, in October 1970,
and it got off to a very bad start for me personally. I knew
it was my last race, and I thought I'd do the announcement
properly; I decided to issue a press release. It was the only
time in my life I've been serious about a press release and
we spent a long time wording it and arranging for it to be
embargoed until after the race on the Sunday. Associated
Press had the news on the Wednesday, ignored the embargo
date and on the Thursday morning it was all over the pages of
the daily papers from London to Sydney and New York.

When I arrived in Mexico on the Friday morning and
found out what had happened I was unbelievably furious.
It had all gone completely wrong, and it spoiled the whole
weekend. I had wanted to get practice and the race over
before everyone heard the news and began hounding me,
and I was so incensed with the newspaper people that I
found myself doing stupid things on the track that I shouldn't.
I know I was in a terrible state on Friday, driving over the
kerbs, setting up a fast time, certainly, but going on the grass
and all sorts of mad things. Most unlike me. I don't believe
in losing my temper when driving, but that day I didn't care.

It was so disappointing, not just annoying. Once Associated
Press had let the news out, everyone had to go along with
it, of course. We had all sorts of things planned in Australia
—a big Press conference on the Monday after the race, which
Ampol were putting on for me, and the whole thing got shot
down. All our plans went haywire. I really did feel like saying:
'That's it; I'm going to keep on driving.' In fact if Betty had
been there that Friday night I might have decided to tell her
I *would* go on.

But by the Saturday morning I had become resigned to it,
and by Sunday I regarded it as just like any other race. I

was quite relaxed. I had talked to a few friends and they had made me see that there would be other things in life that could take the place of motor racing, that good things often come out of what seems bad at the time. So I started the race knowing that I would regret my decision, but not fretting that it was my last race. It didn't affect me at all—until the engine went!

I felt very disappointed then because I was in third position behind Ickx and Regazzoni in the two Ferraris, and a good distance in front of Denny Hulme in his McLaren. There was no way I was going to catch the Ferraris, but I felt satisfied with my position. I was concentrating on making sure the car was going to finish, and it was going like a bird. But unfortunately a casting broke inside the engine, which let the oil pressure go suddenly, and within seconds the engine was destroyed!

That really did hurt actually, having the engine blow up at that stage. I was disappointed that my career should finish that way. In fact, when I rolled into the infield I wasn't even interested in getting out of the car. I just sat and thought: 'Well, to hell with it. I couldn't care less, I've finished with it. I don't want to know any more; it isn't worth it.' For the first time I felt glad I had given it up. I wanted to get out and kick the car and just walk away and forget about it.

It would have been nice to come back to the pits and talk to the boys, but I hardly talked to anyone. I felt thoroughly mixed up and cross that the engine had gone when I was in a certain third place. The race had been a bit fraught anyway, with people running all over the road and some of them lying on the very edge of it—it was the worst race from that point of view that I can ever remember.

I remember taking a long time to change out of my racing gear, and I remember putting my helmet away in a plastic bag and saying: 'For the last time'—rather gloomily. My son, Geoffrey, and Elizabeth Hayward, the motoring writer, were helping me clear up all my stuff. They'd been keeping a lap chart and timing for me, and now they tried to make me feel more cheerful by teasing me a little, and saying that my helmet wouldn't stay in the bag very long, knowing me!

One Door Closes

Ron Denis, my chief mechanic, packed my driving bag away in a crate of things to be shipped home, so I promptly whipped it out again and said: 'Just in case I need it some time!' I was already starting to feel better, and though I was maybe living in a fool's paradise, I had the feeling that there was some hope left—that I might go on driving *somehow*. I told you I was all mixed up.

Later we all went to the prizegiving, which was a Ferrari benefit, with Pedro Rodriguez receiving a special award for being the highest placed Mexican driver. The World Champion's award was handed over to Dick Scammell, Lotus Racing Manager, who was not very happy about taking it, not unnaturally. No one mentioned me at all, and I thought, so that's the way it all ends—just like a damp squib. We wandered off to have a pot of tea—a not unusual habit of mine—and chewed over the weekend's happenings in a sober manner.

Subsequent events at home and in Australia made my decision absolutely concrete for me, and also made me a lot happier than that last night in Mexico. But it was still exceedingly difficult to take in properly that I had retired, that I would be leaving for Australia before Christmas, to settle with my family back in Sydney where I came from.

My life has simply been to drive racing cars. Having to play out the last act, drive the last laps and leave all my friends was almost more than I could bear.

CHAPTER II

An Australian Youth

As I have set out my last days of active race driving and my greatest moment of honour in painful detail, I must now begin to fill in the forty-five years that led up to them. A man may not appear to have much in common with his ancestry or his early way of life, but a man is what his childhood and his parents made him, and they are the product of their fore-bears. My ancestry is a mixture of early Australian stock and London's dockland.

My grandfather, my father's father, emigrated with his family from London in 1885, when he was sixteen. He had been born in Bow, and was very proud of being a Cockney. He was the eldest of quite a family, and his life revolved round the East End. He would talk about the East India Docks, the West India Docks, and the Mile End Road as if those were the boundaries of his world. When the family went for a long holiday they went to Epping Forest, and the South side of the Thames, apart from Gravesend, scarcely existed for them.

His father was a shopkeeper—a fariner—not a word used much nowadays. He dealt in flour and bread, and pollit and sharps, and all the various grades of wheat from the coarsest to the finest.

My main source of stories about my grandfather is my own father, of course; and the story he remembers best was the terrific disappointment felt by my grandfather when the family arrived in Melbourne. The port was exactly the same as Tilbury or Gravesend, or any other place he had been to. He had expected to be met by bush rangers leading kangaroos on strings or something, and he was violently upset

22

before they left England that they wouldn't buy him a red shirt and a holster, and then let him go off on a horse into the bush as soon as they landed! You can imagine how he felt when they reached the other side of the world only to see that it was not much different from London or any other city. Just another dock in another town.

However, he worked in Melbourne for a time and then went up to Mildura where some Americans, the Chaffey Brothers, were developing a big irrigation scheme, probably the first of its kind in Australia. He was apprenticed to engineering there and met my grandmother. When they married there was a very bad financial depression in Australia, which was only relieved by the discovery of gold in a big way in Western Australia. So my grandfather, with two baby boys—one of them my father—went West. He didn't go for gold itself, but because he felt that where there was gold there would be work. He had given up the idea of engineering by then and had become a chef, and, of course, there is always work for a chef where there are hard-working hungry men.

After that they went backwards and forwards across the country as anyone in those times had to if they wanted work and they had a young family. You had to go where you could find a living.

My own father's earliest memories date from the time my grandfather bought a grocer's shop in Adelaide, when Pop was nine. He took a fairly active part in the business because kids started to work early then—very different from today. After that he spent nearly all his life in a shop. He met my mother, May, in Adelaide but they moved to Sydney and settled eventually in the suburb of Hurstville. My mother took care to see that her family followed her there, and my grandfather had settled in Melbourne, so we had a large number of relations in both cities.

I was born in Hurstville, which is about ten miles south of the centre of Sydney. It was quite a big town, really, a growing suburb on the main railway line south. We lived in a bungalow type house on McQuarie Street. The railway had gone through about twenty or thirty years before I was

23

born on April 2 1926, and when I was quite small the electrification and undergrounding of the railway in Sydney itself made quite a difference to transportation. We lived very close to the station and the electric trains started to come through; then, when they got very near to Sydney itself, they went underground. I was mad about trains, especially the old steam ones, and some of my first memories are of the railway and watching the trains go by.

It was a good place for a kid to live. The city was near enough, and easy to get to; Cronulla Beach was a bit to the south of us and the sea came close to us by creeks and bays, channels and rivers. You are never far from the sea anywhere in Sydney and at that time there was still plenty of open ground undeveloped to the south and west of Hurstville.

My father used to work pretty long hours in the greengrocery business; he would go off to the markets at 5.30 in the morning, then go to his shops, and come home quite late at night. So in my early days I didn't see a lot of my father.

We had a reasonable-sized garden at the back of the house, and down at the bottom was a peppercorn tree which was my favourite climbing place until I fell out of it one day and nearly broke my neck. Most of the time, though, it served as a refuge. Every time I got into trouble and Mum used to chase me I used to zoom down the garden and climb the peppercorn tree; I wouldn't come down until she promised not to hit me. Actually, I didn't get thumped much. I used to get the odd belting off Pop, but it wasn't often that they could catch me. Mum was the one who used to drive all the 'dos' and 'don'ts' into me in the early days.

Australia is an ideal place for anything outdoors, even in the winter when it can be pretty cold at night, but it is mostly warm and clear during the day. It really has a wonderful climate, which is perhaps its greatest asset. Whether I like being outdoors because I lived out there, or whether I would have been an outdoor man anyway, I don't know. But until I came over to England I used to be out of the house many more hours than I was in it. I used to get myself into continual trouble by wandering off and going exploring.

An Australian Youth

My cousin, Ken, and a couple of friends used to go off on their pushbikes, a thing I wasn't allowed to have, and I used to follow as best I could on my scooter. One day we ventured all the way out to Cronulla Beach for a swim, which was every inch of twelve miles from my home. I went all the way out there on a scooter hanging on to the back of a bike. That was about the furthest I travelled in that manner, and when my parents found out about it they were justifiably worried—and cross.

But I was always wandering off. I often had my father come looking for me with a big stick. Literally. Luckily, I used to sight him first and when I saw him coming I used to head for home, zoom off down the side of the house, which used to have a bit of a gradient at the side and a concrete path by a fairly big lawn at the back. I'd whizz down there with a big broadside into the shed, and then disappear up the peppercorn tree until it had all cooled down again.

Later on I had a tricycle. One time I got into so much trouble they took the seat and the handlebars off it—so I learned to ride it with no seat or handlebars. I steered it with the pedals, by my feet, and sat on the bar. After a few days of that they decided they might as well give me back the seat and handlebars, but I didn't want them any more. It was more fun the way it was.

Of course, what I really wanted was a two-wheeled bike like my cousin Ken's, but they were considered dangerous—probably because of the way we messed around on them. Then we gained a bad reputation at home with billy-carts. These were really just four wheels and a plank, and you steered with a loop of rope. My first-ever races were on these things, and we used to race down Patrick Street. It was a hill, a main road, and there were lots of side streets and crossroads. Billy-cart racing was forbidden by parents—all parents—because it was so dangerous, but the races used to go on just the same.

I was an only child, but it never bothered me. There were so many other kids who lived in the street, and they all used to come to my place or I was living in their places. I can't remember ever being lost for company, where children were concerned.

My first school was Hurstville Primary School which was within walking distance; half a mile or so. I hated my early days at school. I was four when I first started—I was going to be five in April, but the autumn term began in February after the summer holidays; we used to have six weeks holiday at Christmas—all back to front for people who live in the northern hemisphere.

We had male teachers exclusively because there was no way a woman could control the kids out there! And I know I always wanted to get out to play or get into mischief somewhere else, so I never really enjoyed school until I went to the Technical College.

My main interests in those days were cars, steam engines, trains—and making things. I used to have a good Meccano set and later I ventured on to model aeroplanes. We made these with balsa wood and glue—we didn't have kits in those days, just strips of balsa wood we had to cut off ourselves and elastic bands to wind up the propellers.

Then there was swimming—I suppose we get to take the beaches for granted in Sydney. When the pushbike era came on—when I was about ten, I eventually persuaded my father I couldn't live any longer without a bike—we used to go riding off every weekend, swimming. Or we'd go further down the coast to a place called National Park which was on a river about 25 miles from Sydney, and we used to take lunch with us and have picnics. It was always a group of us, about five or six boys, never girls, and we did that for quite a few years. I must have done thousands of miles on a bike.

I tried pushbike racing once, which I was told was a pretty stupid thing to do. There was a cycle track only about a quarter of a mile from our place, the Hurstville Oval. I used to go down there and watch the races before I was old enough to do any racing seriously. They had the odd race for people like myself who were keen and interested without being professional riders. We used to do a lot of cycling round the track itself. I tried a race one night and finished fourth. There were only four in it!

An Australian Youth

One of the main things I remember from the early days was that my father was a keen motorist. He took delivery of our first car the week I was born, and he and my mother were so excited about having their first car and their first child in the same week that my father always reckons there was some pre-natal influence at work which made me into a racing driver! Whether that is true or not, the car was a 1926 Willys Knight open tourer with a canvas top. We had that car for about ten years, and I know my father used to let me steer it from a very early age, sitting on his lap and just taking the wheel. I know there is a photo of me, at about ten months old—certainly I couldn't walk—sitting up there with my hands on the wheel. I can't pretend to remember that. In fact, it was our second car that I really recall clearly. It was a Chrysler 77 and a particularly good car; it was quite easy for me to drive at reasonable speeds.

My father had a man working for him whose job it was, among other things, to wash the car every week. Pop used to drive it round to the backyard and leave it there for the man to wash when he had the opportunity. Well, I couldn't resist the temptation. My father or mother would look out and see four or five of my friends watching with envy while I drove the Chrysler to within an inch or so of the fence and then reversed it. The first time I did that, and let the handbrake off, very confidently, I went rolling straight through the lattice fencing. That was before I could reach the pedals.

My father started teaching me to drive when I was about twelve. We went down to a piece of common land where we used to go with our pushbikes and catapults and chase birds. The land was being developed and they'd put the dirt roads down but there were no buildings at that time. During the second and third lesson—it was a Sunday—a policeman suddenly appeared from nowhere, a very uncommon sight in those parts; then a second and a third policeman. I began to get nervous when the tally mounted to five, and I was quite convinced they were after me for driving a car when too young to hold a licence. So Pop and I changed places rapidly. There was a bit of panic on as Pop thought they were looking for me too. But it turned out they were only looking for a two-up gambling school; that's a bit like a game of dice, but they use pennies.

My father also had three trucks for the green-grocery business which I used to drive round the yard occasionally. One was a Chevrolet and one a Dodge, but the third was an Albion, a 1925 model. It was delivered with solid front tyres, but got converted later to pneumatic tyres all round, which was a big deal.

Incidentally, people have often commented upon the fact that we use American cars in Australia and New Zealand, almost as though it were treason. Well, before the war I would say at least 90 per cent of the vehicles, in Australia at any rate, *were* American. England just didn't make cars and trucks to suit the conditions. Australia is a very big country with some rough terrain, and America had similar conditions. British cars were very rare in those days.

But that is a digression. Truck driving became my next ambition, and I used to work for my father every weekend, getting pocket money for working in the shop itself and driving down to the markets with him so that he could let me drive home – long before I had a licence. The war made this more possible, I suppose.

I was thirteen and five months old when the war began. I'd just had my first big trip away from home about ten days before the war started. My grandfather lived in Melbourne, and my cousin Ken and I were put on a train in Sydney and travelled the 500 miles down the coast to Melbourne. My grandfather showed us all round the city which had so disappointed him fifty-four years earlier, and while we were staying with him the war broke out.

It wasn't long after that that petrol rationing started and the 'squeeze' began; my father had two of his trucks converted to charcoal burners. For the Chrysler he was allowed four gallons a week, and of course he had petrol for the trucks as well. But it was a saving if you could use charcoal. The burner, which was a big affair, was bolted on at the front or the side of the truck, and the charcoal created a gas which was fed into the carburettor. We used to have to stoke it up, of course, but it would run all week and then, during the weekend, I would have to go round with my father and clear out the clinker from the bottom of the burners. All the charcoal used to matt together and turn hard, which knocked the performance down. The burners had to be cleaned out thoroughly, and I used to go home looking like a black slave!

I had moved from the Primary School to a Technical College by that time. I chose a technical rather than a more liberal education because I was happiest when I was making things. They taught basic, practical engineering, which consisted of three main subjects—metalwork, which was using lathes, files and hacksaws and working at a bench; woodwork, which meant all sorts of carpentry, making furniture; and technical drawing. I was good at all those things but nothing else. I suppose my maths could have been worse, and I used to scrape through on my English and geography, but history . . . ! That I used to hate, especially English history. What could it possibly mean to us when they used to talk about the Magna Carta and stuff like that? Anyway, rightly or wrongly, I hated it.

Geography was more fun; I was always interested in the rest of the world. In fact, I have always had a great desire to travel—so much so that I used to stand and stare out of the window at home and wonder whether I'd ever see the rest of the world. I really did. The kind of life we led and the hours Pop used to work didn't give us much chance to get away except for a few holiday trips in the May holidays. We had a few fishing trips up at Taree and we'd always take my cousin, Ken. I suppose we were more like brothers, except that he was only six months older than I was.

The holiday trip that I enjoyed most of all was one that we made to Lord Howe Island, 450 miles north east of Sydney. We went on an old tug called the *Marinda,* which was not a very big boat, and on the way we ran into a terrific storm. We arrived at the island half a day late because we had spent the time facing into the storm and the *Marinda* wasn't capable of going forward. In fact we were probably getting washed backwards most of the time. Everyone on board was sick, except me.

When the Flag Drops

I can remember nearly going overboard on that trip. I was riding a tricycle round the decks, and as the boat rolled I went downhill in a big way and crashed into the rail. I damn nearly went over into the sea! I never dared tell anyone, of course, but it put me off riding the tricycle until the storm abated.

When we arrived at Lord Howe Island it wasn't possible to land on the usual side, where the coral reef is, because it was too rough, and we had to go round to the other side where they lowered the lifeboats, put everybody in, and then the local people carried everyone ashore, because there was nowhere a boat could land on that side of the island.

It was a wonderful place for swimming and fishing, because it had a beautiful lagoon. I had my first taste of speed boats and water skiing there. Well, it wasn't water skiing exactly — just a flat board towed by a speedboat. Anyway, we spent a whole week swimming in the lagoon and speedboat skiing, until one evening we went down to the little wharf from which we had been swimming and two of the local people were down there with lights, fishing. They caught four sharks off the end of the wharf, and though they assured us that these sharks were harmless — gummy sharks, about 5-foot long, I suppose — and the fishermen reckoned they were the only variety of shark in the lagoon, it rather took the shine off our swimming from then on!

The other pleasure which was spoilt for us was walking round the island. It was all right in the daytime, but we went out one evening with torches and started walking down one of the bush tracks. Suddenly we came across a great big spider's web, which they used to spin out in the night, and there was a spider hanging in it the size of a saucer! It was big enough to catch birds and eat them! I don't mind spiders normally, but this type was the biggest I have ever seen, and it was frightening.

We stayed at Wilson's Guest House on the island. One of the Wilson family had tried to sail a boat from Sydney to the island and never, ever made it. They had big fires going on the island every night in case he turned up, but he must have been overturned in a storm, because he was never seen again.

An Australian Youth

But, in spite of the spiders and the Wilson tragedy, it was still the best holiday I ever had; I only went there once. Maybe I'll go back someday. It is funny how you can travel all over the world and never get back to the place where you were happy as a child because it just never seems convenient. Perhaps it is just as well, it might be changed beyond all recognition.

I was always extremely interested in anything that moved, from steam engines to aeroplanes, so it is not so surprising that after scooters, tricycles and pushbikes, my next great passion was the motor cycle. Apart from swimming, my only other sport was tennis, but I could see I was never going to get anywhere with it so I didn't take that much interest. I couldn't say I was at all athletic — you should see my cricket! I could never claim to be anything like the world's idea of the all-Australian sportsman.

Anyway, I liked engines and mechanical bits and pieces best of all. So when I left school at the age of fifteen — I should have stayed on another three years but I'd had enough of school — my first job was in an engineering shop in Sydney. That lasted just three weeks. I arrived there thinking I'd be right in the thick of it from the start, using the lathes and so on. But I found myself sweeping floors and running messages, and after three weeks I couldn't see any possibility of getting any further than that for a long, long time. The people there were pretty old, and it looked to me as though one of them would have to die before I moved up to the bench to do any real work! I decided that was no good to me, so I left and went to work in a garage. This was the garage that looked after my father's cars and trucks — Ferguson's in Treacy Street, Hurstville.

While I was working there, I came up to my sixteenth birthday. Ken had had a motor bike for six months by then and, as always, I had to keep up with him. My father helped me to buy my first bike, a little 350 Velocette. I was overcome with pride and satisfaction as I joined Ken and the rest of the gang.

It wasn't long before I used to do all my own repairs on

the Velocette. I took it apart and put it together again, found out how everything worked, and then went into business buying and selling motor bikes. That was my first private enterprise, I suppose. I sold my bike and made a profit on it, and I thought: 'This seems an easy way to make money.' So I started to buy motor bikes that wanted quite a lot of work done on them, and used to do it myself. I sometimes had the whole thing stripped down on my mother's back verandah, which she used to get a bit upset about. Then I'd paint and enamel it and sell it at a profit. Sometimes I managed to make £15-£20, sometimes £50; about 20 per cent on most deals if I worked hard—because the only way of making a decent profit *was* by putting the work into the job. Simply buying and selling again would be much more difficult, and anyway I used to enjoy repairing a machine, overhauling it and putting it all back in first class condition.

I did thousands of miles on motor bikes. For six months I rode pillion with Ken, and I think my parents decided it was more dangerous riding on the back of his bike than having one of my own. It had taken them so many years to let me have a pushbike that I was staggered when they consented to let me have a motor cycle. At weekends a whole gang of us would go tripping all round the place—up to Newcastle, which was about 100 miles away, and all the seaside resorts between Newcastle and Sydney, and down the coast to Wollongong quite often, or to Port Kembla and Kiama. These were the romping grounds 100 miles either way, north or south of Sydney.

I didn't go inland much at that stage, not until I started driving a car the following year, when I could get my licence at seventeen. Then we used to go west, shooting, mainly. We went hunting kangaroos and foxes at a place called Cobar. There was a road between Cobar and Willcannia which ran more or less north-south. We would take a compass with us and just ride out into the scrub miles off the beaten track, where there were no roads of any description. We used to take tents and camp overnight, which I really enjoyed.

I was pretty well off working at Fergusons. Harry Ferguson was a particularly good mechanic and he used to run the

My first motor car

Johnny Schonberg driving the first 'Brabham-built' car – the midget racer on its first outing at the Sydney Showground.

Allan A. Gerard

Geoffrey Brabha[...] at the wheel of [...] Cooper Bristol, s[...] wearing its Red[...] Special livery, Australia, 1953.

Souvenir Snapshots

My first race in England – the Cooper Alta at [...] Easter Meeting, Goodwood 1955[...]

Geoffrey Goddard

And the Cooper [...] from the rear.

workshop. I worked under his direction for three years. When I started there, the war was already into its second year, which meant that labour was pretty hard to come by. I wasn't apprenticed at the garage and Harry Ferguson was also spending a lot of time running the spare parts side of the business. This meant that I was left to my own devices quite a lot; I probably gained a lot more experience in the three years I worked for them than I would have in ten years in a garage in normal times. I had the satisfaction of being able to do pretty well any repair on a motor car.

During the war there was a big shortage of spare parts, so I learnt to improvise, and I think this is why you get a pretty good mechanic from Australia. Their basic training is better than anyone gets over here.

Apart from the improvisation that had to be done at that time to get cars back on the road, I found myself, in addition, working with my father's trucks at the weekend, trying to help keep them on the road. The petrol shortage meant that we had to use the charcoal burners which didn't do the engines any good. My evenings and other spare time, mostly at weekends, was spent overhauling and repairing my motor cycles. My time was completely used up by all these activities, plus a little motor cycling; oh, and I was doing a Mechanical Engineering course at college two or three nights a week as well. I'd forgotten that. It was the Kogarah Technical College, and I completed two years out of the three year course. The third I never completed because I joined the Air Force in 1944 when I was eighteen.

When I joined the RAAF my first month was spent on initial training at Cootamundra, which is about 120 miles from Sydney, in the winter. It was quite cold living in tents —the Spartan existence. But the worst problem I had to contend with was the food. I must admit I have always been very finicky about my food, and I had to adjust to eating in Air Force canteens. In those days I was very, very thin, and for that first month I thought I was going to die of starvation! In fact, I put on about half a stone, which was a bit mystifying; it was probably all the exercise.

After the initial training I was sent off to Dubbo, which

was really an RAAF stores, and I was only supposed to be there a month awaiting a posting to a station 'somewhere in Australia'. But the weekend before I was due to be drafted I went down to Sydney by train. Of course, I still had a motor bike at home, and I went off to see Len Ainsworth, one of my mates in the nearby suburb of Bexley. While I'd been away he had bought an old sidecar for thirty shillings and had hooked it onto the side of his motorbike. Now, I had only ridden solo machines, never one with a side car, so naturally I had to try it out.

I went off on it, along Forest Road towards Sydney. As you leave Bexley there is a fork in the road, a Y junction, and right in the middle of this Y is a telegraph post and a mail box, which are about two feet apart. Well, when I arrived at this particular junction I went to take the right-hand fork, but as I turned to go that way, the bar which held the sidecar on to the front of the frame just broke. It was rusted right through. So the sidecar tried to go down one road and the bike down the other, the net result was that I went straight through between the telegraph post and the mail box! And as I went through I banged my knee and cut it quite badly.

Luckily that was the only injury I had, but I should really have had stitches in it; instead of doing that I just got Len's mother to put a bandage on it. That evening I had to travel 200 miles on a train back to Dubbo. The next morning I appeared on parade and started to feel pretty wonky on that leg. I managed to survive the first two days, but obviously the leg was getting worse and I finished up going along to the medical unit just to get someone to look at it. I spent the next seven days in hospital with water on the knee and other complications.

During that seven days my posting came through, but I couldn't leave. The next posting took weeks, and I had to stay in Dubbo. They had to find me some kind of job to do when I was out of the hospital, and I was assigned to driving a travelling crane in one of the big stores.

Eventually my posting came through and I went off to Adelaide, where I spent three months doing my initial training as a flight mechanic. I had desperately wanted to learn to fly when I was in the Air Force, but they had stopped taking aircrew and decided they needed flight mechanics more than pilots!

The worst part of those three months in Adelaide was the fact that I had no wheels to get around on. I had to travel by train or bus, which didn't appeal to me at all, and as soon as I got my next posting, to Melbourne, I bought a motor-bike. With this means of freedom at my disposal I was able to travel at weekends and see quite a bit more of my grand-father's city.

We lived in pre-fabricated huts on the sports arena of the Melbourne Show Grounds. I really enjoyed this course as I worked on aircraft engines in a practical way and also studied the theory side of how they worked. This course was of great benefit to me in my motor racing later on.

After the Melbourne course was finished I got posted out to an operational training unit at Williamtown, about 130 miles north of Sydney. There were two flights of aircraft involved, one Beaufighter unit and one Mosquito unit. I spent the first few weeks on Mosquitoes and then got trans-ferred to Beaufighters, on which I spent the rest of my time there, just about two years in all.

I managed to do quite a lot of flying while I was there; not actually flying the aircraft myself, of course, but being allowed to go up in them. The mechanics who had worked on an aircraft were allowed to go up on the test flights after the work had been carried out. It was here that I just missed out on my first opportunity of being killed in a plane. I was very lucky.

Our Chief Pilot was Wing Commander Crombie, whose job it was to train or convert rookie pilots on to Beaufighters. Now, the Beaufighter was quite a tricky plane to fly, and I had a lot of time for Crombie, and looked upon him as the best pilot at the base. So I always did what flying I could with him.

One morning I went down to the flight hut after carrying out some work on an aircraft that had to be test flown. Wing Commander Crombie came down and said he was going to do the test flight, so I promptly put my name down to go with him. There was a log kept of all the flying that was done called the EE77 – and this had to be filled in with the pilot's name, the crew's names, time of take-off and all the rest of it. I was to be 'crew'.

Well, he went off back to the Officers' Mess for some reason, and didn't return for ages. While I was waiting I got involved in a game of cards with a few of the boys in another hut not far away; we were hiding, of course! While this game was going on Crombie came back and as I wasn't ready or even visible, he took the tractor driver – the chap who drove the tractor that pulled the aeroplanes around the airfield.

So I missed out on my flight. We heard them take off, and about half an hour later the plane came back over the top of us with only one engine running; the other was feathered. What had happened, apparently, was that he had taken one of the rookie pilots up with him as well as the tractor driver. He was a very new pilot who had just arrived at the aerodrome to start the next Beaufighter conversion course. The Wing Commander was demonstrating how you feathered one engine, and when they got the engine into a feathered position the battery exploded for some reason. They didn't have the power to feather the propeller back again, and when they came overhead we knew they were in trouble. We were dead worried about what had happened in the engine, as it was our responsibility. We rushed out to watch the aircraft land.

The Beaufighter was a tricky aircraft to fly on one engine. If it was flying slowly, with the undercarriage and flaps down, and you dropped an engine, you could never pick it up; it just stayed down until the aircraft hit the ground. And this is what happened.

The Wing Commander, who had done many thousands of flying hours, night fighting over London, for instance, was perhaps just a bit blasé, or not concentrating totally. He was in the circuit, and another aircraft was landing and he had to wait for it to land. Somehow or other he must have swung it round the wrong way, and dropped the *dead* engine. We were amazed – it was so unlike him. The next thing was that the plane went straight down, and crashed about a quarter of a mile off the end of the runway.

We all went tearing off, running across the fields to get to the wreckage. Luckily the plane didn't burn, but it shows how stupid you can be at such a time — the aircraft held about 900 gallons of fuel, and the fuel tanks burst. Not only that, but they had crashed on a rubbish tip, and I don't know to this day why it didn't catch alight. When we arrived on the scene we dashed into the wreckage to get the people out, and it was ages before it dawned on me that we were standing in four or five inches of petrol. The whole ground was covered with fuel and it would only have needed one spark and we'd all have been incinerated in a flash.

The rookie pilot was walking around in a daze and had no idea what had hit him. He had a few bumps and bruises but had evidently been thrown clear.

The Wing Commander was dead. He'd been thrown out but had hit his head very badly on one of the engines that had been torn out of the wing. He must have died instantly. The tractor driver, who had gone up instead of me, was still in the aircraft and we had to smash all the glass in the back to try to get at him. He was jammed down in the well where you climb up to get into the navigator's seat. The thing that had saved him was that, just before impact, when he realised they were going to hit the ground, he had braced himself against the cannon bins which are immediately in front of the gunner. He was a very powerful chap, and he had braced himself so hard he had pushed the back out of the seat, and fallen down into the well. This saved him from being flung forward and probably killed.

Anyway, we smashed the glass and got him out, and by this time the ambulances and fire trucks had arrived. Both the rookie pilot and the tractor driver survived, though the loss of Wing Commander Crombie was a big shock to us.

It was pretty lucky I'd been playing cards that morning. I wasn't very strong in those days, and there was no way I could have pushed the back out of that seat as the tractor driver had done. I'd have been thrown forward and been killed for sure.

CHAPTER III

My First Attempts at Motor Racing

When I first came out of the Air Force in 1946, I looked around a bit vaguely for something to do. My grandfather had a house with a fairly large plot of ground, and my uncle was a builder. So I got my uncle to build me a workshop at the back of my grandfather's place, and began working on the cars of the neighbourhood. By now, however, I was not quite so keen on being a mechanic and wanted to expand into engineering. I had always had a leaning towards engineering rather than just working on other people's cars, but my experience wasn't great. My training had been cut off by going into the Air Force, so that side of my small business started off rather slowly.

I was fortunate in having a friend called Bill Armstrong who had retired from engineering but had a little hobby shop of his own in Blakehurst. He spent a lot of time teaching me most of what I know today, either at his place or mine. Incidentally, when I say engineering I mean work that was mainly done on the lathe — nothing very grand.

Then came another piece of good fortune, as it turned out. I met an American, Johnny Schonberg, who had married a local girl who was a friend of ours, and had settled in Sydney as soon as he was discharged from the US Navy. His Australian in-laws owned a produce and carrying business, and when we heard about a disposal sale that was to take place in Darwin, we decided to fly up there and see if we could pick up some trucks and tools and so on. I thought there might be some machinery that would be useful for my workshop.

My First Attempts at Motor Racing

There was no direct flight from Sydney to Darwin, so we had to make a hop to Brisbane and then onwards. We got to Brisbane on the Monday morning, but the plane to Darwin left on Tuesday, so we had an overnight stop in Brisbane. While we were sitting around in the hotel, reading the papers, Johnny suddenly shot out of his chair and said: 'Good God, the race meeting that was supposed to be on last Saturday night was rained out, so they are holding it tonight.' I knew Johnny drove midget cars in Sydney, but I'd never seen him drive and I'd never even seen a midget car. So Johnny jumped at the opportunity to take me out to the circuit to see what they looked like. He immediately got me organised to go out to the speedway circuit with him, because he knew all the drivers, and knew they'd be up at the track to work on the cars. So we went out to the track in the afternoon, met some of the boys, had a look at the midget cars, and arranged to go back to the meeting that night.

I was very interested in the cars, looked at them with staring eyes, asked all sorts of questions, but thought they were a bit on the rough side. They were all dirty and looked as though they had been shot-blasted. I soon found out why — when I saw them race that evening I realised it would be a bit difficult to make them look like pretty motor cars, as they spent most of their time sliding around in dirt and cinders. It was very similar to speedway motor bikes only on four wheels. Anyway I was reasonably impressed, enjoyed the night's racing and thought they were all lunatics. It frightened me to death watching them come haring down the straight and hurtling into the corner all sideways and rubbing against one another and so on. It didn't give me any immediate desire to jump into one and try it next day!

We went off to Darwin the following morning, and we brought three trucks and a utility back with us, plus a lot of machines and tools and things. We had a semi-trailer, so we put one truck on top of that, and strapped it down. The other truck had a fairly big table top and we stuck the utility on the back of that. So two of us brought back four vehicles, no problem at all.

We also bought some ·303 rifles and ammunition, and

blasted everything in the countryside on the way back, including kangaroos, foxes and things. We started out from Darwin at about six in the evening, as we'd been advised not to drive in the daytime because of the heat, and the tyres on the trucks were not all that good. The roads get terribly hot, and the tyre pressures build up. It was actually a bitumen road all the way from Darwin to Alice Springs and from Tennant's Creek west to Camooweal. In the early hours of the morning we were getting pretty tired so we decided to stop at the side of the road and have a couple of hours' sleep. We came to a place where a grader had made a big drain off the edge of the road so that water could run away when it rained, and we parked the trucks on this nice level area. We had a couple of stretchers with us that we slung under the semi-trailer, and went to sleep.

I was first to wake up in the morning; the sun was shining brightly and it must have been up for some time. I looked up, and there were three aborigines standing beside the trailer holding great long poles that looked like spears. I got out of bed rather quickly. They were making all sorts of signs and trying to talk pidgin English, and I got the message that they wanted a smoke—they were just after cigarettes. While this conversation was going on, Johnny heard voices and woke. He looked up and saw me standing with three aborigines who were apparently carrying spears, and he sprang up so quickly that he bashed his head on the underside of the trailer, which knocked him right out! He had a bump on his head for days afterwards. He obviously thought upon waking that we were in danger, and I didn't have time to enlighten him. When he came round, I gave him the message that all they wanted was cigarettes and I've never seen anyone so keen and eager to give away cigarettes in all my life. So the aborigines went on their way with whole packets of cigarettes, and we went on to Sydney.

We reached home with our trucks and bits and pieces; and the first thing I did when I got back was go to a couple of midget races in Sydney that Johnny was driving in. I was definitely interested by that time, but more in how to improve the cars than anything else. After watching a few meetings we decided we'd build a new car for Johnny to drive. I spent quite a bit of time looking at all the other cars, trying to sort out their good and bad points, so that we could try to make a better car than any that were in existence at that time. With the help of a few people around the district, including Ronnie Ward, who was also a midget car owner and built his own cars, and Bill Armstrong, we started on our first racing car. It took four or five months to build, and cost around £A400, a lot of money to us in the 1946-7 season.

We used a 1000 cc JAP engine to start with, which promptly blew up and gave a lot of trouble. We then got in tow with Art Senior who used to be one of Australia's motor cycle aces and had his own machine shop in Sydney. He helped us modify the engine, and at the same time to make it bigger by boring it out to 1100 cc; we raced this for the rest of the season, notching up a couple of wins.

The chassis was tubular; we had a Morris Cowley steering box, we cut a Morris Cowley gearbox in half to make it a two speed box and we used a Harley Davidson clutch. Up front we had semi-eliptic leaf springs with a straight axle. Amilcar hubs supported the wire wheels. It was quite a good little car, but we decided that the engine wasn't man enough for the job. We thought it was time to make an engine of our own.

By this time I had my own engineering shop in working order, and we made crankcases and flywheels, con rods and cylinders and cylinder heads, and put together a 1350 cc engine. The only parts of the original engine we used were the two rocker boxes that operated the valves. This engine was an extremely successful one and it was raced for several years.

We completed one season with Johnny driving, and when the next season was coming up Johnny just drove in the first one or two events. His wife was giving him quite a problem, desperately wanting him to give up racing. He decided he should go along with her wishes, and we were left with a motor car and no driver, so I thought I'd better have a go myself. Johnny took me down to Tempe mud flats and gave me a few lessons on how to drive a racing car, then we went to the Paramatta Speedway, where I entered my first race.

At the drop of the flag, not knowing what it was all about,

I was staggered at how much dirt and rocks were flying, and I found this the most difficult part of starting to learn to drive a midget — how to cope with all the flying dust and cinders. Within a short time it made your goggles so dirty you couldn't see through them, and we used to start off in a midget race with five or six pairs of goggles on. The glasses we used were actually anti-gas goggles, very thin cellophane things, and every now and then, when they got so dirty you couldn't see any more, we used to pull the top pair off and start again. It took me two or three nights to get used to this and to be able to swallow the dirt; on the third night, after running last in all the races the previous two nights, I started to get a feeling for it all. In the feature race, they start twelve cars with the fastest at the back of the field, which is the opposite to what we do in road racing, and I was starting on the front row, being a new boy at the game. Much to my surprise at the end of the race I was still up there!

Notching up my first win on the third night gave me a lot of confidence and from there on I was able to mix it with the best of them. Then I started racing at the Sydney Showground, and on my first night there I won all three of the races that I started. That was the main Sydney Speedway, run by Empire Speedways, and this was all good publicity because in those days they seized on the label, 'Youngest driver in midget racing, blah, blah, blah!' It went down well in the local newspapers.

In my first season I won the New South Wales Championship at the Sydney Showground. I don't really know why — I suppose I just had a feel for it. It is a completely different sort of skill from driving a Grand Prix car, but it was good training. You have to have quick reactions, in effect you are living on your reactions. It was a good training ground for the rest of my career. The tracks were just oval circuits, and the car was virtually out of control all the time — or perhaps I should say just on the verge of being out of control. A lot of people spun, and many people had terrific accidents — it is a dangerous sport. I was lucky to get through nearly six years of it without getting upside down in the car. I think I was about the only driver of that period who hadn't been upside down umpteen times. We had roll hoops and they were actually built into the car; they weren't external ones. From the safety point of view the midgets were better constructed than road racing cars were for many years afterwards. We not only had a roll bar at the back of our heads, but we wore safety belts, always. In fact to drive without one would have been suicide.

Midget racing is a very popular sport in Australia, especially in Sydney, and they used to import American drivers each year, and they would mix it with us during the season, which created quite a lot of interest. You could get crowds of up to 40,000 people. At the same track they would have motor cycle racing and motor cycle and sidecar—these were called 'outfits'—racing.

Interstate racing was very popular. Quite a few of the drivers would go from Sydney to Adelaide or to Melbourne, or up to Brisbane, and vice versa. The Sydney track had two systems for scoring points, one for handicap and one for feature racing. I won one or both of these every year all the time I ran. The big ace in those days was Ray Ravell and, the first season I was racing, there was a nice gold watch for the winner of the points score for the year. And I beat Ray Ravell by one point, which was a pretty bitter blow to him.

I found that I spent every minute of the day working on the midget or making bits and pieces for it, and the evenings racing it. It took up as much time and energy as any racing I've ever done. One week I went to a meeting in Adelaide—my father always used to come with me on these trips—and I don't know if I was just getting fed up with the amount of work involved or what, but I was definitely considering giving up midget racing. I was already looking at road racing and wondering what I could do there.

Well, this particular night in Adelaide, I was leading the South Australian Championship, and with about three laps to go, when I was holding so big a lead that nobody could possibly get by me, the engine destroyed itself—threw a rod, just about cut itself in half, and then caught fire. I rolled into the centre of the Show ground, and there was the midget, all burning, the engine all broken, and I decided: 'Well, it's not worth it.' Mind you, that engine had done a terrific job for us really—it lasted quite a few years of racing.

After I'd decided to finish with midgets I wasn't sure what to do next. My father was still in the greengrocery business, and every now and then there used to be shortages of certain fruits and vegetables. He'd been looking at the situation in South Australia, and he decided that if only we could have a big semi-trailer we'd be able to buy stuff in South Australia and take it across to Sydney to sell. I thought this was a good idea as well, so we went out and looked at semi-trailers—I thought that instead of midget racing I'd go into the trucking business with my father.

We went round Adelaide looking at advertised trailers, and came across a beautiful 'semi' that was absolutely ideal for the job. We made the chap an offer for it, went away and thought we'd bought it, but when we went back to take delivery we found the chap had sold it to someone else for more money than we had offered, although he had agreed to take our offer the day before. So our dreams of starting this great new business came to nothing; we weren't able to go on with it right then because we had to get back to Sydney to repair the car for the next race. Once we were home again the idea of trucking slipped by and I got more interested in road racing.

That setback in Adelaide could have completely changed my life. If the chap had accepted our offer for the semi, and stuck to it, I'm convinced my motor racing career could have finished there and then. Such very small events can change the course of your whole life. Apart from dirt track racing, I had competed in some hill climbs with the midget. I had also come in contact with Ron Tauranac when I had a Velocette engine for sale. I advertised and, when Ron came to have a look at it, he saw I had an engineering shop and was able to bring me some work. He was working for the Colonial Sugar Refining Company at the time and they often needed to have stainless steel castings machined, which Ron would get me to do for them. He was also building hill-climb cars at home, with his brother Austin, and I did some machining for them, and made bits and pieces for their cars.

44

My First Attempts at Motor Racing

We always got on well together, although we are very different in many ways. Ron, of course, became the designer of the Brabham later on, and Austin is the manager of my Ford dealership in Sydney. I felt I could rely on both of them completely from the start and it was a stroke of luck that we met in those early days. It was because of Ron that I started hill-climbing, really.

My first event was in 1951. I was invited to Hawkesbury Hill Climb by the Australian Sporting Car Club. Ron was competing with his car which he called the Ralt, but the midget was so much quicker than everything else that it was a big joke. I think on my first run—just going up to look at the course—I took about five or six seconds off the record, without even trying. So they decided there was no way they could have me up there competing on the hill-climb, and said that this was only a 'demonstration run' and that I couldn't possibly hold the record officially because it wasn't a proper motor car that I was driving! And the reason it wasn't a real motor car was that it didn't have four-wheel brakes. This decision made me very angry, so I took the car home and over the next few weeks worked desperately to fit four-wheel brakes on the midget. I was determined to go back and do some more hill-climbs. When the job was done, we took the car down to Rob Roy Hill Climb in Victoria, run by the Light Car Club of Australia, to take part in the Australian Hill Climb Championship. I won it. This was also in 1951. My winning the Championship in a midget was hard for the Australian organising body to accept.

That particular event accelerated my progress into road racing. I can always remember—at the Rob Roy—John Crouch competing with his brand new Cooper Mark V, which was the first one in Australia and supposed to be the ultimate as far as Hill Climbs were concerned. It was a pretty bitter blow to the Light Car Club people that he was beaten by a midget. They had laid down certain regulations that I had to comply with, and the fact that I *did* comply with them made it impossible for them to rub me out. I had to be the winner of the Rob Roy whether they liked it or not; and they didn't like it.

45

But my two brushes with the road racing boys had made me a bit annoyed and encouraged me to think I might do well in road racing. The midget wasn't suitable for this, of course, so I looked around for something else. I found a Mark IV Cooper chassis and started racing it with a 500 cc engine, based on a BSA bottom end and a JAP-type cylinder head which I adapted to fit. But it wasn't long before I was dissatisfied with 500 cc racing—it wasn't exciting enough. So I put a 1000 cc Vincent HRD engine in the same chassis and raced that for a while, until I tried boring it out to get more power, when it began to blow up regularly.

I then bought a Mark V Cooper chassis and raced it with a 1100 cc alloy JAP engine which was fairly new in those days. All this brought me into contact with the Cooper Car Company, with which I was to be associated for the next ten years.

I really ought to mention that in 1951, apart from starting road racing, almost going into the trucking business and not quite making it, I also got married.

I had known Betty Beresford for six years. She was a keen speedway follower—motor bikes only. When we first started going out together, long before I started driving midgets, I used to take her to the Sydney Sportsground on Friday nights and watch our local speedway heroes on their bikes. (Frank Gardner was one of them.) Betty actually came from Katoomba, fifty or sixty miles from Sydney, and I came in contact with her via a friend of mine who used to live in Donald Street, Hurstville. I used to go down to visit him on my motor bike—I seemed to have a motor bike glued to my seat at all times in those days, just after the war—and Betty would come down from Katoomba to stay with her aunt, who lived opposite my friend. She later came to live with her aunt and worked in Sydney. She actually liked motor bikes and riding on them so I took her to the Sportsground on the back of my bike.

When I started midget racing later she wasn't able to complain too much because she already knew what it was all about. In fact, when I started my engineering shop I used to have her working on the lathe, making electric motor spindles by the hundred. I tried to make her as useful as possible! I even had her cleaning the midget and polishing it—it is incredible what women will do when they want to please a man!

Anyway, we eventually got married after a six-year courtship. At least by that time she must have known the kind of life she was letting herself in for.

My next car, and the one in which I began to make my name in road racing, was a Cooper Bristol, later to be known as the Redex Special. Of course, this car cost a lot of money—brand new it cost £A4,250 in Australia, which would have been far beyond my means. This particular car had been bought in England and shipped to Australia, but before it arrived the owner had committed suicide. The Cooper came up for sale in his estate, and my father and I, with promise of sponsorship from Redex, were able to buy it. We were lucky to get Redex to sponsor the car. This fact, however, caused a tremendous number of problems in Australia. The newly formed Confederation of Australian Motor Sport, CAMS, were just beginning to feel their feet and be strong in Australia, sportwise. Unfortunately, they were a very conservative body and helped to dampen the progress of the sport because of their attitude to advertising on race cars. Just because advertising hadn't yet started in England, they felt it shouldn't start in Australia! Of all the places which needed outside sponsorship for the sport, Australia was in the greatest need. Cars of this type were very expensive because they had to be imported from England. The only way people *could* afford to run this type of motor car was to get some sort of sponsorship, and this was frowned on by the ruling bodies. Every meeting of CAMS included an argument on this subject, and eventually they tried to stop me racing altogether. We were forced to take the words Redex Special off the side of the car, which was a great blow as far as I was concerned, because we lost our sponsorship over it.

This was one of the main reasons why I went off to New Zealand to race. I was so fed up with CAMS and their outlook and the way they were running the sport, that I went to

New Zealand in 1954. In January I raced in the first NZ International Grand Prix. By that time I was known nationally, as I had won the Queensland and New South Wales Road Racing titles in 1953, but I was not very friendly with officialdom. In any case, the New Zealand Grand Prix in January 1954 brought me into contact with international drivers like Tony Gaze, Peter Whitehead and Ken Wharton. I finished sixth.

During 1954 I also tried my hand at a Trial, which is, as its name implies, something of an endurance test rather than a rally. This was the Redex Trial, which took the contestants right round Australia through all kind of climate changes, over all kinds of terrain. It had a reputation for being a car-breaker, and so we found it.

I was driving a Holden for a General Motors dealer in Penshurst, and my co-driver was Harry Gapps, who was a mechanic from the dealership run by two brothers, Bruce and Alan Savell.

We drove to Darwin on reasonably good roads, but then we had to drive from Darwin to Hall's Creek, and Hall's Creek is way out in Western Australia. It took about thirty hours' driving to get there, we were supposed to average a certain speed as well; on top of these problems my co-driver got some sort of bug and was sick for the entire trip. Not only could he neither navigate nor drive, but he was of absolutely no assistance whatever on that particular section. So I drove thirty hours non-stop myself and fortunately lost no points. It was dusty and dirty as we were riding over dirt roads all the time.

At Hall's Creek there must have been more flies than anywhere else in the world; you couldn't even open your mouth without getting it full of flies. It was about 115 in the shade — you are way out in the desert there. I was staggered that anyone ever went to live there in the first place. This was a rest point where we had about six hours off, but there was very little to eat or drink. The only way we could get away from the flies was to light a fire — we had to do that to make a cup of tea anyway. So there we were, with the temperature 115 degrees in the shade, sitting as close to the fire as we could.

48

My first outing with the twin-cam Formula 2 Cooper at Goodwood, 1957.

The Kentish Trophy, Brands Hatch, 1958 – Mike Hawthorn hands it over to Stirling
Moss, supported by Rob Walker (left), with a little advice from me (right).

H. Drovetsky, Australian Consolidated Press

Going through Cottage Corner in the Cooper Monaco sports car, Aintree 1959.

My big shunt at Lisbon with the 2½-litre Cooper in the Portuguese Grand Prix, 1959.

My First Attempts at Motor Racing

The next stage was to Broome, which is on the west coast, from there down to Port Hedland, and on to a gold-mining town called Marble Bar, which consisted of about three houses, a pub and a general store. From there we were to drive over some difficult country to Meekatharra. We headed out of Marble Bar at night, following Tommy Sulman in a big Humber. We were supposed to be in front of him, and I was sitting fairly close on his bumper bar hoping to get the opportunity to pass him.

About twelve miles out of Marble Bar we came to a creek crossing which had no water in it whatsoever. It just had a sandy and rocky bottom. Suddenly this big Humber in front gave a great lurch and apparently his differential, or something underneath his car, had hit a big rock and hooked it right out of the ground, leaving it sitting in the middle of the creek bed ready for me. It was impossible to turn right or left without having a worse accident, because there was a drop on either side. So we hit this rock in the biggest possible way. It knocked the whole front assembly off the car—all the front wheel assembly, cross member, wheels and everything all hanging on to it. It not only knocked it off, but it all rolled back underneath the car, and the front wheels were underneath the front doors, which wasn't quite standard. We couldn't get out on one side because the wheels had the door jammed.

So there we were sitting in the creek bed with two wheels under the front doors and we realised we were blocking the whole Trial! Five or six cars soon arrived on the scene and they couldn't go past. We had to wait until sufficient manpower had arrived so that we could literally lift the whole car. We put people all round it, lifted it and carried it bodily to the end of the creek crossing, which must have been twenty-five yards or more, and they just dumped the car on the side of the road. Then all the people got back into their own cars and drove off. So there we were, all on our own.

It was twelve miles from Marble Bar and the middle of the night. There was nothing we could do till daylight, if at all, so we went to sleep in the car, still on our own; nobody worried about us or came looking or anything like that. The next morning we got out and looked at the damage, and it was obvious that there was no way we could possibly fix this thing without big, major workshop repairs. We sat for some time wondering what on earth to do. No one came by – the trials cars had all gone through and it was not a much-frequented part of the world. I decided I had better walk the twelve miles across the desert to Marble Bar and try to get some help. So, like an idiot, I left Harry in the car and set off.

After five or six miles the buzzards were starting to circle round overhead waiting for me to fall down. The sun was so hot it was unbearable, and I could see mirages everywhere. I reckoned I would definitely have expired somewhere on the way to Marble Bar if I'd gone on walking. Luckily, in the distance I saw a little ball of dust coming towards me, and it turned out to be the first car that had come that way for about twelve hours. Anyway, this car arrived on the scene and there was I walking along in the middle of the desert where you could see for miles in both directions, and the occupants were a bit curious about me.

As chance would have it, it was a Trial car. They had had trouble further back and had got themselves going again. It was a Ford from Perth, with four people in it. They were finished with the Trial and were calling it a day and motoring back to Perth. They stopped and looked at me, then looked in both directions to see where my car was, and wondered how on earth I came to be standing out there thumbing a ride. They were going in the opposite direction anyway.

I explained what had happened and they decided they couldn't leave me in the desert for the buzzards, so they drove me into Marble Bar, left me there, and went back on their way to Perth. After walking around Marble Bar looking for someone to talk to, I eventually found a local garage which was just a little tin shed with an old model car in pieces inside it but nobody working on it.

While I was trying to find the somebody who might have been working on this car in this little tin shed, a jeep pulled up outside. The driver was a chap who worked for the Blue Speck goldmines and he had come into town to get something or other to take out to the goldmine. Of course, I started chatting to him and telling him what had happened to us in the Trial and where the car was and asking how we could get a message to someone on the other side of Australia, which all seemed pretty difficult. As I explained, there was nothing much in Marble Bar. He convinced me I was wasting my time walking around the place, because nobody there was going to help me. I was under the impression that if I could get some oxygen bottles and some means of welding, we might get our car back together again. We both drove off to the goldmine which was a few miles out because he said they had a set of oxy bottles there. When we arrived I found that these oxy bottles were about three times the normal size — they were around eight feet tall. I shall never forget these two bottles standing there, towering over us.

Near one of the mine shafts there was a scrap heap of old bits of steel. I went fossicking all through this to see if I could find some stuff to make sub-frames and I got together all the bits and pieces of metal I could find that might help. I also collected a welding rod and these oxy bottles, which we put in the miner's jeep and then drove back to the car.

That evening I arrived back with these oxy bottles and everything. We had already decided we would have a go at fixing the Holden as soon as possible. On the way out there this chap in the jeep had said: 'You don't want to worry about it. We have all sorts of troubles like this out here in the Bush. I will give you a hand and we will probably get it fixed in an hour and you will be on your way.' Of course, when he arrived there and took one look at the car he said: 'Well, er — um — er, I have to go, actually!' And added: 'You *are* in trouble, aren't you?' Very helpful.

My co-driver had been sitting in the car all day trying to keep cool. It was in the rules of the Trial that we had to take enough provisions with us to last us for seven days if we were in a jam. They checked at control that you did have these provisions on board for sure, because situations like this could happen to anyone and you could be stuck for days. We looked like being at the creek crossing for days, too.

We had a look around the car just before dark, and started

to get a few things ready so that we could start work early the next morning. Not long after sunrise we got the car jacked up, removed the wheels from underneath the doors and put them approximately where they should be. We found that the sub-frame which holds the engine had gone back about nine inches, and the radiator was pulled back around the front of the engine and looked like a banana. We happened to have a spare radiator with us in the boot, so we took the old one off and put the new one in a place where it would miss the fan, then found there was nothing to support it for about 8 inches because the sub-frame wasn't there any more!

So we had to make a sub-frame to support the radiator, and then we had to make brackets down from the sub-frame which was all bent upwards, and try to weld the front cross member and wheels in a place I thought they ought to be by sighting them up against a tree stump! All the metal that I had brought from the goldmine was very useful, and we actually had a hacksaw and a big hammer and other odds and ends on board. We worked for five or six hours on this and eventually got a pair of front wheels on it that we thought would carry the car, and then we started hooking all the steering up and found that the ball joint had literally been pulled right out. We took a long time wondering how to put that ball joint on and have it stay there.

Away in the distance we could see a fence, which looked as if it were made of good, strong wire. So we took a pair of wire cutters, walked as far as the fence, and snipped some pieces of wire out of it. Then we went back and tied the ball joint on with wire — made a nice job of lacing it all together.

At about four o'clock in the afternoon, when the heat was terrific and I was sweating away welding underneath the car, my co-driver shouted: 'Hey! There's somebody coming.' This was the second car that had come by in two days. The place was getting really busy.

It was another jeep. The chap in it had been up north somewhere buying horses and was now on his way home. He had a big ranch about fifty or sixty miles from where we were, just off the main road — or what we called a main road, really a dirt track—and he pulled up, looked out and said: 'Geez! You boys seem to be in trouble.' An understatement. He walked over to look at what we were doing, and we explained about the accident with the rock. While we were talking he stood there gazing at those oxy bottles which stood about three feet above the car; he was completely mystified, and at last he couldn't resist it any longer, he had to ask, 'Excuse me,' he said, 'but how did those bottles get there? I can't see any way you could put them in the car.' So we explained patiently about the other chap with the jeep who had left them with us, and I said: 'Now you are here, maybe you can help us with a problem. This other chap is coming back in two days time, to see how we are getting on and to pick up the oxy bottles. And we are almost ready to move out.' We had got the car fixed in about eight hours, altogether, and we planned to get it rolling in the next half hour.

Well, he knew this chap from the goldmine, whose name was Kennedy, and he said he'd wait until we'd finished welding and take the bottles to a pub which was on the road Kennedy would have to take to get back to us. He said he'd leave them on the verandah of this pub, and he knew there was no way Kennedy was going to drive past that pub!

So that was what he did and he also asked us to call at his ranch on our way by. We crept off in the 'repaired' car at about 10 mph, wondering whether the wheels were going to stay with us or not, and it seemed to keep going all right. They weren't aligned, of course, not within a foot, but they made us mobile, at least. But there were terrible noises coming from the engine. What had happened was that the sump was all pushed in at the bottom, and the con rods were hitting the sump. We had to stop, take off the sump, straighten it out with a great big hammer, and put it back on again. Then we found that the whole sump was warped and twisted and we couldn't get it sealed against the block. Oil was leaking out between the sump and the engine, so there was a terrible leak which we couldn't do anything about. We did thirty or forty miles before we came to the pub the ranch owner had spoken about, and we ran out of oil twice on the way. We had

53

some oil with us in the car, but we were obviously going to need a whole lot more. We bought up as much as they had at this pub, five or six gallons, put it in the back, and every twenty or thirty miles we had to top up with oil again.

We were glad to get to this chap's ranch—or station, as we call them in Australia. His was a sheep station. They were expecting us and had killed a sheep in our honour. His wife was a real country woman, accepted us filthy, oily creatures with open arms, and cooked us an enormous dinner. That was the first proper meal we'd had in days.

We headed off that evening, after the heat had subsided, and started creeping down towards Perth, which was 1,000 miles from where we shunted. Exactly 500 miles from Perth, just halfway, was a place called Meekatharra. That was the only reasonable town, in fact the only place at all, between where we shunted and Perth. The steering broke three or four times at least on that journey, and we ran right out of oil before we reached Meekatharra. We could see the town, actually, about fifteen miles away in the distance, but we weren't able to go any further. We sat by the edge of the road for three or four hours, until eventually someone drove out of the town towards us and we flagged them down. As luck would have it they had a quart tin of oil in the back, so we bought this, poured it in and staggered into Meekatharra with the oil light flashing as it ran out again.

Once we were into the town there were several places where we could buy oil, but we reckoned we couldn't go on the other 500 miles with the car in this condition, and we'd better do something about it. The thing we needed most was a new sump, but there were plenty of other things we could do with —the fan belt had chewed itself up because it was all out of line, the radiator was leaking where the brackets supporting it were not good enough and had pulled the tank off the bottom of it, and we'd been pouring in 'Barr's Leaks' and stuff trying to keep it going. So we decided to stop in Meekatharra and see how we could improve the condition of the Holden.

By now four or five days had gone by since we crashed, and nobody in Australia knew where we were. Apparently ll sorts of messages were flying about, but as far as the people at home knew we had just plain gone missing, and the Trial was almost over. At least Meekatharra was a reasonable sort of town with a telephone and a few mod cons like that, and after waiting an hour we eventually got a call through to Sydney. My father was on the other end and he nearly came through the line! Where were we, where had we been, were we all right, why didn't we let them know, and so on. We told him all the dramas and that we would be in Meekatharra for a day or two to repair the car so that we could drive it the last 500 miles to Perth. We arranged to meet him at the General Motors dealership in Perth where we would have to get the car properly repaired. He said he would get to Meekatharra if he could, and hung up.

We took the car apart and had a good look at it. The engine was pretty sick; it had lost a lot of power and there was a lot of blow-by in the sump, which didn't help things. We rang the General Motors dealership and found they had had spies out everywhere trying to find where the hell we had been for the last week. They were quite pleased to hear from us and agreed to put a new sump and some other spares we needed on a plane and, in fact, they just managed to catch the one that was leaving the same day; so we received these bits in the evening. We got the new sump on and did a lot of other repairs and then found that one of the wishbones had cracked and was just about to fall off completely while we were working on the car. We couldn't go on with it in that state, so we rang Perth again. They agreed to put a new wishbone on a plane, but there wasn't another flight due in for another day. By that time I had taken the wishbone off and welded it all up and reckoned it was good enough. So we decided to be on our way.

We got the car all loaded up and ready to go, started it up and drove it round the block—and found it wasn't running properly. The spark plugs were starting to foul up, and we couldn't get it firing on six cylinders. We wasted the rest of the day trying to make it run better. By that time the plane was due in a couple of hours, so it seemed sensible to wait for it. Apart from the wishbone there were other things we might need coming with it. We drove out to the airport—just a little grass strip, really—and the aeroplane landed, the door opened and out stepped my father. If we hadn't waited for the bits and pieces Pop would have arrived in Meekatharra and found us gone.

Now Pop became the third member of the crew and we drove down to Perth. Those 500 miles were reasonably good, but bumpy, and the car was still getting through a lot of oil. It wasn't leaking, but the engine was obviously burning more oil than it should. The air cleaner was pretty bad, too. It had been knocked about in the shunt, so didn't fit properly, and must have been leaking round the element. All the dust and grit from the roads had been going through the engine and wearing it pretty badly.

We arrived in Perth all right and went straight to the General Motors workshops. We stayed there three days and renewed the whole front of the car from the doors forward. We put new cross-members in it, and a new radiator, and had the mudguards repaired. We replaced all the under-gear, the sub-frame, the suspension, the brakes and the steering. We took the engine out and took the head off it; we still had another 2,500 miles to go to Sydney. The bores were actually worn 19 thou, so obviously it wasn't possible to do much with *that*. And it would have been a bit much to ask them to supply us with a new engine. What we did was go out to their reconditioning shop and find a block that was reasonably good, only about 6 thou wear on it. We took that, but used the original pistons, put in new rings and bearings, a new sump and gaskets, made it all nice and oil-tight and put it back together again. It ran like a charm, like a newey. We drove out of there truly as though it were a new car.

Pop had decided that the trip from Meekatharra to Perth over all those bush tracks was about enough for him, so he said he would fly the 1,500 miles to Adelaide and wait for us there. (We had relatives in Adelaide and knew where to look for him.) We had a pretty trouble-free run right across to Adelaide, picked up Pop and drove back to Sydney. We arrived there about two weeks after the Trial had finished!

I thought the Savell boys would be livid when I got back,

but they were tickled to death. They'd had a report from the dealership in Perth as to the condition of the car when they first saw it, and told them what had been done to it to give it that extra 1,000 miles into Perth. They reckoned it was a pretty good sort of feat. They were quite pleased to see the car get back at all, and when we returned it to them it was in reasonable condition, because we had renewed virtually the whole of the front of it.

I enjoyed all of that trip, really. It was a good experience — it was a challenge. But I haven't been on a Trial since.

Apart from that excursion, I really concentrated on road racing from 1953 onwards.

I raced the Cooper Bristol for two years in Australia quite successfully, at circuits near Surfer's Paradise in Queensland, Mount Druitt, Orange, and a couple of circuits in Victoria. Then it was time to go to New Zealand once more, and in January 1955 I competed in the second NZ Grand Prix. This time Prince Bira arrived with the 250 Maserati, and won it.

At that meeting I met two people from England who were to be very important to me — Dick Jeffrey, who had just taken over the Dunlop competition side, and Dean Delamont of the RAC, who eventually convinced me that I should come to Europe. We sat in a car practically all night talking about it. We had been to a party at the house of Reg Greason, one of the organisers, and I had a car in New Zealand that I had borrowed for the trip, so I offered to drive Dean back to his hotel. And there we sat, outside the hotel, while Dean answered my many questions. He didn't bat an eyelid at being kept up all night, and painted a very rosy picture of racing in England. Being young and enthusiastic, I was carried away. When I went back to Australia, I had made up my mind that I wanted to race in Europe, at least for a year, to see if I could be competitive among the world's top drivers. Little did I know what I was really up against — I was very gullible and very much out of my depth. But I soon learned!

CHAPTER IV

The Raw Recruit

I came to England on my own early in 1955. I didn't bring
Betty or Geoffrey, who was only a toddler then, because I
was going out into the great unknown and before I sent
for the family I wanted to make sure I was doing the right
thing. Betty flew over to join me later in the year.

I made my first big mistake before I had even left Australia. I thought that the Cooper Bristol couldn't possibly
be competitive in England, where I imagined everything to
be very professional and racing to be of a far higher standard
than at home. So I sold the Cooper Bristol to Stan Jones in
Australia, and bought a Cooper Alta from Peter Whitehead
while we were in New Zealand. I'd never even seen the car,
but it had a twin-cam engine and all the rest of it, and I was
sure it had to be better than the 2-litre Bristol. When I got
to England I realised how wrong I had been. The Cooper Alta
wouldn't keep running for more than five minutes.

The first race meeting I attended in England was at Goodwood—the Easter meeting. I went off to do my first deal in
motor racing in Europe—with John Morgan, of the BARC.
The deal he offered me was double what I expected. I didn't
admit this to him, but I know I was very appreciative. In
Australia they paid a driver scarcely enough to cover his
travelling expenses.

At that meeting I had my first opportunity to display my
talent for running out of fuel. I had a few problems *getting*
it in the first place. I went into one of the fuel tents and asked
for some petrol for the car. They told me that unless I had
a contract I couldn't have any; 'I don't want a contract,'

said. 'I simply want to buy some fuel to go racing!' Apparently that was not on.

So I wandered in to see old Reg Tanner of Esso, and he helped me. I worked out on paper how much fuel I needed, but I missed out by two gallons. Sure enough, with three laps left to go I coasted into the pits with a dry tank, and then couldn't get the engine to start again.

I received my first big mention in the motoring magazines after that meeting. Gregor Grant of *Autosport* was particularly kind, and mentioned 'the Australian's spectacular cornering giving the crowd a thrill'. He went on to say: 'This Aussie is certainly a presser-onner, and possesses remarkable control over his car. More will be heard of this young gentleman.'

Well, there wasn't much to write about after my second meeting, at Ibsley three weeks later. I was running fourth — Salvadori was leading — when on the penultimate lap the engine expired. It was obvious that it was a waste of time pressing on with that engine, so I went to Bristol, bought an engine from the Bristol people, and fitted it into the chassis.

I had been working on the car at Peter Whitehead's place at Chalfont St Peter, but now I moved down to Saltdean, near Brighton, where Bob Chase had a big garage. He let me work there for a few months while I installed the Bristol engine, and took the Alta back to Geoffrey Taylor in Surbiton. He was the man who made the engine, and I hoped they would be able to put it back together. They did, eventually, come up with the engine completely modified, using a new type of cylinder block, but it was too late to use it again that season. I took it back to Australia with me at the end of the year and sold it.

At some time between Goodwood and Ibsley I met John Cooper and established a friendship which was to last to this day. One of the first experiences I had in which John was involved, and which shows how helpful he was to me, was when I drove the Cooper transporter down to Goodwood. I was supposed to go down to try out his first rear-engined car with a Coventry Climax engine. I don't know what happened to the regular transporter driver, but I know I was elected to drive it, and I went belting off down the road from

59

Dorking towards Goodwood. In the distance every now and
then I heard bells ringing. 'Gee!' I thought, 'I didn't know
they had bell birds in England.' After quite some time
had a really good look in my rear view mirror and there
was a police car trying to overtake me. I finally got the message—they had bells on the front of the police car. I had
never seen one with bells on it, they don't have them in
Australia.

So I ground to a halt, the police got out of their car and
wanted to know my name and address and to see my licence
I gave my address as care of the Cooper Car Company, 24
Ewell Road, Surbiton, so it wasn't too long before a big
official letter turned up at Coopers. John couldn't wait to
ring me up and say: 'Your bluey has arrived. What are we
going to do?'

'I don't know,' I said. 'What is the form in this country?'

John thought quickly, and came up with an idea: 'I tel
you what is the best thing,' he said. 'I'll just write on the back
of the envelope that Mr Brabham has returned to Australia
and his forwarding address is unknown.'

He did this and posted the letter back to the police and
I've never heard a thing since. I hope I won't now! But that
was typical of John. I suppose I began to know him really
well around the time the changeover took place from 500 cc
racing to the 1100 cc sports car with that first Climax engine
This particular car was very successful, and I tried to convince
John we could make a racing car out of one of these sport
cars; I started to work for Coopers about halfway through
1955. I wasn't exactly employed by them—I wasn't paid any
money by them—I just worked there fiddling around with
their cars in any way I could. I eventually twisted John's arm
into letting me build a sports car with a Bristol engine in the
back. I was still based at Bob Chase's garage then, and that
was when Betty came over. We stayed with Peter Morrice
one of Bob's mechanics, for a couple of weeks and then
moved to a flat in Surbiton. It was in Ewell Road, and we had
the upstairs flat in the house of a Mrs Stott.

At the International Trophy race, according to *Autosport*
I apparently gave the spectators 'good value' with my fast

cornering in the Cooper Bristol, and I finished seventh. I remember that I felt pleased simply to be driving with people like Moss, Hawthorn, Collins, Salvadori, Prince Bira, Jack Fairman and others who had, only four months earlier, been just names to me. And the cars — Maseratis, Vanwalls, Connaughts, Ferraris — it didn't matter too much that I started from the back of the grid!

I think it was around this time that the 'Kangaroo' Team, six Australians with DB3S Aston Martins, was formed and first raced. Tony Gaze, Dick Cobden, Les Cosh, Tommy Sulman, David McKay and myself went to Hyères for the 12-hour race and collected second, third and fourth places. The Ferrari that won blew up on its lap of honour. It was a good start for a team that consisted of a dentist, a stockbroker, a journalist and three oddly assorted racing drivers. Unfortunately, that was my first and last race with the Kangaroos, and the Team itself, which looked so promising at Hyères, was not to last very long because the Le Mans disaster of 1955 put a stop to many meetings in which they were entered. That was my first experience of driving in a team of any kind.

The next time was as a reserve driver for the Bristol team at Le Mans. That first encounter with Le Mans should have been enough to put me off for the rest of my life. It started, for me, with the team forgetting all about me until fog was coming down on the Mulsanne Straight and it was getting dark. Then I was sent out, never having driven on a race track with headlights before. I didn't like it much, and it was just as well I was not needed for the race, because 1955 was the year of the Le Mans disaster. That is the kind of event that it is best to try to forget.

We were by then working seriously on the rear-engined Cooper Bristol, and we managed to get it finished the night before the British Grand Prix, which was run at Aintree that year. We rushed the car off, virtually half-finished, to try to compete. Unfortunately on the morning of the race the clutch packed up, and I had to start the race without a clutch. Eventually I think the engine overheated and expired a few laps from the end. Stirling Moss won the race in a Mercedes-

Benz and Fangio was second. In fact, Mercedes took the first four places!

Anyway, that was the first time the new car was run. We got it working properly again and I went to Snetterton for the Formula 1 race a few weeks later. It rained, as it often does in August in England. The Vanwalls of Harry Schell and Ken Wharton were way out in front, but I had a marvellous battle for third place with Stirling Moss and his 250 Maserati. They called it 'a classic contest' in the motoring papers, and it was certainly a landmark for me. If it hadn't been for that race I might have gone back to Australia for good. I remember I fairly threw that car about on the wet track, passing and being passed by Stirling, and then re-passing him. We raced in very close company for about sixteen laps, then the track started to dry and with four laps to go I spun off when in front of Stirling, collecting a lot of grass and straw; I went on to try to catch Stirling again, but it was too late. I finished fourth. The car went well in that race, and I felt *I* had gone quite well. So I decided it would be worth coming back to England the following year. We put the car on the boat and sent it back to Australia, and in November I took it to South Australia and won the Australian Grand Prix. I sold it while I was out there, and the profit I made from selling the car financed my trip back to England the following year.

The fact that I thought the 250 Maser was the best car around led me to make my second big mistake in buying cars. I was carried away by having a few pounds in my pocket, and started negotiating with Ken Gregory to buy Stirling's Maserati while I was still in Australia. When I reached England early in 1956 the deal was almost complete. It had reached the stage where I was just about to hand over the money, so I went up to Tring to see the car. The Maserati had raced the previous year with Dunlop disc brakes, and they were the first disc brakes I had ever seen. When I reached Tring I found they had been taken off and the original drum brakes and wire wheels had been put back on the car. This upset me considerably, and eventually Ken and I fell out over it and I didn't buy the car. This was a pity, because

The Raw Recruit

I'm sure I would have been better off with that car. In fact, I'd have been better off if I hadn't bought a 250 Maserati at all. But I thought at that time that if I was going to get anywhere in motor racing I simply had to have one. Little did I know what I was in for.

Somebody mentioned that BRM had one to sell—the ex-Collins 1955 car. So I went to Bourne and ended up buying it. It was in a terrible state. Of course, it looked very nice in the workshop and there wasn't time to try it. I was pretty dim in those days. But the biggest drama was to come. Apparently the car had not had Purchase Tax paid on it, and in those days it was about twice what the car was worth. I took delivery of the car and was told it wasn't possible for me to drive it in this country—first it would have to be exported and brought back in again!

I had a transporter by this time, an old Commer; I loaded it up with the Maserati and the bits and pieces, drove down to Newhaven, and exported it to the Channel Islands. This complicated process was the only way it could be done. The paper work on which BRM had temporarily imported it into England had to be cancelled, and the only way to do that was to export the car.

I shall never forget that day. It was so foggy you could only see a few yards, and as we neared the Channel Islands I saw some rocks looming out of the mist within what seemed to be touching distance of the boat. That really scared me. We did eventually land at a wharf, but I never saw the Channel Islands. The car had to be transferred to another boat that was leaving within an hour, so it was taken off and wheeled across the wharf to where the second boat was tied up. It was so foggy I never even saw the end of the wharf. But we got it back to Newhaven.

As they lifted the car out of the hold, the sling slipped and started to come off a rear wheel. I was up on deck watching the unloading, and as the Maser swung across at least 60 feet above the wharf my heart stopped beating and my blood stopped circulating. I just stood there petrified waiting to see my car drop out of the sling and come crashing to the ground. Later I wished it *had*, because it was insured and would, on the whole, have been of more value to me in a tangled heap.

I drove it away on the import side, and from then on I could drive it in England. I finished third in the Aintree 200, but I think that was the *only* race I ever finished in that car. It was in such a bad condition that I could have spent all the year repairing it. At the *Daily Express* Silverstone meeting in May, my first race in the ex-BRM car, I had the unpleasant experience of being black-flagged for an oil leak. It had been smoking for some time, and I came into the pits once, but went out again until I saw this ominous black flag being hung out for me. The only successes I was having were with the Cooper sports car, and Formula 1 seemed as hopeless as ever. So I decided the only thing to do was to take the engine back to Maserati's to fix.

I didn't get away to Italy until after the British Grand Prix, which was won by Fangio in his Ferrari. I sent the engine to Maserati's, and I went across to Germany by plane and bought a 1500 Borgward Combi which Betty and I picked up, with our son Geoffrey, and drove on down to Modena. We arrived there on the date when the engine was supposed to be ready, and it was. But the price, which had been estimated in advance, turned out to be much more, and took virtually every penny we had with us. We loaded up the engine, but had a pretty thin time on the way home. Luckily we had our tickets booked on the ferry, but our great worry was whether we could afford enough petrol to get to the coast.

We drove back to the ferry living on a loaf of bread or two, and that was it. Time was tight because money was tight, and we very nearly had a big accident as we neared the coast. I was belting down one of those narrow French roads when the biggest truck I ever saw pulled out of a side turning on the right. He saw me, but just kept on going. I learned later that the idea in France is that you have to give way to the man on your right, but it was no time to be learning things at that stage. I had this Maserati engine in the back of the Combi, and if I had hit him we would have been killed for sure, because the engine would have just squashed us against the truck. So I had to put my foot on the gas and try to beat the truck from cutting me off. I went up on the kerb and over the top of a bank and round the front of this truck, missing everything by inches, coming down on the road on the other side, not having hit anything, and continuing.

We got to the coast in time for the four o'clock boat — the *Lord Warden*. We had to search for the docks in the thick fog, and we got lost more than once. The boat was just about to move out when we got there, but we were lucky to be one of the last five or six cars on. I remember walking round the decks wondering how on earth this boat was going to find England when you couldn't see more than 100 yards.

We worked out that we had just about enough money left for a bowl of soup in the restaurant, so we went and ordered some. I had just finished mine, and the boat had only been going about an hour when all the engines stopped. I remember looking across at Betty and saying: 'Crikey, I don't like this. Why have the engines stopped in the middle of the Channel?' I stood up and went over to a window, but I couldn't see a thing except fog. It was incredibly thick. The next moment the engines went into reverse, and I felt even more uneasy. I had just reached our table but before I could sit down we had run straight into the side of another boat. I went sprawling across the table and the noise . . . ! We were right next to the kitchen, and every plate, cup and saucer came crashing to the ground. Everybody was lying on the floor, bowls of soup, roast beef and what-not on top of them, women were screaming . . . you've never seen such a mess. The impact had pushed the front of the boat back about sixteen feet, and I thought there was no way the boat could stay afloat. The crew were rushing around trying to pacify the passengers, so I slipped round the back of everyone with the family and up onto the deck. We could see the outline of a boat drifting away from us in the fog — a boat about twice our size. Of course within seconds it had disappeared and we never, ever saw it again. I don't know the name of it, but I found out later that it had its engine room flooded and was forced to go aground near Dunkirk. It actually had to be towed aground because it was sinking.

I was beginning to think we had better look for some

65

lifeboats when I suddenly remembered that the Maserati engine and the Borgward, on which we had spent our last penny, were down in the bottom of the boat. I could then picture the thing· in a great big heap stuck up the front of the boat. I thought: 'My God, this is really the end!' I wanted to go down and look at the car, but of course the crew wouldn't let us go down. They didn't allow us to move around the boat or do anything until they knew how much damage had been done. Passengers weren't allowed below until we reached England.

I was ready to jump overboard with frustration, when some man came staggering up from the bottom deck and I nailed him as he came through the door. Luckily, his car was right behind ours, and he gave me a good idea of what to expect. The damage wasn't too bad. He had got himself a flat tyre as he came aboard, and he was down there changing his wheel. ·It was an old car which had a wheel bolted on at the back of the car, and he had the car jacked up, had gone round to the back to take the spare wheel off, walked round the side again and was just about to put the wheel on when the crash came. It was pretty lucky he wasn't actually between the cars because when the boats collided his car came off the jack and all the cars hit one another pretty hard.

There was a big performance at Dover while they wrote down all the damage to the cars. Ours wasn't too bad—both bumpers stove in, and things like that. As it happened, I never competed in the Maser again anyway, mainly because we couldn't afford to at the time. Financially I was in terrible trouble, and there was no way that I could afford to take the car to a meeting, let alone take the risk of blowing it up again or crunching it. And that is when I first started driving for John Cooper in works sports cars.

The new Formula 2 Cooper had already won its first race, in the same programme as the British Grand Prix at Silverstone, beating the hitherto almost unbeatable Colin Chapman in his Lotus, and being the only true Formula 2 car in the race. It had been designed with the 1957 1½-litre Formula in mind, using a 1460 cc Coventry Climax fire-pump engine.

The Raw Recruit

At the August Bank Holiday meeting at Brands in drenching rain, I competed first of all in a sports car event, two heats and a final, and had a great dice with Mike Hawthorn in the first heat, and with Reg Bicknell in the final. I was second both times in my Cooper Climax, while Roy Salvadori, with whom I now came into close contact as he was the regular number one for Coopers, crashed his and broke two ribs. Driving in a lot of pain, he won the Formula 2 race, was third in the first part of the Formula Libre event, and was then taken to hospital. I was put in the car for the Formula Libre final, and finished third. I found it a very good car to drive.

We took two Formula 2 cars to the Berlin Grand Prix at Avus, which is a very fast circuit with a steep banking. Richard von Frankenberg had the most horrifying-looking accident when his Porsche went straight off at the top of the banking; he wrote off the car, which caught fire, and fractured his skull. It is surprising anyone could survive going over the top there, but he was lucky. We were not very competitive because of fuel problems, but we came home fifth and sixth; I led Roy for a change.

We went next to Oulton Park for the Gold Cup and here we had a rather good meeting. Tony Brooks, Roy Salvadori and I were on the front row in our Coopers with Colin Chapman in his Lotus 11 Le Mans. Tony's car was entered by Rob Walker. Salvadori went ahead and pulled out a big lead, while Tony and I duelled for second place. Right in the thick of the battle I had a fuel pump lead come adrift and by the time that was put right I had lost 4 minutes. But we carried off the Team Prize and Roy won the Gold Cup, so Charles and John Cooper were very happy. I suppose that was the beginning, really, of the great days that were to come for the company later.

At Imola, in a sports car, I finished second to Castellotti. Roy and Castellotti were having a big dice and Roy's engine blew up for some reason. It was at that race that I first met Jo Bonnier who was having his first drive in a works Maserati sports car. When Roy dropped out Jo was on my tail and we worked up a really good struggle for second place. About four or five laps from the end I remember coming round towards the finishing line and there was a car that we were lapping for the second or third time, right in the middle of the road. I was still leading Jo by about a car's length, so I went round the outside of this chap on the right; he pulled over to the left and shunted Jo straight off the road. That was one of the most monumental shunts I have ever seen! I remember watching it in the rear view mirror. Jo finished up against a telegraph post and I thought no one could survive a crash like that. I went on to finish second, and Jo was all right, thank goodness.

Incidentally, at that meeting I got my first taste of what life might be like as a Cooper works driver. They had taken a third car down to Imola for another Australian called Alan McKay to drive, and at the end of practice his gearbox broke. We were using Citroen gearboxes at the time which were pretty weedy and I had to work all night getting this car going again. The gearbox was split and I had to weld it up, repair all the gears, and put it back together. The crown wheel and pinion had gone as well. So I worked virtually all night and didn't go to bed at all. In the morning John came down and the car was just about complete and everyone wanted to get to the circuit. My car hadn't even been looked at. By the time we started the race I was ready for bed, and I had just begun to realise how much hard work motor racing could be.

At Brands Hatch, in October, there was a Formula 1 race which was won by Archie Scott-Brown driving a Connaught, and a Formula 2 race in which I drove the Cooper against Tony Brooks's Rob Walker car. I did fastest lap, but I was put out of the race after only eleven laps because a piston went. However, my fastest lap was a new Formula 2 record, and I think people were beginning to take me a bit more seriously, at last.

When I first came over there were a lot of jokes made about my style of driving and the way I hung out the tail of the car rather like a midget racer on a cinder track. And being a fairly silent Australian, I came in for some good-humoured banter from John Cooper, who used to pretend to strangers that I had just emerged from the bush and didn't even know how to hold a knife and fork! I went along with all this, and got a lot of laughs out of it. The British didn't seem to know much about Australia, except that the inhabitants were all descendants of convicts. That is right, of course, but what used to worry *me* was that I was back in the country where they all came from! But seriously, by the end of 1956 I felt that I was quite at home here, and that I had perhaps made enough of a mark on the racing scene to come back for another year.

I had the old Maserati running again long before the end of the European season, but I didn't race it because I didn't want to spoil my chances of getting into the Cooper works team the following year. At the end of 1956, in fact, I made a deal with John that I *could* drive in the team *if* I came back from the 'down-under' series. That was another time of decision — should I go on racing or not? Going on meant that I would be committed to trying to get to the top, to reach the heights where Moss and Fangio and Hawthorn and Collins belonged. I didn't know if I could do it, but before I left for Australia I decided that I would, indeed, be back and have a go!

CHAPTER V

The Race to the Top

I didn't compete in the 1956 Australian Grand Prix at Melbourne, having sent my car direct to New Zealand, but I won the Argus Trophy Race for Sports Cars in the Cooper Climax after an exciting race, and then watched Moss show everyone else how to go Formula 1 racing in his Maserati; He won the Grand Prix easily. Then we had an inaugural meeting at a new circuit on Philip Island, which had taken many years of perseverance on the part of a band of enthusiasts to become reality. I drove my 1½-litre Cooper Climax sports car in both events on that gloriously sunny summer's day in mid-December, and won them both. So I enjoyed my Christmas.

I had already made an entry for the New Zealand Grand Prix and was supposed to drive my Maserati. However, John Cooper had made it clear that he would like me to use both the Coopers I had taken over and then sell them afterwards. So when I got to New Zealand I had to go and see the organisers and try to persuade them to let me use the Formula 2 Cooper instead of the Maser. I succeeded.

It was at this meeting that I first came to know Bruce McLaren; I was introduced to Bruce and his father by Geoff Wiles, the New Zealand Redex top man, as a matter of fact. I was looking after the cars in Geoff Wiles's back garden, and Bruce's father brought this young lad around and introduced him to me. Bruce was a very keen youngster who read all the right books and probably knew more about engineering and racing cars than I did. I shall always remember how enthusiastic Bruce was, looking at the Coopers and talking about them. At the end of the season Mr McLaren bought the single-seater sports car from me, and Bruce drove it with great success after I left—when the New Zealand series was finished. We raced all through New Zealand, of course, at Christchurch and Dunedin and Ardmore.

I also met Phil Kerr for the first time on that trip. Phil was a keen trials man and used to drive a Ford Zephyr in competitions. He used to talk of coming to England one day, and it was a bit of a toss-up between him and Bruce as to who should have the 'Driver to Europe' award in 1958. When Phil *did* come, he became the manager of my Chessington garage and my racing manager.

The worst thing that happened in New Zealand during that 1956-7 racing season was the death of Ken Wharton. I had known and admired him for a long time, and I was right behind him at Ardmore when he went off the road and was thrown out of the car, a Ferrari. Ken had made fastest practice time for the Formula 1 race in his Maserati, but before the Grand Prix there was a saloon car race and then one for the sports cars—Ken led this from the start with me hanging on behind him. We stayed close together until, on lap 18, he went into a corner particularly fast, went inside the marker bales, hit a barrier, and shot up into the air. Ken was flung out but died of his injuries. The accident looked bad and I found it quite difficult to go on to win, but there was nothing else to do but carry on driving. It cast a gloom over the Grand Prix, which was won by Reg Parnell in a Ferrari. I was tenth in the Formula 2 Cooper after innumerable heating troubles and pit stops.

The Ferraris were the stars of the season. They were 3½-litre, sports-engined, Super Squalo cars especially contrived for Formula Libre events such as this. Reg Parnell and Peter Whitehead cleaned up between them that year. At Christchurch Peter Whitehead won for the third successive year and I was second, ahead of a 4½-litre Ferrari. That little Cooper was a great car, and the sports car won again as well. Both Coopers certainly impressed the locals, and we sold them a great many similar cars during the following years.

Reg Parnell, who had announced that he was to retire from

driving after the New Zealand races and become Aston Martin Team Manager, won at Dunedin and I was second, twenty seconds behind. I kept up with him until I had to take to an escape road (!) and was unable to catch Reg again. Dunedin is a round-the-houses circuit, very tight and only 1.7 miles long.

Early in March 1957 we had to go to Western Australia for yet another Australian Grand Prix because they had fixed the '57 date for March. This was a bit disconcerting because we had only run the last one less than three months before. I finished third in the Formula 2 Cooper, while our Australian ace, Stan Jones, won in a Grand Prix Maserati from another Aussie, Lex Davison in a Ferrari. Several days later the decision was reversed and Davison was declared the winner with Stan second. The race was run in terribly hot weather and, as the road had recently been resurfaced, there was a lot of grit about. And to add to the confusion, the tubular steel pits blew over—twice! After all that it wasn't surprising that I was quite looking forward to getting back to Europe. In fact, when Rob Walker sent me a telegram suggesting I should meet him in Syracuse and that there would be a car there ready for me to drive, I jumped at the chance. All I had to do was present myself on a certain day for practice. This all sounded great, so I got on a plane from Sydney and landed in Rome, where, for some reason, the plane to Syracuse was cancelled. There were several people I knew standing about at the airport, Harry Schell (then a BRM driver), and Alan Brinton, the motoring journalist, among them. We decided that the best way to get to Syracuse was to go by train, so we dived into a taxi and went back into Rome, to the railway station. We booked tickets down to Sicily, and I took a sleeper because it was a long trip.

We took off all right, and during the night the train came to a halt at a station. I remember looking out of the window where there was a light shining on a sign—it was in Italian, so I don't really know what it said. Anyway, I went off to sleep again, and in the morning the sun was beaming in through the window. I looked outside—and there was the same sign still hanging there!

The Race to the Top

I couldn't believe it at first. There were people walking up and down the platform, and there was Harry Schell rushing up and down and waving his arms about. Apparently there had been a derailment down the line and the train had spent the night there. This was now early in the morning on practice day, and we had to get to Syracuse somehow. Alan and I left the organisation of this in the hands of Harry, who disappeared up the platform and came back to tell us that he had organised a taxi. You should have seen it! I don't know how long it had been a taxi, but it must have been the very first one in Italy. The wheels had 19-inch or 20-inch tyres, and it looked as if it might do 35 mph flat-out going downhill. But it was all we had, so we climbed in and staggered away towards the South prodding the driver constantly and saying 'Syracuse!' in urgent tones.

It wasn't long before we had a puncture. The three of us hopped out of the taxi and had the wheel changed almost before the driver realised what had happened. He had just about got his dust jacket on when we leapt back into the car and began prodding him to go faster. So we arrived at the water's edge where we had to cross on the ferry to Sicily — the ferry boat was just coming in. We paid off the taxi driver in a hurry, got aboard the ferry, and then began to wonder what on earth we were going to use for transport on the other side.

Harry suggested we start with the Captain and work down to see what help we could get. Luckily the Captain took in this big sob story about drivers wanting to get to a race in time, and he said he would radio for a hire car to meet us on the other side. Sure enough, when we disembarked, there was a little Fiat 1100, so Harry signed the papers and we were about to drive off Harry taking the wheel again. I'll never forget the poor chap who owned the car, pleading with Harry Schell: 'Please, please treat it like a baby. It is brand new!'

The little car only had about 20 or 30 kilometres on the clock, and I can remember to this day the screeching of tyres as we left this poor bloke standing there watching his car being driven flat out, straight up the middle of the road. He

73

wasn't the only one who was worried. When Alan and I saw Harry making for the driving seat, we both made a dive for the back door and got jammed, each trying to get there first. I won, and Alan had to sit in the front and sweat this out. I sat in the back with my two feet braced at each side of the car and hanging on to the straps at the side. That trip is something else I'll never forget! The Fiat was driven flat out all the way to Syracuse.

Harry was definitely one for the girls, and we came into one town very fast and drifted round a corner to find two pretty girls standing at the side of the road. Harry had to let the car drift right over, and nearly ran over their feet. As we went by one of the girls leaned over and spat right across the window. The look on Harry's face — he just couldn't believe that a female could treat him like that!

Eventually we reached Syracuse where Rob was waiting. I'm sure he never realised the problems we had getting there.

The race itself was considered to be a convenient dress rehearsal for the forthcoming big battles at Monaco, Spa, Rouen and elsewhere. There were two Vanwalls, three Connaughts, two Ferraris, seven Maseratis — and three little Coopers. The public nicknamed them 'Topolinos'. One Connaught, Les Leston's, was destroyed by fire during Saturday's practice, which caused a bit of a stir. The race, naturally enough, was dominated by the really big machinery. The two Ferraris of Collins and Musso were first and second, with Moss's Vanwall third. I came sixth out of the seven finishers!

Just over a week later I was back in England and running at Goodwood. By this time some new, up and coming stars were joining Moss, Salvadori, Fairman, Brooks and Co. Stuart Lewis-Evans surprised everyone by winning the Formula 1 race in a Connaught, Ron Flockhart had joined BRM alongside Salvadori, Archie Scott-Brown was in a Connaught and Jim Russell in a Maserati. Archie would have been one of the greatest Grand Prix drivers if he had been allowed to race regularly in Formula 1. Because he was born with a deformed arm, he was considered unfit to drive and not allowed entries abroad, although he won so many sports car races it would be difficult to count them.

The Race to the Top

I came fourth in the Glover Trophy race in the Formula 2 Cooper and beat Salvadori for only the second time ever—it must be admitted that he retired his BRM. After this outing I suddenly achieved fame and notoriety at Monaco before and during the Grand Prix. I made some dramatic pictures for the photographers, but it wasn't much fun for me.

The Coventry Climax engine eventually got stretched to 2.2 litres just prior to going to Monaco, and then came a series of coincidences which brought attention to Coopers and to myself and the Walker equipe.

I was late getting to Monaco, it was virtually a new car, and when I went out in it during the second practice session I found the brakes had not been bedded in properly. It was getting near the end of the practice session and I was eager to get out there—same as usual in Monaco, big panic to do a good time as soon as possible in case it rains on the Saturday and you don't qualify. We'd been fiddling about trying to get the brake ratios right, and now I shot out to achieve my good practice time, arrived at the top of the hill, and the brakes locked up. The road had a terrific camber sloping away to the right, and I got off line for the left-hander round by the Hotel de Paris. I found myself in the road where it drops off to the right and wasn't able to make the bend. I went straight into the barrier, which was made of sandbags and telegraph posts. The photographs make it look as though I've knocked a post down, but in fact I knocked it *up*, and as it went up I went under it. It crashed down on the bonnet of the car right behind my head. That put the car into an irreparable state by quite a bit. However, a Rob Walker Cooper had been taken down for Les Leston to drive but the engine had blown during the first practice. As we had an engine but no chassis and Rob had a chassis but no engine, we installed the 2-litre engine in Rob's chassis, which I subsequently drove, much to Les Leston's annoyance.

Anyway, we had quite a good run during the race, and from being thirteenth fastest in practice I was running third with only three laps to go when, going up the hill to where I'd crashed on the Friday, the engine stopped. The fuel pump drive had failed, I discovered later. I coasted over the top of the hill and down past the station to the waterfront, and came to a halt just before the tunnel. In those days I didn't like to be beaten, so I got out of the car and pushed. I was eager! I pushed the thing through the tunnel down to the chicane, up to the Tabac corner and along the harbour side to finish sixth — and last. Out of all those Vanwalls, Connaughts, Ferraris and Maseratis, only Fangio (Maserati), Tony Brooks (Vanwall), Masten Gregory (Maserati), Stuart Lewis-Evans (Connaught) and Maurice Trintignant (Ferrari) finished — and my little underpowered Cooper. I think in view of the opposition that that car was marvellous on the Monaco track.

The worst thing about pushing the car home wasn't so much the exhaustion as losing third place; and the really scary part was going through the tunnel with all these powerful great cars screaming past in the near dark! However, I received the biggest ovation I'd ever had from a crowd up till then.

Monaco 1957 was a dramatic race all round, with three of the favourites going out on the third lap. Moss was leading and setting up a cracking pace in his Vanwall, and Collins in his Ferrari had streaked past Fangio's Maserati to take second place. Fangio, Brooks and Hawthorn were third, fourth and fifth. Coming down towards the chicane on the third lap, Stirling came tearing out of the tunnel at high speed and braked hard. But he couldn't possibly get through the chicane, and chose to go up the escape road rather than into the harbour! Unfortunately, a barrier of telegraph poles had been put across the escape road for some idiotic reason, and as Moss hit them they flew into the air and came down on Pete Collins, who was trying to get through the chicane. He couldn't make it and hit the quayside barrier of strawbales, sandbags and poles, *very* nearly going into the harbour.

Fangio managed to tip-toe through all this mess and take the lead, which he kept till the finish, but Tony Brooks almost stopped to avoid trouble, and Mike Hawthorn, who was right on his tail, hit the Vanwall, knocked a wheel off his Ferrari, and joined Collins's wrecked Ferrari among the telegraph poles. Tony kept going in the bumped Vanwall, but was never in the running for the lead.

Moss, Collins and Hawthorn wandered back to the pits almost hand in hand, swinging their helmets, pretending it was a big joke; but there must have been quite a few thousand quids' worth of damage left behind them, actually. Two Ferraris and a Vanwall . . . ! I was behind them, of course, and I can only remember a big cloud of smoke and dust and straw everywhere, big black lines reaching right down past the chicane. They were quite lucky to get out of that, really.

That meeting was the start of Cooper's success in Grand Prix racing, because the cars began to show signs that they were worth going on with. Journalists called it 'the fantastic little Cooper', and when you consider that it was using fuel tanks meant for the 1500 cc engine, that I had had to make a pit stop for fuel, and would still have been third at the finish except for the fracture of the fuel pump drive, well, yes, it was fantastic.

As for my 'performance', this is what Gregor Grant had to say in *Autosport*: 'Brabham's effort in pushing his crippled car nearly a mile to the finish was warmly applauded. The little hill at the tobacconist's kiosk nearly defeated him, and when he finally reached the finish line, the Australian was so exhausted that he could not hear what was being said to him, nor could he utter a word.' Knowing myself fairly well, I'd hazard a guess that it was more likely I didn't *want* to talk, not that I couldn't. But it was a race I shall never forget.

We had a good weekend at Whitsun. For once it was sunny and warm, although it was a bit windy, and we were racing at Brands Hatch on Sunday and Crystal Palace on Monday. At Brands Coopers showed up well again, scooping up the Formula 3 and Formula 2 races, and only losing out to Colin Chapman in the up to 2000 cc sports car race. I won both parts of the Formula 2 race, beating Roy Salvadori — something I always enjoyed doing.

The next day Roy and I had a terrific carve-up at Crystal Palace. Roy won the first part of the Formula 2 race while I remained right on his tail for the ten laps, then in the second

77

part I broke the circuit record going all out to take the London Trophy. Coopers won five out of nine events that day, the Formula 2 Lotus still being relatively new and having teething troubles. They had no such worries with the sports cars, however! The Lotus Eleven must have been one of the most successful cars of all time, and it was always good value to watch Colin driving one himself. Graham Hill in those days was an up-and-coming challenger but had quite a reputation for spinning!

All in all, that was a profitable weekend, and we went off to Montlhèry the following week with plenty of enthusiasm. It wasn't exactly a major meeting, but the Prix de Paris for Formula 2 cars was a notable race. Mike Mac-Dowell and myself had a good duel, which I won, and I remember 'Jabby' Crombac winning the 1100 cc sports car race in his precious Lotus. Jabby and I became good friends and remained so. Sometime that year he took me to a factory in Paris to see if we could do something about our Citroën gearbox problems. This factory made the four-speed conversion we were using, but they also made gearbox casings for Citroen. I went down to the foundry and I can remember trying hard to explain to them what we needed in the way of a stronger case. The 2-litre engine was too powerful and used to break the gearbox constantly. I finished up with all the patterns spread out on a bench, and I recall putting plasticine on them and scraping out cores and so on. We made about six gearboxes, all cast with extra strengthening ribs, and came home with all the bits and pieces we needed. It seemed to do the trick, but the following year we used the same case and I made a new bellhousing for the front of the gearbox which incorporated drop gears. This way we could change the final drive ratio without changing the crown wheel and pinion; we had been having great difficulty in sorting out our gear ratios.

I shared a car at Le Mans that year with Ian Raby, and we finished thirteenth overall, and third in our class. It was the Ecurie Ecosse year, with Ron Flockhart and Ivor Bueb winning magnificently in their Jaguar. Lotus caused a major sensation by winning the Index of Performance category

The Race to the Top

with a 750 cc car, depriving the French—and Panhard in particular—of something which had been a traditionally French preserve. Jaguars took the first four places overall, blowing off all the Ferraris and Maseratis and Aston Martins.

We seemed to be in France a lot that year, and I learned about two words of French. One of these was *'jambon'* and the other *'bifteck'*. I always put my food first! After that came *'essence'*, another great necessity of life. Our next Grand Prix was the French, at the new circuit of Rouen-les-Essarts. The whole meeting was typically French, right down to the three men starting the race—one to count the seconds on his fingers, one to be official watch-watcher, and one to drop the flag. The track hasn't really changed much, except for the addition of safety measures, and we all thought it was a pretty good place, I remember.

But the thing that impressed me most was Fangio's driving. This was the second or third time I had had the opportunity to drive with him in a race, and he was one of my idols. He was the chap I looked up to and tried to learn from. I can clearly recall going down through the esses after the pits at Rouen, and Fangio sweeping down and passing me on the way through. He had fantastic control over that car— the Maserati. He had all four wheels drifting all round the corners through those tight bends, and that was when Fangio impressed me once and for all as the greatest driver I'd ever seen. He really was *that good*.

He won at Rouen that year, with three Ferraris behind him, Musso, Collins and Hawthorn. I was seventh. The other thing I remember from the French Grand Prix was Ron Flockhart's accident. He lost the BRM coming round the bend into the pit straight and he had a really big shunt. I was behind him when he went off and I just couldn't believe that Ron would be able to walk away from that. He did, though. Incidentally, right from the early days, Ron was a chap I could go and talk to and get advice from. I found him a very likeable sort of person, and we got on very well together. Later he started teaching me to fly, and he used to tell me all the things I was doing wrong. He was an experienced pilot and let me take over the controls—but that is another chapter.

The British Grand Prix at Aintree that year made motor racing history, Moss bringing home a British car, the Vanwall, to take the chequered flag. Brooks shared the glory, because it had started the race as his car; but his leg injuries from Le Mans had not healed, and when Moss's engine blew up, Stirling ran back to the pits, took over Tony's car, and proceeded to win the race! This from ninth place. As for me, my clutch decided to stop functioning when I was in seventh place.

Over the August Bank Holiday the motor racing photographers show me crouched over my steering wheel in the Formula 2 Cooper as usual. Lotus were now winning virtually everything in sports car racing, with the Eleven in various forms, while Cooper seemed to have a stranglehold on Formula 2. Making Formula 2 cars was a very profitable business for John and Charles Cooper and we had plans, quite tentative at that time, for going into Grand Prix racing seriously the following year. The Cooper had obvious advantages, although it was down on power. The rear-engined lay-out, left over from the old 500 cc days, made it a very controllable car and put what power it had on the ground. I found I could hang the tail out to what would seem to an onlooker a frightening degree, without ever losing control of the slide. In all the photographs of racing in 1957 and '58, the Cooper looked really tiny beside the bulk of the Ferraris and Maseratis and BRMs and Vanwalls, and so it was.

We went to the German Grand Prix in 1957 and I was pretty impressed with the Nurburgring. We had two Coopers entered in the Formula 2 section of the race, one for Roy Salvadori and one for me. Roy put up the best practice time for Formula 2 and was on the fourth row behind the Maseratis, Ferraris, and so on, while I was right behind him on the fifth row.

The Nurburgring was very bumpy in those days, and very difficult to learn. The surface played havoc with suspensions, and tyre wear was greater than normal. But the thing that everyone will always remember from that Grand Prix was,

David Phipps

The Cooper Climax heads for victory at Oporto in the Portuguese Grand Prix, 1960 –
'The first really good Grand Prix car they produced.'

Piloting the De Havilland Chipmunk from Fairoaks with Wing Commander Arthur
in the back seat, 1959.

News Chronicle

Thumbs up for a safe win at Zandvoort – the Cooper in the 1960 Dutch Grand Prix.

Me working on a 1960 Formula 1 Cooper.

once again, the absolute mastery of Fangio's driving. Roy went out with suspension failure and I had gearbox troubles, so I got the chance to stand and watch for once.

Fangio had set up fastest practice time of 9 minutes 25·6 seconds in his Maserati, three seconds faster than Hawthorn (Ferrari), five seconds faster than Behra (Maserati), and nine seconds faster than Collins (Ferrari), all of whom were also on the front row. He let the Ferraris go ahead, then passed them and took the lead on the third lap, pulling away immediately. By half-distance he was practically on his own, but on lap twelve he came in for a tyre change and for fuel. The Ferraris shot past, and then Juan Manuel set off in pursuit. It was at this time that I retired at the pits and watched the drama unfold. I remember watching the board and listening to the commentary while Fangio broke the lap record again and again. He threw that Maser around the Nurburgring like no one I've ever seen before or since.

The lap times came down from 9 minutes 41 seconds to 9 minutes 20 seconds and the Ferrari pit hung out 'faster' signals to Hawthorn and Collins. Fangio had just regained 35 seconds in two laps, he was sideways all round the circuit, but under perfect control. He drew relentlessly nearer the two Ferraris and, on the third lap from the flag, the commentator nearly burst with excitement. Fangio had achieved what had seemed impossible before that race – he had brought the lap record at the 'Ring down to 9 minutes 17 seconds! In those days that was a fantastic time, and it was another occasion when Fangio impressed me as a really great driver. (He was forty-seven then.) He won the race from the astonished Hawthorn and Collins by three seconds.

Salvo and I went to Pescara next with the Formula 2 cars. This event counted towards the World Championship, and there was quite a little problem being thrashed out in the top layers of motor racing. It seemed as though Fangio had the Championship in the bag for Maserati and, as Enzo Ferrari had steadfastly refused to enter any more Italian road races because of bad newspaper publicity, poor Luigi Musso was frantic, because he still had a chance of tying with Fangio in the Championship. It was a terribly long shot, but Ferrari eventually relented and let Musso have a car. Hawthorn and Collins were not at all happy about this, but the Italians were delighted!

Pescara is one of those places we don't see much of nowadays, a course through villages and mountains and so on, where you run on a road with houses and chickens and people all adding to the roadside attractions! It was about 16 miles round, and the first lap was quite something. Fangio spun on someone's oil and Musso went into the lead. (It took ten minutes to complete a lap, and in the long interval everyone in the stands began to fight and police were called in to restore order.) Roy knocked a wheel off the Cooper on a milestone, Moss took the lead from Musso, Fangio dropped back, and there were six retirements before the halfway mark. I found myself driving a pretty lonely race, because there were only about seven of us left on the 16-mile circuit after Horace Gould went through a fence and came to rest inside a chicken-house.

At the Cooper pit Roy had elected himself signaller. I remember him walking out into the middle of the road and the first signal he gave me said: '*I am going swimming*'—in other words: 'The best of luck mate, I'm off!' So there was I, touring round the mountains and villages in the sunshine, with the car going beautifully. I worked out I'd be in a reasonable place as I started on the last lap—about fifth or sixth. Then—you'll never believe this—I ran out of petrol.

As the car went coasting along I wondered what I should do about this, miles out in the country, when I saw on the righthand side of the road a petrol station. There were a few people standing there, and the car seemed to roll naturally into the forecourt and up to the pumps. I parked alongside a pump attendant. He sprang about six feet into the air, rushed round and got a hose, and before I knew what had happened he had a few litres of petrol in the car. So I started up the engine and finished the race!

Incidentally, Stirling won in the Vanwall, with Fangio second and Harry Schell third. I was seventh, three laps behind. It had been an unusual sort of day, to say the least, but the biggest drama was to come.

The Race to the Top

Roy had driven down to Pescara in a little Hillman, and I was elected to drive back—at least, that is how it seemed. When I came out of the hotel the only seat left in the car was the driving seat. Tony Brooks was in the front passenger seat with his future wife, Pina, and John Cooper and Salvo were in the back. I assumed from this that I was the one who was supposed to drive. I wasn't sure why.

We started off for London going up the east coast of Italy, and there was a motor scooter going along the road in front of us. I was getting all sorts of comments from the back seat about passing the motor scooter but the scooter at the time was passing a big truck. I thought, I cannot go past now, I have to wait until the scooter gets past the truck; but the motor scooter was only doing the same speed as the truck and I was going to take a long time to get by. Eventually, I was just passing this poor chap on the motor scooter, and as I went by Roy leant over and grabbed the steering wheel and we nearly sent this poor bloke off the scooter under the lorry. *Now* I know why I am in the driving seat, I thought. If anything happens it is all down to me for sure.

We drove along a bit further and I looked in the rear mirror and this chap on the motor scooter was really upset in the biggest possible way. He was flat down over the tank trying to catch us up so I thought the best course is to get out of here quickly. We drove as fast as we could but before long, blow me, there was a hold-up in the road and we had to stop. I shall never forget looking in that rear view mirror and seeing that motor scooter coming up behind us and thinking: 'This is going to be lovely!' He pulled up at the side of the car and what he didn't realise was that it was righthand-drive. He leant in and got hold of Tony Brooks's arm and started tearing strips off poor old Tony who had really had nothing to do with it. The hold-up started to disappear then and I was able to drive off with this chap holding on to Tony Brooks's arm. Eventually we broke free but I didn't get very far before I had to stop again. This bloke soon arrived on the scene and was twice as furious as he was before. He drove around to the front of the car and started to write down the number of the car in a notebook, and trying to talk.

We just looked at him. In the end he got so exasperated that he spat into the car (seems to be an old Italian custom) all over Tony!

At that moment the road got clear and I managed to drive off again and I thought: 'I hope we never see this chap again!' The next hold up was a big convoy of trucks that was bringing all the police from Pescara—they had been posted all round the circuit. There were two big truckloads and a long queue of traffic behind them so Roy and Tony decided the only thing to do was to get past *everybody*. I didn't feel that game in those days. I was only just learning what it was all about. Then I looked in the rear view mirror and saw this motor bike coming along again, and I thought: 'I am not going to take this any more.' I put it down a gear and rushed along the side of this queue of traffic until we came to the big truckload of police. When I got there I just chickened out. There were four or five cops on motorcycles escorting this lot and *nobody* was game to pass, and *I* wasn't going to pass. Tony had had enough by this time. 'There is only one thing to do,' he said. 'I will drive.' So, without losing our position on the grid, we changed drivers whilst going along. When Tony got to the seat he said: 'Pass me my gloves.' And once he had put his gloves on, I can assure you it was a pretty hair-raising ride. We overtook the trucks and nearly knocked all those police off their motorbikes and I remember looking out of the rear window with these four cops chasing us with their sirens wailing. It was raining at the time and Tony just left the cops behind. This was my first introduction to continental driving.

Another thing I learnt from Salvo was that, when we went to Germany, he didn't always put me in the driving seat. When we were in a hurry Roy drove. He always used a Volkswagen. I didn't know why but I learnt. The reason he had a Volkswagen was that it was the only thing he could fit between the wheels of a transporter he was trying to overtake when another transporter was passing us going the other way. John Cooper would disappear under the seats and I had to tell him when it was all over and he could come up again. When Roy went across the top of a hill passing somebody I thought it was ridiculous and couldn't help commenting to

84

Roy about it. 'Roy,' I said, 'it is very dangerous to pass a car when you are coming to the crest of a hill, and how do you know there is nothing coming?' And he turned round to me and said: 'Boy, there is all the footpath not being used yet!'

CHAPTER VI

Still Climbing

1957 was the year when British cars first began to win races against the Italians. There was a lot of talk—and a lot of writing—about the tables having been turned against Ferrari and Maserati, and how the green cars would now come into their own, and so on. And it was true. Connaught, unfortunately, withdrew from racing and had to sell out, and the Cooper was only just beginning to be taken seriously as a Grand Prix contender. Most people's hopes were therefore centred on Tony Vandervell and his Vanwalls, and on his drivers, Stirling Moss, Tony Brooks and Stuart Lewis-Evans.

The Championship had been decided before the Italian Grand Prix—Fangio and Maserati had won—but the coming of the Vanwalls caused plenty of excitement in Italy and, when practice had finished, there were the three green Vanwalls on the front of the grid, with a solitary Maserati, driven by Fangio, alongside them. We were not competing at Monza for various reasons, the main one being lack of power on that fast circuit. It would have been a waste of time competing. But I was there as a spectator, and I have a vivid memory of the start.

There was Tony Vandervell with three cars on the front row, and the heat was as intense as the excitement. Everyone had their engines running except a Ferrari on the second row which wouldn't start. Naturally the Italian chap with the flag wasn't going to start the race until the Italian car was ready. This took quite some time and eventually one of the Vanwalls started to boil. I can remember watching Tony Vandervell looking at his cars—he was standing about level with the

86

front row—and he looked underneath the car that was steaming a bit and saw the water coming out of it. He jumped up in the air and roared off up the road towards the starter, who was standing there holding the flag beside him, *still* waiting for the Ferrari to fire up. Well, Tony rushed up, grabbed the bloke by the arm, lifted up this arm along with the flag and pulled it down again. That started the race, and they all roared off into the distance!

Apart from being typical of Tony Vandervell, it turned out to be the right move because Moss won the race. It was Vanwall's third big victory of the year, and the second in Italy. The British Press really went to town over that. Tony Vandervell was later awarded the Ferodo Trophy, which is always considered to be one of the top honours in the motor racing.

Bruce had been driving the 1500 cc Cooper sports car his September that year, it was the turn of the BRMs. The Ferrari, Maserati and Vanwall teams did not attend, so BRM dominated the event and Jean Behra won and set up a new circuit record. In fact, BRMs finished one-two-three, and I think I was fifth, but it wasn't a day I particularly enjoyed so I don't remember it too well. I prefer to recall Goodwood and the BARC meeting, in which I drove the 1500 cc Cooper Climax and set up a new lap record. It was about now that Coventry Climax started racing in a big way. Since Alf Francis had been able to increase the capacity of the 1500 cc engine to 1750 cc, they said they would construct one or two 2-litre units for the following season for use by Cooper and Lotus. Rob Walker would be running a Cooper in 1958 for Maurice Trintignant to drive. *We* were hoping to do a full season's Grand Prix racing for the first time.

The racing year used to come to a temporary halt in those days, and unless you were off on the Temporada series or the 'down under' races, you could have a fairly peaceful time from October till March, working on new cars or improving last year's model. I never stayed in England for the worst part of the winter, but this year I had two more major races to compete in after the Italian Grand Prix. One of them, the Oulton Park Gold Cup Formula 2 race, carried a first prize of £1,000 and a real gold cup for the mantelpiece. I was especially happy to win that race by over half a minute from Cliff Allison in a Lotus. It was the biggest prize I had won up to then and the money certainly helped.

The Moroccan Grand Prix was held on a new circuit about six miles from Casablanca and reminded me quite a bit of Zandvoort, designed as it was amongst sand dunes, with the grandstand and finishing straight parallel with the sea. Anyway, all the big teams were there, and Roy drove the works Cooper while I drove Rob Walker's. During the race my car broke its gearbox, so we had a look at it in the pits and decided we couldn't go on as the gearbox had really had it. We pushed the car behind the pits and this signifies that you are disqualified or that you don't intend to continue in the race. So the car was parked there behind the pits for quite a few laps, and the other runners were dropping out like flies. And we thought: 'Well, we are going to miss a place like this!' – so we decided to fix the Cooper.

We jumped over the rails, went round the back, and actually put in a new gearbox. This took a long time. But eventually I put on my gloves and crash helmet again, got in the car, drove down the back of the pits and out onto the circuit when no one was looking. I wondered if I could get away with it. I drove round for a few laps before they realised I was back in the race; then they came along and gave a message to Rob that I was to be black-flagged in. Of course, Rob started arguing and wouldn't have it. So the Clerk of the Course, who happened to be poor old Toto Roche, had to get out the black flag and get on with it. The sun was getting pretty low and the cars were coming out of the sun down the straight, and he was peering at them and trying to find my car. He had the black flag in his hand, and every time my car came along Rob would tap him on the shoulder and start talking to him, trying to convince him that he was doing the wrong thing. This went on for two or three laps, and Toto had really done his biscuit; so he swung round, looked up the road and waved his black flag violently at the first car that came by. It just so happened that it was Fangio, the World Champion, who was fourth or fifth at the time.

Still Climbing

Toto Roche had not remembered to hang out a car number with the black flag, so next lap poor old Fangio came into the pits and there were about eight or nine Italians jumping up and down and waving Fangio back out onto the track again, and Fangio asking: 'Why the black flag?' The crowd was going wild and in the end Fangio rejoined the race. (I don't think he would have come into the pits except that he had a bit of a conscience about some assistance he had received out on the circuit after he had spun and stalled.) The Walker pit then called me in, but there was great commotion in the crowd, a lot of whom thought it was rather admirable to have crept out again after changing the gearbox behind the pits. But rules are rules, and I came in, probably with a bit of a grin on my face. But I don't suppose Fangio or Monsieur Roche were very pleased with me! Behra won the race in a Maserati.

In December the news broke that Maserati were withdrawing from motor racing, which was quite a blow. They were pretty well broke, mainly because there were several million lire owing to them from other firms. This left Fangio, Behra and Schell without a drive for the following season, and Stirling Moss had to look for another sports car to drive. There were other things that forced them out of business — the following year would see the change to 'Avgas' instead of methanol-fuelled cars; the Ferraris were already coping with this new problem and seemed to have it solved, judging by their speed at Casablanca. Maserati were behind on this and had been spending money developing a V-12 engine — which was a failure — and a V-8 for their sports cars when the limitation on this category was changed to 3 litres. We were all sorry to see the famous 'Trident' cars go.

I stayed on in England for Christmas that year and went to Boxing Day Brands. It was cold but fine and all the people who had had enough of eating and drinking and of their relatives took the opportunity to get out into the open air. There was a very big crowd to see the seven events.

I won the Formula Libre race in Rob Walker's 2-litre Cooper Climax and captured a new circuit record of under 59 seconds — remember, the circuit was rather smaller in those days. The car went exceptionally well. I then flew to New Zealand and on January 18th 1958, in the beautiful warmth of New Zealand, I won the New Zealand Grand Prix — at the fifth attempt!

This was the year that the New Zealand Grand Prix Association started their 'Driver to Europe' scheme. They paid a young driver's fare to England, and he was then expected to make a name for himself. Bruce McLaren was one of the first contenders, and I was actually on the committee to decide which New Zealand driver to send. As I already knew Bruce and thought a lot of him, I naturally recommended him, and he was chosen. The rules governing our choice stipulated that whichever youngster was chosen to go on this scheme must not only show his ability on the track, but must also be a suitable 'ambassador' for New Zealand. I think no one would argue that Bruce was probably the best ambassador his country could ever have found, even if they had searched through a far wider field than motor racing.

Bruce had been driving the 1500 cc Cooper sports car his father bought from me the year before. He drove our second 2-litre car in the Grand Prix and came to England in the New Year to join the Cooper organisation, partly as a mechanic, partly as a driver. He was then twenty years old, and had a fine driving record, though he had very little luck in the 1958 Grand Prix. He had a late start owing to a gearbox problem, made up ten places, and then retired when the gearbox selector mechanism failed. But he had driven well enough for the judges to vote him into going to Europe.

We had a lot of trouble with gearboxes throughout that series of races, but by February the new Cooper Formula 1 and 2 car had made its appearance at Surbiton, and had an improved gearbox in which we could use a ZF limited slip differential. In addition a pair of quick-change spur gears were fitted between the clutch and the gearbox, which enabled us to change the axle ratio to suit the circuit. The front suspension was new, using adjustable Armstrong spring-damper units, the engine sat lower in the car, and two twin-choke Weber carburetters were now being used.

Still Climbing

Meanwhile, back in the antipodes, I had a nasty moment at Teretonga Park when I was trying to catch Ross Jensen in his Maserati. I had been working on the car up to the last minute and I forgot to change from ordinary shoes into driving shoes. I was closing on Jensen, and was hoping to make a real race of it, when, just as I was preparing to go through the 90-degree left-hander before the main straight, the welt of my walking shoe caught between the brake pedal and the accelerator. Instead of making the bend I went straight on, and I thought I was going to end up in the crowd. I freed my foot just in time, and regained the circuit, shaken, and determined never to forget to change my shoes again. Jensen won, Bruce was second, and I charged through the field a bit to finish third.

Now we were well into 1958, which wasn't a particularly good year for Coopers. We were still getting ourselves organised to go Grand Prix racing, and it wasn't really until the end of the year that we believed we stood a chance for the following season. By then we had ironed out all the major problems, got the gearbox sorted, and learned a lot by experience. But at the beginning of the year we knew we wouldn't stand a chance at circuits like Reims or Monza.

As usual, I began my year at the Easter Goodwood meeting, which was memorable for two things—Behra's big shunt in a BRM (both Behra and Harry Schell had gone to the BRM team) and my wheel to wheel duel with Graham Hill in the Formula 2 race. Jean Behra *demolished* his car at the chicane, clouting the brick wall, and was lucky to be only slightly hurt. Moss, in his Rob Walker Cooper, I remember now, threw a connecting rod and *I* spun on his oil. There is a picture of me facing the wrong way, looking lost in a cloud of smoke!

The Formula 2 Lotus were now competitive, and Graham and I had a battle royal. We were only inches apart most of the time, I squeezed ahead of Graham, and then he retook the lead and stayed there till the last lap. I tried everything I knew to get past him, and eventually took to the grass at Woodcote to get to the chicane first and come out of it first. So I won, but only just! It was a taste of things to come, for this was to be the first year for Lotus in Grand Prix racing. Drivers were Cliff Allison and Graham Hill, and they made their debut at Monaco.

Of course, Stirling was the man to beat in those days. He was easily the quickest driver around, and there was only one catch; he didn't really know how to save the car. While he was going he used to get the utmost out of the car, but it rarely got to the finishing line. If the car lasted he generally used to win. I had quite a few dust-ups with Stirling, and I enjoyed beating him a few times at Brands. Beating Stirling was really something. In 1957 and 1958 Moss was really at the top of the tree as a driver, and he was the ultimate goal — beat him and you felt you'd achieved something. I never had the same feeling about beating anyone else.

One of our best tussles was at the next race meeting in the spring of 1958, the Aintree '200'. Stirling was having trouble with a slipping clutch, and I had been delayed in the pits for nearly a minute to fill my radiator with water. But Stirling was well in the lead when I set out to catch him — if I could. During the last few laps I was creeping closer and closer, and I was preparing to take Moss on the last lap if it was humanly possible. I managed it when we were within sight of the finishing line, and I didn't think there was anywhere that he could overtake me again. But Stirling had plenty of talent in reserve always — he got alongside me at Tatts Corner and took a fractional lead as we came up to the line. He finished exactly one-fifth of a second ahead of me!

At Monaco Moss was in a Vanwall and Maurice Trintignant drove Rob's first car and Ron Flockhart his second. Trint won the Grand Prix. He drove very well — he was fantastic, actually.

The weather was marvellous that year, except for the early morning practice session on Friday, when it rained and Moss had not qualified his Vanwall by the end of the session. I found myself on the front row of the three/two, sixteen-car grid, just one tenth of a second faster than Trint, and alongside the BRM of Behra and the Vanwall of Brooks. Stirling qualified on Saturday for the third row.

The race started on the harbour side of the pits then, and

Still Climbing

I remember there was an almighty traffic jam on the first lap as we went into the Gasometer hairpin. Salvadori, in the other works Cooper, went wide and there were all sorts of incidents going on in the crush while we took avoiding action. Behra went into the lead, and as we came out of the tunnel for the end of the first lap it must have looked good to British eyes, because the order was BRM, Vanwall, Cooper (mine), Cooper, Vanwall, Vanwall, BRM. After all that green paint came the first red car, Hawthorn in his Ferrari. Unfortunately, I had to stop at the pits because an anti-roll bar link fell off. It looked then as though Hawthorn could win, with Moss second and Trintignant third, but things were to change. I was a lap behind by then and all my hopes of winning were gone. Moss took the lead only to come into the pits with a misfiring engine, and then Hawthorn's petrol pump ceased to work. This left Trint in the lead, and his consistent driving, lap after lap, now paid off. He simply kept going steadily to the finish, and as he is a Frenchman, you can imagine the cheers of the crowd as he took the chequered flag. I finished fourth, and I shall always remember little Trintignant in the equally tiny Cooper driving his lap of honour with a big laurel wreath round his neck so you could hardly see more than his hand raised to wave at the crowd. It was a good win for Cooper and for Rob Walker, and both were the main topic of conversation for weeks to come.

The Dutch Grand Prix at Zandvoort was notable for the dominance of British cars, with Moss winning in his Vanwall, taking the lead in the World Championship table. BRMs were second and third, and Salvo was fourth.

Most of my successes that year were in Formula 2 races, but there was one sports car race that deserves a mention. I partnered Stirling in an Aston Martin DBR1 at the 1,000 Kilometres of the Nurburgring. Mind you, Stirling drove thirty-six out of the forty-four laps, which is why we won. I was also partnered with Moss for Le Mans, and luckily it was Stirling who was driving when the engine blew up on the first evening, and not me!

The Belgian Grand Prix was not exactly a raging success for anyone but Tony Brooks in his Vanwall; Ferraris ran away with the French Grand Prix at Reims, as anyone would expect, although I did manage to get myself on to the second row of the grid in the Formula 2 race, only to throw a con rod on the line! I finished sixth in the Formula 1 race behind Collins, whose turn it was to push a dead car over the line. The two outstanding things at that meeting were Behra's great performance in the Formula 2 Porsche and, on the bad side, the death of Luigi Musso, who was Italy's only star driver at that time. He was killed when he was simply trying too hard to keep up with team-mate Hawthorn, which made him take a corner too fast and crash.

It was Peter Collins's Ferrari which walked away with the British Grand Prix, while Stirling's Vanwall retired with engine trouble. Hawthorn took second place and fastest lap, so he now took the Championship lead over Moss. Roy drove his Cooper very well to finish third, and people began to look upon him as possibly one of the few top Grand Prix drivers. My reputation was more for Formula 2 in those days, and my sixth place at the British didn't thrill me. But it was all good practice.

Roy drove brilliantly again at the Nurburgring, but the whole Grand Prix was overshadowed by the death of Peter Collins. It was so totally unexpected. As with all great drivers, we tended to take it for granted that Pete didn't make mistakes — we always get upset, it goes on happening, but we never get used to the shocks.

I had a slight argument with Bonnier's Maserati on the first lap — we were both a long way down the field but we both wanted the same piece of road at the same time and we touched; I ran into the back of his car and knocked off the oil tank. There was oil all over the road and I went off on it, clouted a bank and squashed the front of the Cooper. So I wandered back to the pits with the car looking very second-hand and shorter than usual! Roy went on to finish second to Tony Brooks's Vanwall, and Bruce McLaren won the Formula 2 section of the race. John Cooper did one of his victory rolls in front of the pits as Bruce came by.

Those were the days when we had to move heaven and earth to get away from Germany as quickly as possible and

94

get home for the August Bank Holiday Brands Hatch meeting. There were times when we staggered into Heath Row sometime after midnight, might snatch a few hours sleep and then turn up at Brands bright and early the next morning. Luckily I can survive with very little sleep, and my race at the Ring had not lasted long, so I managed to win the Kent Trophy for Formula 2 cars after two 21-lap parts, both spent dicing with Stuart Lewis-Evans.

At the Brands meeting for the Kentish '100' Trophy, Stirling and I fought one of the fastest and closest races ever. We broke all the lap records in beautiful, sunny, warm weather, Stirling in the Rob Walker Cooper Formula 2 car and me in the works car. I won the first part and Stirling the second, but he took the trophy on aggregate, and Mike Hawthorn, being suitably light-hearted, presented Stirling with the cup—after swigging most of the champagne himself. Mike was one of the most colourful drivers of the time and someone I used to look to for pointers on how to drive Grand Prix cars. And by now it looked as though Moss might lose the Championship to Hawthorn unless the last two events went his way.

I shouldn't have bothered to go to the Italian Grand Prix. I was on the next to last row of the grid, but at the start I somehow became involved with Gendebien's Ferrari, which stalled on the second row. I crunched the Ferrari hard in the rear, broke my suspension, and was out of the race before I really began. Brooks won in a Vanwall, ·Stirling retired early, Hawthorn was second, and now had an eight point lead over Moss for the Championship. The system of awarding points at that time was complicated and tended to make it more profitable to go after places than outright wins—not that anyone was driving *not* to win, but that was the way it panned out. The Monza result left Moss an outside chance, and the deciding race would be Casablanca.

Stirling needed to win the race and set fastest lap, in order to take the Championship, while Mike only had to finish no lower than third. Well, Stirling did his bit right. He won the Moroccan Grand Prix *and* set fastest lap; but Mike was second, and clinched his crown.

95

When the Flag Drops

While all this high-powered drama was going on at the front, we Formula 2 drivers were ploughing on, trying not to be worried by the fact that we were being lapped with monotonous regularity. It was really a bit dangerous to have some of the locals in such an important event in slow cars. I clinched my particular Championship, the Formula 2, by winning that section of the race while Bruce came second. The worst thing about the meeting was the terrible accident to Stuart Lewis-Evans, whose Vanwall crashed and caught fire. He died of his injuries, and the accident had a profound effect on Tony Vandervell. He became ill himself soon afterwards, and decided to withdraw from racing altogether. We were to see no more of the Vanwalls.

I was disappointed with my Formula 1 year, but I hoped that the coming new 2½-litre Coventry Climax engine would put us in a stronger position in 1959 than we had been in with the 2-litre and 2.2-litre during the past two years.

Sometime in the autumn Juan Manuel Fangio announced his retirement from motor racing. We had seen nothing of him since the French Grand Prix at Reims, so we had become used to his absence by the time the announcement came out. He assured everyone that he would never be seen on the circuits again, and was making a clean break. He chose Reims as his last race because he had first raced there upon arrival in Europe. He was forty-seven. When I retired I, too, wanted to break off cleanly although for different reasons from Fangio; I was not tired, nor did I have less interest in motor racing. I just felt it was, all round, the best time. Fangio's Press statement included the following words:

'It is most difficult to know when to call a halt, but I sincerely believe that my own decision is a wise one. I can now look back on a career of many successes, and congratulate myself on the fact that I had the sense to give it up when I was still regarded as being in the top flight of drivers, and not just another "old man" trying to recapture the skill of his youth.'

I would like to think that I was in a position to say the same.

Lotus 24 in the Monaco Grand
x, 1962 – I had to keep my
d in while we worked on the
Brabham.

d Phipps

e first appearance of the Formula
Brabham Climax at
rburgring, 1962.

id Phipps

The Brabham at Indianapolis in 1964 – the year of the big crash

Roy Billington and I working on the Coventry Climax V8 engine

Still Climbing

So that was the 1958 season over, but I had been doing other things than racing cars during the year. Betty and Geoffrey and I had settled into a house in Dorking, and were making England our permanent home for the time being. Naturally, I had to look round for something to do with my spare time left over from working at Coopers, driving sports cars, Formula 1 and Formula 2. I took up flying.

CHAPTER VII

I Discover I Need Wings

I became interested in flying mainly because at that time Ron Flockhart was a good friend of mine, and came to visit us quite frequently. He used to fly a little Auster aeroplane down to Surrey from Scotland, and I went to a few meetings on the Continent with him in that plane. He started to teach me what he knew about flying, and I think the few trips I did with him at the end of 1958 swayed me into learning to fly.

Whatever time I could spare from Coopers I used to rush out to Fairoaks and take a few lessons. The chap who was teaching me was Wing-Commander Arthur, who had many thousands of hours of flying to his credit. I was learning in a Chipmunk, doing circuits and bumps, and one day he suddenly got out of the aeroplane and said: 'Now you have to do a circuit on your own.'

This was a big moment—my first solo—especially as I had only done a total of five hours flying up till then. I managed to achieve the circuit without drama, and from there on I got really serious about it. Before I actually got my licence I decided to buy a plane, so I bought a Cessna 180 and did my last few hours of training in that. I had to do 40 hours of flying, and as I had done 30 in the Chipmunk the last 10 were done in the Cessna. I had already done a couple of venturesome things, like rushing up to Coventry one day and getting lost on the way. So I landed on an old airfield and asked some farmer bloke where I was. I wasn't far from Coventry, as it happened, but I was under the impression I was miles off.

I Discover I Need Wings

I did my check-out with Wing-Commander Arthur in the Chipmunk belonging to the Club. We went down over Guildford doing spins and loops and so on, and the check-out made my licence complete. I think that was on a Tuesday and on the Wednesday we set out in the Cessna for Oporto.

I took my wife and Dean Delamont on the trip and as usual took off from Fairoaks. The weather was marginal and far from good. We went to Eastleigh and cleared Customs there, and when I took off from Eastleigh they said the wind was from the north, less than 5 knots, which is virtually nothing. (In those days, incidentally, I had no navigational aids and it was a big map reading deal with a map on your knee, looking for railway lines and rivers and that sort of thing.)

Anyway, we set off in dead calm and flew over the Isle of Wight heading for Nantes, which takes you across Cherbourg. About half way across I realised that the sea underneath me wasn't any millpond; in fact it was all white tops and the wind was blowing quite strongly from the west. Not knowing anything about the wind speed, I had to make a big rough guess, then made a correction which was not enough, and when we were due to arrive over land the visibility was rather poor—only ten or fifteen miles. Cherbourg never appeared, so then I didn't know whether I was going down the right-hand side or the left-hand side of Cherbourg. So we kept flogging on, and eventually found land half an hour later than the ETA, missing Cherbourg altogether. We managed to locate the right railway lines and set a new course for Nantes.

We finished up in Nantes all right, cleared Customs and refuelled. The weather report wasn't too good for going on, but we pressed on and went down the coast to Biarritz. We landed there but weren't allowed to go on to Portugal because it was quite bad over the mountains. I persuaded them to let me go on as far as Bilbao; the weather was so bad we were flying on the top of the water, following the coast around, looking up at the cliff tops. Dean and Betty were sitting in there looking completely unconcerned, and there was I, wondering if we'd ever land again. Actually, we did land at Bilbao and, when we checked the map, we found we could go down a valley there without going over the top of the mountains, but before leaving we had to refuel again.

I went out to the BP chap and asked for some fuel. He let out a bit of a gasp, rolled out a dirty forty-gallon drum from the long grass, fetched a dirty old pump and pumped the fuel into the aeroplane. Heaven knows what was in it. But we flew off and went up this valley with mountains towering up each side, and when we came out on the other side of the mountains the weather was dead clear, so we sailed on down to Oporto, no problem. In fact, on the way back, one of the John Webb 'Webbair' flights was about to leave Oporto at the same time as us, and we actually raced them to Bordeaux for a fuel stop. And that was my first trip abroad in my own aeroplane.

Not long after I had bought the Cessna 180, Charlie Cooper bought a house down in Cornwall. John went down there for a week's holiday, and suggested that I went down to see him. So he marked the house on my map and also marked a field where I should land—he said he'd pin-point it with a big white sheet or something. He would be there.

So I set off, found the house all right, and flew over it. John gave his usual big wave and Betty and Geoffrey waved back, and I went across to the field and flew around for a bit. John came up to the field and held up a towel to give me some idea of which way the wind was blowing. After a lot of fumbling he got it up in the wind, and I could see the direction. Unfortunately, this field was sloping down to a creek running into a main river. And the tide was out. It was a sea of mud, and this field ran down into it, except that there was a fence before you reached the mud. The wind was blowing completely the wrong way, which meant I had to land *uphill* with the wind behind me, or land into the wind going *downhill*. So I had about five or six goes at trying to land in this field and there was just no way. Eventually, on the last run I tried to touch down, downwind, but I was obviously going too fast. The wind was blowing very, very strongly when we came over the fence, and although we had minimum airspeed, the actual aeroplane speed across the ground was very high. Of course, this meant that if I had touched down I would have gone through the fence at the top part of the paddock. There were a couple of big trees right at the top on the departure side so I really put the throttle on and tried to go over them. I had to lift a wing over the top of one tree—just missed it by a foot. Betty didn't realise what was going on; she was busy looking out of the window at John. She didn't see the tree at all.

We decided there was no way we could land in this field. The next big problem was where we *were* going to land and how could we get the message to John? We decided that we would go to St Morgan, which was the nearest place on the map which was a proper aerodrome. So Betty wrote out a little note on a piece of paper. We thought it wasn't feasible to throw a piece of paper out of an aeroplane—he wasn't going to see that—so we looked round the aeroplane, and Betty's knitting bag was there with all the wool and stuff in it. We chucked out all the knitting, stuck this note in the knitting bag, flew back across the field, and tried to bomb John. I said to Betty: 'Right. Now!' She said: 'What did you say?' And I said: 'Now!'—but whilst she was saying 'What did you say?' we had gone that few feet too far, and instead of bombing John the bag went into the mud just outside the fence.

John's next job was to wade out in the mud and get this bag with the message; he waved to us that he had got it OK and we headed off for St Morgan. It was an RAF station and I didn't have the frequency in the aeroplane to talk to the tower, so the problem was telling the tower I wanted to land and getting a message back from them. I flew down past the tower, wiggled my wings, and put on my navigation lights. I did this about three times before they eventually gave me the green light to land. That was fine, except they had one big runway which was about two miles long and there was a BOAC 707 landing and taking off and doing circuits and bumps at the time.

The crosswind was about ninety degrees to the runway and much too strong for an aeroplane like mine to land on the main runway. In fact, the 707 was nearly shunted every time it hit the ground and almost scraped its wing on the tarmac. I reckoned it was too dangerous to land and the only other runway into the wind had big crosses on it meaning it was disused. Half of it was dug up at the other end and there was only one section of it about 300 yards long that was possible. I came down, much to the disgust of the tower where the occupants were all staring down on me as if I were mad. When I touched down the wind was so strong the aeroplane wouldn't stay on the ground. We were virtually stationary, just touching the wheels on the runway, and eventually two people came out and held the plane on the ground while I knocked the power off.

Luckily they were air crew from the RAF station. They realised I couldn't get the thing on the ground, because it was almost stationary and still hovering. They had to literally come and pull us out of the air. I would have turned upside down on the main runway in the crosswind for sure. We tied the aeroplane down and went over to the tower to wait for John to turn up. About half an hour later he arrived on the scene so we went off and had a quiet couple of days with John . . . except he got us into trouble, got his boat all tangled up in the ropes, tore a propeller off, and a few other things. Quite an exciting weekend really. When we had to leave the weather was much better and the wind wasn't blowing and we took off in 100 yards on a two-mile runway!

Later in the year when we went off to Germany to race Formula 2, I took Ron Flockhart, Betty and Geoffrey with me in the plane. I was supposed to race in Germany on the Sunday and at Brands on the Monday, and for a start we had a big drama getting into Bonn Airport because it was all foggy. When I eventually got in touch with Bonn they wouldn't let us land there because the weather was too bad, so they passed us over to an RAF station near Cologne. There we had our first experience of a radar approach which I thought was quite exciting, and eventually they put us on the end of the runway. We left the aeroplane there and went off to the Nurburgring, but when we came back to get the plane early on the Monday the weather was bad again which delayed our departure. We left eventually, but had quite a problem flying around Europe dodging this really bad weather and crossing the Channel. The idea was for us to land at Biggin Hill then drive to Brands Hatch, but by the time we arrived at Biggin Hill there wasn't time to drive to the race as it was due to start in 15 minutes! John Cooper and Charles were pacing up and down waiting for us to arrive, so we *flew* to Brands and circled around there to see if we could find somewhere to land. We picked out a paddock which was only about 100 yards from the gate and landed in the field right by the trees. We rushed up to the track just in time for me to get into the car for the start of the race — which I won. After the meeting finished we decided we had better find out who owned the field we had landed in and go to make our apologies. It turned out it belonged to John Hall, who owned the circuit. We had to go to see him, and he was very nice about it. Many aeroplanes have landed at Brands since then, but I think we were the first.

The next plane I owned I bought in Los Angeles from Lance Reventlow. We were on our way out to New Zealand at the end of the year and we went to a party at Lance's place; while we were there he took me out to show me his plane, which was a Cessna 310. I liked it, eventually bought it from him and had it ferried to England; I used his plane for the next three or four years.

When I had been flying for about two years, *Flight* magazine decided they would like to do a story on drivers and other people in Grand Prix racing who flew aeroplanes. Colin Chapman by this time had a Comanche, and John Cooper was learning to fly as well. He had bought himself a Piper Tripacer and Innes Ireland had his Bonanza, so *Flight* organised a day at Fairoaks to come and take some photographs of us all, air to air photos, flying, and messing around with our planes generally.

Of course, the day they fixed was very windy — not only windy, but very bumpy weather for flying. But there we all were, and photographers waiting, so we thought we'd better get on with it. Colin Chapman went up first and flew all round having his picture taken, and then John Cooper and myself were about to go off. Now, Charlie Cooper was there with John's son, Michael, who was about five or six, I suppose. John wanted to take Michael up with him, but Charlie absolutely put his foot down and refused to let the boy go. He said it was too windy and too dangerous, and that was that.

John had his licence, but he was not very keen on going far without someone being with him. So he had organised himself another pilot — I think he was with Dan Air at the time, flying big aeroplanes — to go with him. Then Colin decided he'd go up with John, too, so he got in the back, and we took off, me in my Cessna and the others in the Tripacer. We flew alongside each other and had our photos taken, together and separately and from all angles. Then, coming back to the airfield, John's plane was in the circuit and on final approach, so I decided to go round one more time till I could land. When I looked back to see whether they were on the ground or not, there was the Tripacer, right in the middle of the aerodrome, standing absolutely vertical on its nose!

There was quite a panic on then. I landed and taxied over to where the plane was, and there was poor old John's plane all bent and twisted, petrol pouring out of the wings. Charlie was jumping up and down and having a great 'I-told-you-so' session, and John and Colin were having a big conflab worrying whether John had paid up his insurance policy or not. Apparently John was just coming in to land when he decided it was too bumpy and windy for him. So he tried to pass control over to the other pilot who was sitting beside him; between them they hit the ground too hard. The plane went up a bit, and stalled or something, and came down on its nose. They were lucky they weren't hurt actually. The plane was pretty badly damaged; it had to go away to be repaired and it took about nine months to fix.

After it had been repaired, John got somebody to go with him up to Luton to fetch his plane. It was the same day that there was an Air Fair at Biggin Hill, so he decided not to fly back to Fairoaks but to go to Biggin Hill and watch the Air Fair. So they landed at Biggin Hill, parked the Tripacer, and went off to have a look. When they came back to fly home, they found another plane had taxied up behind John's and chopped all the tail off with its propeller!

John had meant to get home in a hurry, because he'd promised his wife, Pauline, to go out to dinner with her that night. Now he was standing there, looking at his plane with its tail knocked off, so he had to ring Fairoaks and get someone else to come in and pick him up. He was terribly late getting back. He jumped into his twin-engined Mini — it had a second engine in the back — at Fairoaks and roared off down the road to go home so that he wouldn't get into trouble with Pauline. And he had a big shunt on the Kingston By-pass on the way. So he finished up in hospital for a while, which put paid to his flying career for the time being. I don't think he did any more flying at all, actually; it was a fairly unhappy interlude.

The only really uncomfortable incident I have had while flying was when I went off to Reims on one of these two-day race meetings, with the twelve-hour race on the Saturday and the Formula 1 race on the Sunday. We went over to Reims on Wednesday for practice — practice was Wednesday, Thursday and Friday — and I decided to come back on Friday night, have Saturday at home and fly back for the race. I got away all right, but on the way back one engine developed a terrific oil leak. By the time I reached the Channel the engine was just about out of oil; I was heading for Gatwick at the time, and I had to cancel my flight plan and decided to land at Lympne instead. The Channel was full of fog and the weather was pretty bad in general. I called up Lympne on the radio and they decided to bring me in by radar. On the first approach it was so foggy I never saw the ground at all, so I had to overshoot and go round again. Then the engine ran out of oil, so I had to fiddle with that, and do another radar approach on one engine. This was all quite exciting, but difficult too, because I hadn't flown in these conditions on one engine before. I was learning pretty rapidly. On the second approach I could just see the fences as I went across the edge of the aerodrome, and I managed to get the plane on the ground. Then I had the job of trying to taxi the thing across the aerodrome on one engine.

When the Flag Drops

As soon as I reached a hangar, I checked the engine over, but there wasn't much I could do about this oil leak. I filled it up with oil, and realised it wasn't much use going to Gatwick with a dud plane. I might as well fly it to McAlpines at Luton so they could get it put right for me.

I took off from Lympne and headed for Luton, but before I got there the engine ran out of oil again and I had to close it down. So I had another big, one-engined landing session at Luton, when it was almost dark, and I don't relish doing that kind of thing too often.

My method of changing aircraft is simply to try to buy the plane at the right price and sell it without losing any money on it. This I managed to achieve most of the time. I traded in the Cessna 310 for a single Comanche, and later changed that for a twin Comanche which I bought from the Piper dealers in Geneva. That must have been in 1964. It was a fairly new aeroplane, and I sold it at the end of the year and bought a Queenair.

I liked the Queenair for its size, mainly. I bought it from the Coal Board and then employed Roy Coburn, who used to work for McAlpines, to look after it at Fairoaks. That was Roy's main job, to keep my plane in good order, but he used to look after the planes of other people who used Fairoaks and that was how a small business started up which now thrives, with Roy, in Australia. I didn't want to get involved in buying and selling planes myself; I had enough on my plate at the time.

The Queenair was useful because at that time we were racing Formula 2 Brabhams with Honda engines, and I was taking quite a few people to race meetings. I flew Honda mechanics around, and wherever we went we had a plane full of mechanics, and engines, and bits and pieces. So Honda helped me buy the Queenair and also run it — I could never have bought it on my own. It was better at getting in and out of tight places than many other aircraft, provided you didn't have it loaded to the gunnels. If the Queenair was only half full of fuel it would get out of anywhere. I kept it for two years, but when the Honda team finished with racing I sold it and went back to a cheaper aircraft, a twin Comanche. I ran that for a year and then bought a Navajo.

This is a far more economical plane than the Queenair, and made more sense maintenance-wise. The Queenair was better made and a lot safer in many ways for the type of flying that I was doing, but the Navajo was a lot cheaper to run and about forty miles an hour quicker, which saved a lot of time getting to races and back.

Going from Fairoaks to Geneva, for instance, used to take me two hours. Well, by the time you get to London Airport and get on a commercial flight and fly to Geneva you'd be very lucky to do it in two hours. The biggest advantage I found in having my own aeroplane was that it never, ever went without me! It was always there waiting for me, and I didn't have all that trouble booking and switching flights and so on. In our way of life there is no telling a week in advance what day you are likely to leave, or which flight you want. You kid yourself you'll have time to go out to a race meeting the day before practice, but it is almost always the morning of first practice in the end. With your own aeroplane you have a big advantage in these sort of circumstances.

I have never employed another pilot to fly for me, though I have had other pilots go with me on occasions. The only exception to that is the one time I employed Hugh Dibley, who is both a racing driver and a BOAC airline pilot—and a racing car constructor, now. We were racing in England, at Silverstone, and the next day we were to race at Enna. We had to fly down to Rome overnight, and I wasn't going to fly all night and then drive in Sicily the next day, so I got Hugh to come with me. I slept up front while he did the flying. We just managed to get to Rome; during the night he had flown through some pretty marginal weather and the plane picked up a lot of ice—I don't remember because I was sound asleep. Rather than wake me to ask how to work the de-icing equipment, which was located just where I was flaked out, he let me sleep. The plane must have slowed to about one hundred and sixty miles an hour with all that ice on it, and this cut our range down so much that we arrived in Rome with only enough fuel for another half-hour's flying.

I had another unfortunate experience while flying, but it was not in my own aeroplane. My plane was being worked on and wasn't available so I hired a Dove to fly down to Albi for a Formula 2 race. I was taking some Honda people down and my mother and father came over as well. We got down there OK, but coming back we stopped at Toulouse to clear Customs. While we were dealing with that procedure we had the plane filled with fuel and asked the chap to check the oil out. Well, he did this on one side but apparently couldn't get the cap off on the other side, because we found later that the cap was absolutely jammed tight and we couldn't undo it. So he must have given up and gone off.

We took off for London and on the way back I was sitting there just looking at the instruments; I noticed the oil gauge on the right-hand engine flicker a little bit. Once I had seen it flicker I kept on looking at it, and in about ten minutes the gauge started fluctuating, which meant the engine was definitely running out of oil. I couldn't see any visible oil leaks, but when it began fluctuating really badly it was time to stop the engine before any damage was done so I feathered it.

We had a quick scramble through the books to see where the nearest aerodrome was that would let us land, and it turned out to be Tours. We set course for Tours. But the plane was pretty heavily loaded; we had eight or nine people on board and were stacked up with luggage and spare parts and things, so flying on one engine was not going to be easy. We were losing altitude gradually, and we still had thirty or forty miles to go to Tours. By the time we got there we were down to about 1,500 feet. We called the tower for clearance to land and we had to do a circuit the wrong way round because of the engine that was feathered. I didn't want to drop the dead engine — I'd learned about the danger of that in the Air Force. We made a circuit on to the right runway, with the engine feathered up a little, which I think helped a lot.

We had a terrible job getting the oil cap off and had to rush round Tours aerodrome looking for tools; but in the end we got it off, filled up with oil and got home quite easily. But while we had been flying with one engine my mother

I Discover I Need Wings

had been staring out of the window and worrying. A couple of comments about the problem were passed round the aircraft and my mother got wind that something was wrong. So she kept on staring at this dead engine and fussing. In the end I said: 'Never mind looking at that one. The one you want to worry about is the one that is still going!'

On many occasions we got back to Fairoaks late in the evening and as the airfield closed at sunset, I had to learn a pattern to be able to land safely in the dark. Luckily there was a greenhouse just on the threshold of Fairoaks and this could be seen pretty easily at nights, because it used to shine out. Once you had found this glass house you were able to come down alongside it with the landing lights on; the glass-houses were just on your left and the landing lights showed up the trees just past them. Then, if you cleared the trees you could drop down over the top of them and the lights would show up the fence, which gave you a pretty good indication where to touch down on the field.

But one night we came in particularly late; there were just Ron Tauranac and myself in the plane and it was quite cloudy and very, very dark. We made about four or five passes across the field before we eventually convinced ourselves that it was, in fact, Fairoaks. On this particular night it appeared to have fences across the field, and this threw doubt into our minds as to whether it was actually the right place. But eventually we saw the lights on in a school nearby which convinced us that this was the right one. We did our usual pattern to come in alongside the glasshouses and landed OK except that after we had parked the plane alongside the hangar and were going out through the gate we noticed somebody come roaring in on his pushbike, past us, and going along to where the aeroplanes were. At the time we didn't take any notice of this, but apparently one of the local residents was quite upset about our flying around at this time of night over the top of his house making a noise. He must have gone in and felt the aeroplanes till he found one with hot engines; then he took the number of it and reported us to the police. Of course, after a couple of days the police came down to the house and said they had had a complaint which they had to investigate. They asked if I had landed on such and such a night and they gave me a form to fill up which started off by having the usual things like licence numbers and insurance details; and inside it said that the only occasions you were allowed to fly under 500 feet were on landing and taking-off. So the fact that we were landing at the time cleared us of flying over this chap's house at a very low altitude making a noise.

So there was nothing the police could do. Luckily the complaint had *only* been made to the police and not to the Air Registration Board—if it had been made to them, it would probably have gone further. I could have had my licence taken away for flying into an aerodrome which had closed for the night. Nowadays I am more law-abiding.

Something I always wanted to do was to fly to Australia—or back. We had the opportunity to sell the Queenair in Australia in 1968 so I took the chance and flew it out there. First of all there was quite a bit to do for the preparation of the aeroplane. Roy Coburn fitted up all the extra fuel tanks we needed, because we had decided it would save a lot of time if we by-passed India on the way. There were too many problems involved in landing there. We removed the seats and put the extra fuel tanks in the back.

We took off from Gatwick about lunchtime on Monday, 5th February, 1968. For the first leg we set out to go as far as Brindisi with a stop at Bastia in Corsica on the way. On the first leg down to Bastia we put fuel in all the ferry tanks and decided we would try them all out on the way to make sure that when we got to the stretches where we needed them they were all functioning properly. They all appeared to be working pretty well on the way down, so we stopped at Bastia, refuelled and went on to Brindisi. We arrived there fairly late at night, probably about eleven o'clock because we had spent more time in Bastia than we really counted on. We refuelled the aeroplane ready for the next morning, then went and found a hotel to stay the night.

This particular aerodrome at Brindisi is half military and half civil and the next morning it took us about two hours just to lodge a flight plan because the flight planning section was run by the military while all the other red-tape stuff was run by the civil authorities. They didn't seem to work together in any kind of liaison. We spent half our time running backwards and forwards from one side of the aerodrome to the other trying to get all our clearances sorted out, and eventually we got off quite late in the day. We had hoped to press on to Bahrain, which we did, but it was pretty late when we got there. We took off from Brindisi and flew along the Mediterranean coast which was very picturesque and beautiful, with great big mountains on our left. We went across Cyprus and down to Beirut. We had arranged with BOAC prior to our departure for them to assist us with our clearances at all the places at which we were calling.

We were met at Beirut by BOAC representatives, and I am sure without BOAC's help we should have been there for quite a long time. We managed to get off fairly late in the afternoon and then we had quite a long hop to Bahrain. We had to cross over Damascus, for which we had had to get prior permission with telegrams from London and so on before we left. We had had to wait for the replies, too. Anyway, when we arrived over Syria we spent the entire time crossing Damascus talking to the controls down below, going over all the clearances and telling them our addresses, dates of birth, where we had come from, where we were going and just about everything you could name: they wanted to know *all* about us. Eventually we went out of radio contact with them before we knew whether they were going to let us cross or not, but as we were already past Damascus we just pressed on. We expected trouble, but they didn't send up any MIG fighters after us.

It wasn't long before it was dark. I think it was the blackest night I have ever seen in my life. There was no moon whatsoever, and you just couldn't see anything outside the window. You wouldn't have known whether you were up in the air or down on the ground or upside down or what. During the evening a terrific crosswind must have come up, because we were flying at 12,000 feet and we found that we kept getting blown off-course. There were very few radio aids — with quite long distances between them. By the time we got a couple of hundred miles from Bahrain one of the beacons obviously wasn't working and we had to cross it and go to the next one, which meant a long time before we had any fix, and by the time we picked up the beacon we could hardly believe we could be that much off-course. It was the beacon about 100 miles *south* of Bahrain. We eventually got back on the track and arrived at Bahrain about midnight. Once again we were met by the BOAC representative and taken off to a brand new hotel which had just been completed there. This is something we had hardly expected, in fact we had more or less prepared ourselves to sleep underneath the wings of the aeroplane. It was very pleasant after a long day's flying to have the opportunity to sleep in such a nice hotel.

It was so good that we slept on in the morning and were quite late getting back to the aerodrome to check the plane over, refuel it, and get it ready for its next leg. We hoped to go as far as Colombo, in Ceylon, in one hop. Eventually we got away OK. Prior to leaving London we had made arrangements to stop at a little island by the name of Masira which is off the coast of Saudi Arabia. The only thing on the island is an RAF station. We went straight across the desert to the island and when we arrived we were met by the Commanding Officer and quite a lot of RAF mechanics took over the job of refuelling the aeroplane while Roy and myself were taken off to the officers' Mess. We had lunch with them and were really well looked after. We were told some fantastic stories about the fishing there; I was very tempted to stay at Masira for a couple of days, but as we were on a very tight schedule to get to Australia we decided we would have to leave it till the next trip—to which I am still looking forward!

When we had finished hearing all about the fish and the sharks and the big stingrays that they had at Masira and that we didn't have time to go after, we took off—fairly late in the afternoon—for Colombo. This was a stretch across the ocean of just about 2,000 miles. We headed off across this pond and about half-way across we had a drama. We had changed over to one of the ferry tanks of which we had two on board. (When the engines were switched over to the ferry tanks they both ran on the one tank.) We were flying at 13,000 feet and suddenly, out of the blue, both engines went dead quiet. All the noise stopped in both of them at once. Of course, Roy and I banged our heads together, diving down for the fuel taps, because this was completely unexpected; we reckoned we had another three-quarters of an hour's flying on this ferry tank before it would be empty and now suddenly there was no fuel at all. There was a bit of a panic on then to check what had happened. We found that the first tank hadn't emptied, for some reason, and there was quite a bit of fuel left in it. We were now flying on the other ferry tank which seemed to be working quite happily.

By the time the fuel had come through and both engines were running again we had dropped down to 6,000 feet. When both engines had stopped the plane was flying on auto-pilot and with all the excitement of diving for the fuel taps I had forgotten all about the autopilot. The altitude control was trying to hold the plane up when the engines had stopped, and the aeroplane was trying to fall down. By the time I had worked out what was going on, the plane was in a stall condition. I quickly got the autopilot out and we got both the engines running again. The noise was wonderful after all the silence.

We started climbing back up to 13,000 feet, set it on autopilot again and started investigating as to why we had run out of petrol in this ferry tank when we did. We were unable to explain it because we couldn't see how the fuel had run out of the tank. There was a lot still in it. Luckily we had taken a pump with us which enabled us to transfer fuel from one ferry tank to another while in flight so when the second tank had gone down we re-filled it from the first one, which meant that we still had the range of fuel left. As it was a bit tight on fuel for the distance we had to cover over the sea, it was essential that we were able to do this.

Anyway, we flogged on through the night until we passed the tip of India and pin-pointed ourselves on the map. After flying across water so long we were within a few miles of our course, which was pretty good really considering we had done about 1,700 miles over the sea. We tracked out on an MDB beacon at Masira which had a range of about 500 miles, so that pulled us well on our way. Luckily, there wasn't much wind that day so it was fairly easy to keep on course.

We passed the tip of India and set course for Colombo; when we were about 150 miles out of Colombo we decided to try and give them a call on the radio. The range was pretty good that night and we were able to contact them that far out. It was obvious from their comments that they knew nothing whatsoever about our coming. The flight plan we had lodged in Masira hadn't got round to Colómbo by the time we got there. We then had to explain on the radio that we had come from Masira and the flight plan had been lodged; we gave the details of the flight and then there was a silence. After a while they came back to us and said: 'What would be your endurance when you get over the air field?' Which meant: 'How much further could you fly if you had to?' The aerodrome we were flying to was Ratmalana, which we found afterwards wasn't the main aerodrome in Colombo, and we should have gone to the international one which was both military and civil. But apparently they didn't know this at Masira and suggested Ratmalana.

We were 100 miles out when we were asked what our endurance would be when we arrived over Ratmalana, which was a bit mystifying because the weather looked one hundred per cent clear. We couldn't understand why there should be a hold-up. We worked out that we would have about fifty minutes of flying left by the time we landed so we pressed on and arrived over the aerodrome. We were given a clearance to land straightaway on arrival, which was pretty good, because we had been flying for a long time and although we had fifty minutes of fuel left it always seems that it doesn't take long to use it up.

When we came in on final approach we could see why there might have been a delay. The airfield didn't have a proper airstrip, it was just grass. This grass strip was lined down each side with little kerosene goose-necked flares, so obviously they had had their little dark chaps out there lighting them all! They probably didn't think they would be able to get all this done for us by the time we got there. Luckily the flare path was all finished just as we arrived.

I Discover I Need Wings

The actual flying time from Masira was 9 hours and 35 minutes—it's in my log book. We landed and stayed the night at a hotel not very far away but it didn't have any water. I don't know now why, but there wasn't enough water even to have a wash. Next morning we were met by people from Repco who were expecting us and they took us around and showed us a little bit of Colombo in the morning. Then we went back, refuelled and set off in the afternoon for Singapore, which was slightly further in distance than the trip from Masira to Colombo; it was just over 2,000 miles. On that particular route the met report gave us a slight tail wind, but in fact we had a slight head wind.

We were aiming for the most northern part of Sumatra so that we could pinpoint ourselves and because we were doubtful whether we were going to make Singapore. We had two possibilities of landing before that—one at Kuala Lumpur and one at Butterworth. We arrived at Sumatra about an hour late and we were relieved to see it, because if it hadn't come up shortly we would have been starting to convince ourselves we were very much off-course. We pressed on and headed for Kuala Lumpur but we were doubtful about stopping there. We would have wasted quite a lot of time and we were particularly keen to get to Singapore that night. So after passing over Colombo we worked out our fuel and we decided that we would have enough to get to Singapore. On the way down we were able to get met reports, and everything looked pretty good.

We landed safely in Singapore and we were met by representatives of the Motor Club; BOAC speeded up our clearance for us for which we were very, very grateful. It was marvellous to get into bed that evening as it had been a pretty long day.

We spent most of the next morning checking the aeroplane over, and refuelling it. We decided to take out one of the ferry tanks because from there on there weren't any long legs and it gave us a lot more room in the aeroplane. We managed to get all this sorted out by lunchtime and pressed on for Bali. Sumatra is always a difficult place to fly over and the necessary clearances had to be arranged in London before departure. We found out after we left that a clearance had been granted to cross Sumatra but, much to our surprise, when we arrived in Bali the people there didn't know about our coming apart from the flight plan. We didn't have our clearance. They then refused to allow us to depart from Bali until such time as the clearance side had been confirmed!

The situation looked pretty bad, because we had hoped to get to Darwin that evening. We went ahead and refuelled the aeroplane anyway and asked the people in charge of the aerodrome there whether it was possible to get any messages to Jakarta, which was the central point of Sumatra where all cabled information would come from. But there didn't seem any quick, easy way of achieving this so I decided I would go back in and pay the landing fees. Whilst paying the landing fees I was just able to come up with a few extra American dollars as a tip for the chap to see if this could speed things up. It was unbelievable how quickly it all happened then! In ten or fifteen minutes the clearance was all fixed up and yes, okay, away we go!

When we went out to the aeroplane we found there were some five or six Australian people there asking if they could have a lift to Darwin. Unfortunately we were unable to accommodate them, because we hadn't any seats. They had been there three or four days waiting to get on an aeroplane to get out of Bali. At that time there were only one or two aeroplanes calling a week, and they were nearly always full. These poor people were stuck there and probably were there for some time after we left.

We had a pretty trouble-free flight from there on and arrived in Darwin on the Friday evening, just six days after leaving England. We had a similar drama going into Darwin as we had into Colombo. The flight plan from Bali hadn't reached Darwin, and there again it was about eleven o'clock at night when we called Darwin to give them our position; they immediately came back to us saying they had no details of our flight and no flight plan had arrived. We explained we had come from Bali and they immediately came back and said that it wasn't the *first* time somebody had arrived before

116

the flight plan from Bali. So there wasn't any problem, and they cleared us into Darwin before the flight plan arrived.

We stayed the night in Darwin and the next morning we gave the plane a thorough checkover. We had a slight rev drop on one engine, which turned out to be a faulty ignition lead: this we were able to deal with without any trouble and then pressed on with the idea of getting as far as Charleville. But on the way down across Australia we went via Katherine and Mount Isa. When we got to the Mount Isa area there were fantastic thunderstorms and although it was fairly reasonable to fly round these we did have to go a long way out of our way to dodge them. There were clouds going up probably thirty or forty thousand feet and, with all this dodging around the thunderstorms and getting a few headwinds, we were starting to get concerned as to whether we would make Charleville on the fuel we had with sufficient reserve. It was just going on dusk and running out of fuel at night in that area is not an ideal situation.

We decided we would call control and cancel our flight to Charleville and switch to Longreach which was quite a lot nearer to us. We flew into Longreach and stayed the night and then on the Sunday morning—it was Saturday going down from Darwin to Longreach—we set off to arrive in Sydney at lunchtime. When we got there we found the Sydney newspapers had been checking on our trip all the way through, and they had had a little running commentary each day about where we were and how we were getting on with our trip; much to our surprise, when we arrived at Bankstown there was a crowd of people to see our arrival. My wife and my mother and father were quite pleased to see us, too.

The other little flying drama I had whilst I was racing was when I was buying the Lotus 24, which must have been in 1962. It was arranged for me to go up and have a fitting in the Lotus 24 at Cheshunt. At that time they were nearest to Panshanger aerodrome. My aeroplane was being worked on, so I had to hire a plane at Fairoaks, because we had been down testing at Goodwood earlier in the day with a Cooper. Anyway, we drove up to Fairoaks and hired one of the club aeroplanes, a Tripacer. We took off in this thing and flew up to Panshanger without any problem because the weather was quite good; but during the time we were at Lotus a snowstorm had come in which was a pretty sharp, nasty one. It was quite a surprise because it wasn't expected so early.

We took off from Panshanger and had passed the south side of Luton when we could see this weather starting to come in. I was beginning to get worried as to whether I would get back to Fairoaks because the aeroplane wasn't equipped for bad weather flying. In fact, it didn't have what they call an artificial horizon, which meant that there was no way you could fly this aeroplane safely in cloud. It was essential that we should stay in sight of the ground, and I had the idea that if I could get past Amersham and through the valley to the Thames near Henley, we might get back to Fairoaks in time. But the weather really closed in on us, and by the time I had gone over Amersham and was flying up this valley, it was getting obvious that we weren't going to reach Fairoaks. The snow on the windscreen was making it pretty difficult to see and we were then flying alongside power lines – following power lines up this valley. It got to the stage where it just wasn't possible to go any further. So I had to pick out a field to land in. I made a quick decision and a quick run over my chosen field to have a look at it and then make an emergency landing. It wasn't even sunset at the time, but with all the snow clouds and the weather closing in like that it was getting dark long before it should have done. The landing into the field was without incident except that when we landed we didn't know which way to taxi to get out of the place. Eventually we saw a little light in the distance over to one side of the field, so we turned towards it and found it was a house behind a clump of trees. We taxied up there and somebody came running out of the house. His first comment when he came over and saw an aeroplane in his field was: 'My God! I thought somebody was pinching my tractor!' He couldn't believe his eyes when he saw an aeroplane taxiing across his field in a snowstorm. Anyway, he was very good about it all, and took us inside. They had a nice, big fire going and by that time it was very,

very cold and starting to snow quite heavily. We had to ring up and get transport to come and pick us up—just Tim Wall (my mechanic) and myself. Eventually Phil Kerr turned up in a car and drove us back to London.

It snowed heavily all that night, and the next day when it stopped we went back and tried to see if we could fly this aeroplane out of the field, which was a bit of a joke really. When we got up there we could hardly see the house, let alone the field or the plane. It wasn't possible to get it out at all. The snow looked like staying there for quite some time and, as the plane was a Club aeroplane, we had to do something about it. In the end we had to take the wings off and put it on a truck and bring it back to Fairoaks by truck. It turned out to be a pretty expensive trip up to Lotus for a try-out. And I only drove the car five times!

CHAPTER VIII

Achievement

In the winter of 1958, while I was basking in the heat of summer in Australia and New Zealand, we held the Australian Grand Prix at Melbourne. There were two heats of twenty-five miles and the Grand Prix of 100 miles. Stirling was out there in Rob Walker's Cooper and he won the first heat, while I won the second. Moss's engine was overheating, and I got the pole position on aggregate. Moss won by thirty-nine seconds from me but his Cooper was absolutely dry of water at the finish, so he went on his lap of honour with Sabrina (You don't remember her?) in her bright mauve Vauxhall with leopard-skin-covered seats. There was an enormous crowd and people were breaking down barriers and over-loading bridges.

The New Zealand Grand Prix at Ardmore, near Auckland, was quite a big international event that season. It took place in January, and it was obvious from the entry that racing in Australia and New Zealand in the winter was becoming attractive to European drivers. We had Moss, Flockhart, Shelby, Bonnier and Schell, with Bruce McLaren and myself representing the ones who had spanned the gap to Europe: plus the locals. As in Melbourne, there were two heats and the Grand Prix; Moss was leading his heat easily in the Walker Cooper when a drive shaft broke on the last lap. He pushed the car the last half mile to the line, but even if he were to start in the Grand Prix he would be right at the back. I won my heat and set up a new lap record, and then I had a problem. There could only be one spare drive-shaft for a Cooper in the whole of New Zealand, and that was the one I had in my spares kit. I remember making the decision as to whether I should lend it to him or not: I did. And I finished the Grand Prix second to Moss!

He drove a great race. Starting from the back of the grid, he scorched by everyone else on the grass while all those further up the grid were sorting themselves out, and as they went into the first corner he was already sixth. By the end of the race I was in second place and he was coming up to lap me! I just managed to avoid this indignity.

Before I returned to England at the beginning of 1959 we heard some news which shocked us very much. After Mike Hawthorn had won the World Championship, he announced his retirement and, although we were sorry to see him leave motor racing, we knew that such a dynamic character would find something worthwhile to do with his life. Then came the day when we heard that he had been killed on the road in his own 3.4 Jaguar. He was driving towards London on the Guildford by-pass and the inquest decided that he had momentarily lost control. The Jaguar skidded, hit the back of a lorry and then hit a tree; Mike was killed at once. After all those magnificent races and his years on the track it seemed a cruel irony that he should meet his death in such a way.

Meanwhile I was being the eternal runner-up in New Zealand. Ron Flockhart's BRM beat me for the Lady Wigram Trophy . . . always the bridesmaid. But I couldn't have lost to a nicer chap. Then Bruce beat the two of us into second and third places at Teretonga! I thought it must be time to see how the new Coventry Climax engine was coming along in England, ready for our first real onslaught on the World Championship.

The 2½-litre Coventry Climax was probably one of the best engines ever made. It won first time out, and hardly looked back. It was so reliable; it very, very seldom stopped running. Its first outing was at Silverstone in the International Trophy Race. The biggest drawback we had had in previous years was the gearbox, and this was the first year with our Cooper gearbox. It was reasonably successful although it had a few teething troubles. It never really let us down, but it occasionally gave us a few gearshift problems. I think we would have won easily at Zandvoort only I couldn't get second gear, which is essential on that circuit.

Generally speaking, in 1959 the thing that we had going for us was the fact that the car was really small and the Cooper body much better aerodynamically than other Grand Prix cars. It was always pretty quick on the straight as well as being able to get round the corners much quicker because of its lightness. I like driving that type of car anyway. This particular Cooper was a lot easier to drive without throwing it around sideways, whereas with the previous Coopers there didn't seem to be any other way of driving them. They used to be really tail-happy, although they were controllable, and the only way to get them to go quickly was to drive them with the tail out. The 1959 Cooper was the first one that you could make understeer.

Our win at Silverstone on the car's first outing gave us plenty of confidence to go to Monaco. The only problem we had at Monaco with the car was heat, the radiator being in the front and the pedals immediately behind it. The discomfort in that race from the physical point of view was very bad. I remember, when I eventually took the lead, wondering how I was going to keep going to the finish, because the actual brake pedal, clutch pedal and accelerator pedal were that hot I could barely keep a foot on them. The car was pretty badly designed from the cockpit point of view, and we had spent the previous night putting bits of cardboard in place to try to direct the hot air outside, away from the cockpit. Although we had done a reasonable job, the heat was still getting through to the pedals, and I can remember John giving signals that Brooks was beginning to catch me towards the end of the race—I was dropping back because the heat on my feet was almost unbearable. However, I won the Monaco Grand Prix, which was a good way to start the season.

Stirling Moss was driving the Rob Walker Cooper with a 2½-litre engine, and I think his gearbox packed up. He was using a Colotti gearbox then, which was always giving him trouble. It was intended to replace the old Citroen gearbox, which wasn't strong enough to take the $2\frac{1}{2}$-litre engine, but the Colotti substitute cost Moss a lot of races and Monaco was one of them. He and Brooks were my main opposition that year.

The Dutch Grand Prix at Zandvoort was one that we should have followed up with another win. I led the race for quite some time until the gearbox gave trouble, which was disastrous. You desperately need second gear around the Hunze Rug, the twisty corners at the back of the pits, and this I had lost. So Bonnier in his BRM eventually caught me and passed me, and there was nothing I could do about it without the gear. I finished second in that race. For some reason I like the Zandvoort track very much—it is a real drivers' circuit.

That year we had the French Grand Prix next, at Reims. Everyone who was there will remember it as being probably the hottest race day they have ever experienced. It was so hot the road broke up, and great big pieces of asphalt were thrown back by other cars. The Cooper, being so low, seemed to cop more of it than the others, particularly at windscreen height. As I mentioned before, we had terrible trouble with heat in the cockpit, and of course at Reims it was unbelievably bad. I finished up with blisters on my feet. Towards the end of the race we had a pretty dangerous situation. There were several drivers just about flaking out at the wheel and it was only a matter of luck that they all managed to get in to the pits before they collapsed. I was almost at the stage of collapsing at the wheel, so I broke all the windscreen away with my hand to try to get some air. Every car I got near showered me with bricks and stones, and the Coopers were absolutely destroyed at the front. I can remember really fighting to complete the last few laps and keep going. There was a stage when I was really coasting into the corners rather than braking, because my feet were so badly burnt that I could hardly put any pressure on the pedals. When the race was over I had to be lifted out of the cockpit—I finished third.

We don't have nearly as much of a problem with heat inside the car nowadays. The Cooper was the first of the modern Grand Prix cars and naturally came up against new problems. Now a much better job is done to shield the driver from hot air, and the cars are much more pleasant to drive.

Aintree was the scene of the British Grand Prix that year. The big drama of the race was tyre wear. We were all on Dunlops, but for some reason the Aintree circuit was very hard on tyres. The surface of the track had a lot to do with it, but also that year the cars were going so much faster than previously. The engines were developed to a point at which tyres were becoming marginal. We needed bigger tyres and there were none available—little skinny things we had, and there was just not enough rubber on the road to cope with the power and speed.

I got off to a good start and got well out in front in the race, but I noticed at about half distance that my left front tyre was at the stage where the tread was starting to disappear. From there on I had to change my driving technique, because the car had quite a bit of understeer at that meeting, and I had to get it into more of an oversteer situation simply by my driving style. I had to try to complete the race without stopping for a tyre change, because we only had bolt-on wheels in those days and it would have taken a lot of time to change tyres.

I remember John Cooper coming out and holding a wheel out for me to see, because Moss had been into the pit in his BRM and they had found out that the tyres had worn badly.

John was trying to warn me about this problem, but I had known about it myself for quite a few laps and I was already taking steps to finish the race without stopping. We got through with a completely bald front tyre. If I had been chased hard I couldn't have got through without a tyre change; but we weren't the only car in trouble. It was just that I was lucky enough to notice the severity of the tyre wear early enough to do something about it. I won the Grand Prix and Moss was second. Why he drove for BRM I don't really know. Obviously it was something to do with money, but he didn't drive a BRM all the time. He used the Cooper at Monaco and Zandvoort.

Achievement

For the German Grand Prix they decided to use the track at Avus, Berlin, where I had raced before in a central-seat Cooper sports car. That was a shocking circuit; it was just an autobahn with a hairpin at one end and a banking at the other end. The banking in its day was probably quite good, but it was made of bricks and it was already pretty old by 1959. A lot of bricks had sunk and it was very, very rough. The banking wasn't really steep enough for the speeds that we were doing round there, and the G force, coupled with the bumps, was unbelievably bad. Every time you went round the banking you were glad to get to the other end of it; it was a tremendous relief to have got round each time without something breaking on the car or your crash hat coming down over your eyes so that you couldn't see where you were going. It was especially bad for the light cars like the Lotuses. The Cooper was always a strong car which helped us considerably in places like that, and in those days we used to run pretty high spring rates by present day standards. To take a current motor car and put it round that banking just wouldn't be feasible. The days of being able to race a Grand Prix car on a banking as well as on a flat circuit are over. It isn't possible any more. None of the drivers wanted to go back to Avus—well, none of the sane ones anyway. There were quite a few sane ones. . . .

We had two big crashes at that race meeting. I actually witnessed both of them. I can remember being passed by Jean Behra's Porsche after he had slipstreamed me up the straight just prior to going onto the banking. He really went in there very quickly indeed and the car just went out of control; it went up over the top as if nothing in the world could have stopped it. It hit a flagpole right at the top of the banking and Behra must have been killed instantly.

That was tragic, but the biggest shunt I think I have ever seen ended quite happily. Hans Herrmann lost his BRM under braking at the end of the straight at the opposite end from the banking. He went in amongst the strawbales, and I can remember seeing that car so high in the air it didn't seem possible. I had already turned the corner and was coming back up the other side when I saw all these strawbales in the air and the car apparently going into orbit. Hans Herrmann walked away from that accident. He was thrown out and crouched on the road watching the car flying and wondering where it would land!

Tony Brooks won at Avus — I didn't finish the race — so now he and Moss and I were all in with a chance for the World Championship. We ran the Grand Prix in two heats at Avus and I finished the first but not the second. The clutch packed up and there wasn't time to change it between heats.

Then came Portugal, with the race at Lisbon where I had my famous accident! I describe this in detail in a later chapter, so I will simply say that I was overtaking a slower car driven by a local when he suddenly took an unexpected line that put me off the road in no uncertain manner.

The Lisbon circuit was quite a dangerous one really, lots of trees and strawbales and dogs running across the road. In fact I had a pretty nasty experience there just before my accident. A little boy of probably seven or eight ran across the track in front of me, and I had to stand on the brakes and do a little swerving on a very fast part of the circuit. It gives you an awful jolt, because the last thing you want to run over is a kiddy; if it is a dog or something you might press on, but to see a little kid run across the track just as a straying dog would is quite upsetting. So there were two races on the trot where we dropped out and after starting the season so well this changed the picture somewhat. It looked now as though Moss would take the title.

My bumps and bruises and stiffness subsided in time for the Italian Grand Prix at Monza which was another place where we had a problem with tyres. I remember Dunlops bringing down some special tyres with a much deeper tread. They were quite difficult to drive on because of the extra tread, which we hadn't been used to, but they were supposed to be an advantage wear-wise. I think there was a bit of a fiddle on, tyrewise — Dunlops only had a few down at Monza, which they had just managed to scratch out before they went there. Moss and Bruce and myself had them, but there weren't enough for everybody. Moss won, Phil Hill was second, and I was third.

Achievement

I am a fairly patient sort of character, but I must admit the long wait between the Italian Grand Prix at Monza on September 13th 1959, and the United States Grand Prix at Sebring, Florida, on December 12th, some three months later, tried me to the limit.

It was not that I was worried about the result. Frankly, I just did not believe my luck would hold out and let me win the Championship. What was frustrating was that the actual timing, location and importance of the race in the motor-racing world interfered with just about every decision I wanted to make. Everything, it seemed, just had to wait until after Sebring.

I had counted on the 'season' ending with the Italian Grand Prix. My garage at Chessington would have been just about ready for opening by then, so that I could settle down and get it running smoothly before work on the 1960 season started. My lease on a house I was renting in Dorking was just about up, and I wanted to help my wife look around for a new home to buy where we could settle down with my son Geoffrey.

What made it all the more confusing was that there were endless rumours that the Sebring race was foundering. Right up to the time we shipped the cars to America in November, and even after that, we were not certain that the race was definitely on. There were rumours and counter-rumours; some said that Ferrari would not take part on any account and, therefore, Tony Brooks would not have a mount. Tony himself became the centre of another rumour when it was suggested that, because his wife was having a baby, he would retire before Sebring.

BRM and Aston Martin decided not to take part because of the great distances involved. Coopers waited to see what Ferrari intended doing, because to them the race didn't really matter except so far as I was concerned in the World Championship stakes. Coopers had already won the Formula 1 and Formula 2 Constructors' Championship, so there was little point in wasting a good deal of valuable time and money preparing the cars for one meeting and shipping them 3,000 odd miles. In fact, apart from Stirling Moss, I don't think any of us wanted to go to Sebring at all. For Stirling, who for four consecutive years had been runner-up first to Fangio and then to Mike Hawthorn the previous year, this looked like the chance for which he had been waiting.

Eventually, it appeared that the Sebring organizers would get the necessary finance and the entries needed to make the first US Grand Prix since the war a reasonable race. When it became final, I looked back on the season and felt that, even if I didn't clinch the Championship, I had certainly given everyone a run for their money.

After the Monza race everyone in motor racing got down with pen and paper to try and work out the various permutations to see who could win the Driving Championship. Monza had given Cooper cars the Constructors' Championship and, although the over-zealous Italian officials had acclaimed me World Champion at the same time, some ten or fifteen minutes later they blushingly had to admit they had boobed. Even they, I think, did not believe Enzo Ferrari would send a team to Sebring and, apparently, they felt that if he did not go, the race would definitely be off!

When the mathematicians had done their stuff it seemed that any one of three of us could win, and two of us could draw for the Championship after Sebring. The system of points allocation for the driving championship in 1959 was complicated, to say the least. Drivers were awarded eight points for a win at any of the Grande Epreuve meetings, six points for second place, four points for third and two points for fourth. In addition, fastest lap counted for one point. Although I had scored in five out of the seven meetings, up to and including Monza, I could not alter my leading score of thirty-one points at Sebring unless I came in second or higher. The reason for this was that a driver could only count his five best scores towards the Championship.

This did not affect my closest rival, Tony Brooks, who had twenty-seven points. Tony, up until then, had scored only in four events. Stirling had scored in five races, but two of those were singletons for fastest lap. If he won, only one point needed to be deducted from his total.

Achievement

What it amounted to was this. To beat me and make certain of the World Championship, Stirling—who had made a terrific comeback with a win and fastest lap at Lisbon, and another win in the Italian Grand Prix at Monza—had to win Sebring and make fastest lap. If he just won the race and I came in in second place, I would pip him for the Championship by half a point. Second place would give me six points and I could discard one of my third place point scores to attain thirty-three points. A win for Stirling would add eight points, but he would have to discard one of his fastest lap points and so reach a total of thirty-two and a half points. Moss's half point was for sharing fastest lap with Bruce McLaren in the British Grand Prix. The fastest lap for Stirling at Sebring was vital, if I were still in the running at the end of the race.

Tony, on the other hand—if I was placed second—had to win and make fastest lap to draw with me. If I dropped out and Tony won—with Moss in second place, but with fastest lap—Tony would lose the Championship by half a point. So far as I was concerned, to be safe I needed second place, with neither Tony nor Moss achieving fastest lap. It was all very confusing.

To me, that fastest lap was the all-important factor. I felt reasonably confident that, providing the car kept going, I could get my second place. The only issue in doubt was the fastest lap. If I had to go out to get it my car might blow up. It was decided, therefore, that Masten Gregory should go out for fastest lap and help me clinch the Championship. Masten could drive exceptionally fast and it would be worth risking a blow-up of his car early in the race—providing he did capture the fastest lap. But Masten, who had had another accident just before Monza, failed to recover from his injuries in time. This meant that Bruce McLaren would take his place, as it had been decided to have only a two-man team for the US Grand Prix. As it turned out this was indeed fortunate for the young New Zealander, who showed at Sebring that he was worthy of the hopes everyone had in him.

When it finally became certain that Sebring would take

129

place, I was offered a drive in the Nassau Speed Week, held in the week preceding Sebring. As it only meant a short plane trip from Nassau to Sebring, and as I had never previously taken part in a race on that side of the Atlantic, I thought I might just as well accept. Another reason was that I wanted to have a little driving practice before the Sebring race, because of the long gap between Monza and the US Grand Prix. As it turned out, this decision might very easily have cost me the Championship.

My Cooper Monaco, with the 2-litre engine, was shipped down to Nassau in November, and originally I had intended to arrive in plenty of time for at least two of the practice sessions. But, meanwhile, the Esso Petroleum Company decided to make me a presentation of a silver model of a Cooper in London on December 2nd—the first day of practice. Eventually it was decided that Tim Wall, my own mechanic, should go down before me and prepare the car at the circuit. John Cooper intended travelling down with me, as he also had to attend my presentation.

John and I left by BOAC Britannia just before midnight on December 2nd, bound for Nassau. It wasn't a bad trip, but headwinds slowed us down and we arrived two and a half hours late. By the time I had driven to the circuit, some eight miles away, been ticked off by the medical officer and had my papers signed, practice was officially over. The organizers were very good about it, however, and extended the practice period for half an hour.

Tim had the car ready and I hopped in and went for my first drive around the Nassau circuit—it was my first drive on any circuit on that side of the Atlantic. It took me a little time to discover all was not well with the car and I quickly returned to the pits. It didn't take long to find what was wrong. When the car had left England it had been taken down and prepared so that little work on it would be required. When Tim unloaded the car he just gave it a general tighten-up; there was no reason to do anything else.

John Coombs, in whose garage the car had been prepared, had told me the gear ratios had been changed to suit the long 3.4-mile Nassau circuit. The reduction gears, he said, were twenty-five and twenty-eight teeth. They were—trouble was, they were mounted upside down! I was geared for a slow circuit like Brands Hatch, when the Nassau circuit was faster than Silverstone!

We didn't have time to carry out post-mortems there and then. I went out with a car terribly undergeared and tried to get to know the circuit. That night we stripped the gearbox down and changed the gears around. Next day I went to the line in the sixth row of the grid. Most of the drivers, apart from Michael Taylor, were Americans. I didn't know any of them. The race of five laps was for sports cars under two litres.

The opposition was not tough and the first time round I was in third position. The next lap, I got up into second place, and began overhauling Michael. It was on the fourth lap that trouble came. Half-way round the circuit I went to overtake Michael going into a curve, when a stone, thrown up from his wheels, smashed my goggles. The glass in these is safety glass, but apparently the goggles were an old pair and the glass just came away from the central celluloid sandwich. I almost stopped: I just could not see. I whipped the goggles down and tried to drive with one eye, the other stinging like blazes. I finished fourth, with my damaged eye full of glass.

Back at the pits the doctor took a look and rushed me off to hospital, where they extracted as much glass as they could, and arranged for me to see an eye specialist that night. The specialist told me I had been very lucky. A piece of glass had pierced my eye about an eighth of an inch off the pupil. It had cut it badly. The specialist was worried lest there should still be another splinter of glass left in the eye. I was worried also—but for other reasons. If that eye were to play up the following week-end, my Championship chances could be written off.

I rested on the Saturday in preparation for the International Nassau Trophy, the main event on the Sunday. The race was originally scheduled for fifty-six laps (two hundred and fifty miles), but eventually it was curtailed to forty-nine laps and ended at 5.30 pm, because of bad light. Sixty-five drivers took part in the race: they included Moss and Constantine (4.2-litre Aston Martins), Phil Hill (3-litre Ferrari), Ginther (4.1-litre Ferrari), Carol Shelby (new 2.8-litre Maserati), Jo Bonnier (Porsche), and myself in the Cooper Monaco. My eye was still aching when we raced to the cars in a Le Mans-type start.

With forty-nine of the fifty-six laps completed, the chequered flag was held out to Constantine, who won at an average of 87.2 mph. Hill was second, Jo Bonnier third and I came in in fourth place.

I had intended leaving Nassau immediately after the race and going direct to Sebring, but the doctor was still not happy about my eye and persuaded me to stay for a couple of days. There was still this possibility that a splinter of glass was lodged in my eye, but it was so bloodshot that he could not be certain. We eventually left Nassau on the Tuesday night with my eye still a query. John Cooper and I stayed the night in Miami and arrived in Sebring about midnight Wednesday. First practice was the following day.

I went out for the medical examination and scrutineering of the cars on the Wednesday afternoon and took my first look at the track. Back in London, John Bullock, Rootes Group public relations officer, had arranged for me to pick up a Rapier from the local distributors to use during my stay.

As circuits go, Sebring is just a circuit; a curious mixture of road circuit and airfield runways. About one-third of its 5.2-mile length runs through service roads around the hangars of the airfield while the remainder wanders across flat and featureless country. It was dull for both spectators and drivers, and had the appearance of being set up for a driving test in a rally. There were rubber pylons to mark the edges of some parts of the circuit, while the inside of some turns was marked by half-buried tyres, which were not easy to sight.

For such an important race there was no doubt in anyone's mind that the circuit was, to say the very least, second-rate. Tucked away down in Florida, away from the main populated areas of the US, the race had little hope of being a tremendous success. But Alec Ulmann, despite the lack of financial support, certainly deserved praise for getting the first US

World Championship Grand Prix to be attended by such an array of topline machinery.

Ferraris turned up with four cars for Brooks, Phil Hill, von Trips and Cliff Allison. Dan Gurney attended, but only as a spectator. He had his foot in plaster after a go-kart race in which he had driven the previous week. Three of the Ferraris were the Dino 246 models, which had now been fitted with independent rear suspensions and wishbones. Our two Coopers had arrived safely and were fitted, as was Moss's Rob Walker-prepared car, with the new enlarged valve head 2½-litre Climax engines. Despite reports of far greater outputs, these engines were only giving 235 bhp.

While Rob Walker's second-string car, to be driven by Maurice Trintignant, was in more or less standard trim, the Moss car had had its suspension altered. Instead of the normal transverse leaf spring layout at the rear, coil springs were now fitted. On the first day of practice, when conditions were very near ideal, Stirling managed a very creditable three-minute-dead lap, which was never improved on. But to compare this time with my fastest practice lap—which was some three seconds slower—proves little. On the first practice day I was settling in a new car—it was my Lisbon car rebuilt—with all the worries of adjusting suspension and getting the car to handle. The next sessions were held with a strong wind down or across the straight. Apart from that, I always stuck to the theory that so long as I made the front row I did not care what position I was in for the start. There is little use wearing out a car before a race.

Back in England we had been led to believe that the fast circuit was rough and was going to be tough on tyres. Stirling had, therefore, retained the knock-on wire wheels for his rear tyres, but kept the bolt-on alloy type at the front. But a few laps to check tyre wear convinced us that a tyre change would not be necessary, so the alloy bolt-on wheels, fitted to Trint's and our works cars, would not be a worry.

Apart from these four Coopers, there was Harry Schell's privately entered 2.2-litre Cooper Climax, while Mike Taylor's car was taken over by George Constantine, as Mike was ill. The seventh Cooper was from Tommy Atkins's stable—the

Cooper-Maserati driven by Roy Salvadori. Colin Chapman had two Lotus entries driven by Innes Ireland and Alan Stacey.

The remainder of the nineteen cars that started should not really have been there. Admittedly, local colour is good to have, but not in a hotly contested Grande Epreuve, which this was! Some of the cars, however, were interesting. Indianapolis-winner Rodger Ward's 1.7-litre Offenhauser-engined midget looked small, even beside the Cooper. To all intents and purposes it had only two forward gears and twelve-inch wheels, and it was hopelessly out-classed. The car was designed for speedway and although Ward, later in the race, gave an excellent exhibition of dirt-track technique, his car looked out of place. De Tomaso had a 1½-litre Osca-powered Cooper with a new body and somewhat lower suspension, while the much publicised Maserati-engined Tec-Mec was sadly disappointing.

On the first day of practice, when I was trying to set up the suspension, I took a corner wide and ran over one of the half-buried tyres, denting the side of the body. The second day, for the first time in my driving career, I failed to see some oil on the circuit. I didn't stop at a corner and hit one of the rubber pylons, denting the nose. The damage was only slight. I wished it was my only worry for, on the second day, my engine showed signs of over-heating. It was Monaco over again. The head seals were not fitting correctly.

That night we worked late, took the head off and replaced the seals. But it was too much of a risk for me to use that car in the race, so we decided I would drive the car brought over for Bruce. This turned out to be a lucky decision for both of us. If we had not decided to change cars I would probably have put my car away and not practised any more in it. I had driven around sufficiently to get to know the circuit and it would be pointless to wear the car out before the race. When we swapped cars, Bruce decided he would do a couple of laps in my car to see if he wanted to make any adjustments to it to suit himself. He had done only half a lap when the crown wheel and pinion broke! Had I used that car, I wouldn't have completed a lap in the race.

Even so, my troubles were far from over. It seemed that Sebring was going to be a jinx as far as I was concerned.

I took Bruce's car around for a few laps and found it would not handle well at all. When we checked up that night we discovered the chassis was twisted. This car was the one Masten had used at Lisbon; during the race he had hit a kerb, with the result that the frame was now three-quarters of an inch out. We did our best to straighten it, but it was an almost impossible task. I fiddled with the suspension and reset it to suit the twisted frame. Then the brakes started to shudder. Would anything go right, I wondered? Nothing would, it seemed, for having got the brakes working reasonably well we then dismantled the gearbox and discovered the mainshaft was cracked. Luckily, we had a spare gearbox.

Bruce, John Cooper and I worked with Tim Wall and Mike Grohman until 1 am on the morning of the race. There was still a lot of work to be done on the cars when we left, but by morning Tim and Mike had burnt the midnight oil and had almost finished the preparation. Bruce's car was ready and Mike, who was working on mine, had only a little to do on the Cooper I was to drive. For Sebring I loaned Tim to the works team to help out on Bruce's car.

Race day turned out fine, although there was a strong wind blowing across the fastest straight where we were hitting about 165 mph. Before we lined up at the grid there was an Indianapolis style, pre-race march-past of a 'mixed' band complete with 'majorettes', who led the formation. It was all very colourful and we, from this side of the Atlantic, got a lot of amusement out of it.

Originally the grid formation had been: Moss (Cooper Climax), myself, and Tony Brooks in the leading Ferrari. As the cars started to form up, the organizers suddenly 'discovered' that they had failed to notice Harry Schell's fastest lap put up in a 2.2-litre Cooper Climax. Harry was suddenly advanced into the front row along with Moss and myself, while poor old Tony was relegated back to the second row.

The confusion this caused was no one's business. Ferrari's team manager, Tavoni, took an exceedingly poor view of it — particularly when no one seemed to know exactly what this fast time of Harry's had been. His official time until then was 3 minutes 11.2 seconds. Frankly, I just cannot see how Harry in the 2.2-litre car could have managed to make a time of between 3 minutes 3 seconds, which was my fastest practice lap, and 3 minutes 5.8 seconds, which was Tony's. But, despite the commotion it caused, Harry made the front row and Tony went back to row two, with Maurice Trintignant driving Rob Walker's number-two car.

I cannot remember making a bad start during 1959. I think, apart from the French Grand Prix at Reims, I was always a nose in front for the first hundred yards or so. Sebring was no exception. The Cooper pulled away well and I led, probably for the first 100 yards. Then Stirling raced past me like a rocket. As far as I was concerned, this suited me fine. Before the race we had worked out several tactics to suit various conditions that might arise. The final plan could not be put into operation until the race settled down. The main object was to sort out exactly the pace Moss was likely to set for a start and then stay as close to him as I could without going quicker than I thought the machinery could stand. If Moss got a long way in front at the start, I would let him go and have a crack at catching him later on.

There was no sense, to my mind, in chasing Moss with full tanks in the very early stages of the race, because this is the easiest time to break a car. When I saw Moss pass me I almost relaxed completely. The way he went off down the road I just could not believe he would go far. He seemed to have decided to win or bust—and, my feeling was, he would do the latter.

Moss led into the first corner with Bruce McLaren (who must have gone like blazes up through the pack from the fourth row) on his tail. I followed Bruce, with Phil Hill, Innes Ireland, Trintignant, Allison and Stacey just behind. The rest of the pack were well behind. But, having just got over my pleasure in seeing Moss do what I had thought he might do, I nearly had heart failure. I had hardly done a quarter of a lap when my engine started to miss and run on three cylinders. It did this for a few hundred yards, then picked up again and began running perfectly.

Achievement

By the end of the first lap, Moss had pulled out a fair lead from me; I had passed Bruce at the hairpin, and Bruce hung on to my tail. Then, at the back of the field, first Brooks, then a Lotus, called at the pits. Brooks had been involved in a slight shunt with von Trips—who had had his car's nose flattened a little—and had called in for a wheel inspection. Stacey shed a circlip from his gearbox and that left him with only fifth gear; he burnt out his clutch trying to keep going. The Lotus overshot a corner, took to the straw bales, and stalled the engine. Two cars were out.

Moss continued to pour on the coals, increasing his lead over me by some two seconds a lap. At this stage I had nothing really to worry about, providing he didn't get too far ahead. If he did, then either I would have to risk it and go out after him, or else let Bruce get ahead and see what he could do. Then, on the sixth lap, I rounded the Webster Turn, about half-way round the circuit, and spotted Moss off the circuit. As I went past into the lead I assumed he had spun off. When I went through the pits, John Cooper just signalled I was in front, but said nothing about Moss.

Next time round I took another look to make sure Moss had not started up again. His car was still there and it was obvious that he was out. His Italian gearbox had let him down again. Now, my worries, so far as the Championship were concerned, were centred on one person—Tony Brooks. Tony could still upset me. Tony had dropped back to fifteenth place when he called into the pits to have his wheels inspected after the shunt with von Trips. Now he was running ninth.

Up to that time I had never had to overwork the Cooper, and I didn't intend doing so now. I was lapping nicely about 3 minutes 7 seconds a lap, with Bruce about ten seconds behind me. Close on his heels came Allison, who was driving his race of the season; Ireland, Trintignant, von Trips, Hill and Salvadori came up behind with Tony harrying them at the rear.

Harry Schell was out on lap seven with clutch trouble, and Phil Hill followed him a couple of laps later with a fractured brake line. I slowed a little and let Bruce tuck himself nicely in behind me. It looked like being a procession. Allison was still there in third place, leading the three remaining Ferraris; von Trips had brought his snub-nosed car up past Trintignant into fourth position. My lap times lengthened to 3 minutes 10 seconds.

Within a few laps, however, Trintignant overtook von Trips's Ferrari, and Allison started to move up. John Cooper advised me of this from the pits, so I quickened the pace to 3 minutes 7 seconds again and opened the gap between Bruce's car and the Ferrari. Then, on lap twenty, Allison began to slow down and he called in at the pits with a slipping clutch. By lap twenty-three he had retired. Von Trips and Trintignant came up into third and fourth position, with Tony Brooks now in fifth place having passed Salvadori and Ireland. Ireland had spun and had also lost all but fourth gear. Trintignant re-passed von Trips on lap twenty-four and was now chasing up behind us. He was still a long way behind, so I made no effort to put on steam and widen the gap at that stage.

On each lap, John Cooper would signal me the extent of Trintignant's progress. On lap twenty-eight Trintignant was 21 seconds behind Bruce; on lap twenty-nine he was 21 seconds behind. Gradually the gap narrowed: 19 seconds, 15.5 seconds, 13 seconds, 12.5 seconds, 12 seconds. Trintignant, I realized, was coming up fast—he got the fastest lap for the race (3 minutes 5 seconds at 101.13 mph) while he was chasing us, but he was still a long way behind in my calculations. I was judging my race so that both Bruce and I should still be in front at the end. The fact that he was coming up by one or two seconds a lap didn't really worry me.

Five or six laps before the end I increased speed, and Bruce stayed with me. Trintignant still gained a little, but not enough to worry us. I had never driven flat out from the start and, if necessary, I had enough in hand to pour on the coals at the end. The car was running perfectly. I could not see anything happening to rob me of the Championship now. My idea in letting Bruce slip-stream me was that, if anything did go wrong with my car, he could take the lead and beat Tony to the line, for Tony had to win and get the fastest lap to beat me for the Championship. Now it seemed in the bag. I went past the pits and nodded to John Cooper and off we went into that final lap.

I was about a mile from the finishing line, when the car started to run on two cylinders; I was shocked. I just couldn't believe it. I automatically put the gear lever into neutral as the engine went dead—I was out of fuel! We were cornering at the time at around about 70 mph. I coasted on down until we reached the second last corner, when Bruce came along-side me, almost stopping. My reactions were quick and to the point. With much arm-waving and shouting, I told Bruce to get going. Bruce was horrified. He just couldn't work out what was wrong and had vague ideas of stopping to help me! Luckily, he got the message quickly and pressed on. Trin-tignant went past me at about the same time as I coasted along getting slower and slower. Eventually, about five hundred yards from the flag, the car came to a standstill. I thought of 1957 and Monaco. Why must home straights always be uphill? I took off my helmet and goggles and started to push. I remember seeing Tony pass me—he came in third in the race, making enough points to beat Stirling for second place in the Driving Championship. Then I just put my eyes to the ground and kept on pushing. It was hot. They tell me the crowd went wild. Motor cycle cops tried to keep back the crowd . . . it must have been the first time the new World Champion was escorted to the flag by a motor-cycle escort. Frankly, I don't remember a thing, except flopping down on the ground beside the car and reviving myself with a bottle of Coca-Cola John handed me. I lay there for a few minutes while people pumped my hand until, eventually, they helped me into an official's caravan. I flopped out for a quarter of an hour or so to get my breath back. Then it suddenly dawned on me. I'd won. I'd won the World Championship! Although Mike had been the first Briton to win the Championship, I had clinched the double and become the first British driver in a British car to do so! I just couldn't believe it. Bruce was there, smiling away in a daze, and hardly believing his luck. He had not only won his first Grande Epreuve—on the eve of going back to New

Zealand—but also a plot of land in Sebring. We kept on asking him about his 'ranch'.

Then it was bedlam. Reporters crowded in, newsreel men and photographers flashed lights in my eyes and microphones under my nose. I answered thousands of questions. Then one of the London Sunday newspapers telephoned me direct from England. I do not know which one it was, but the reporter asked if I'd like him to tell my wife that I had won. I said yes, but I never got a chance to thank him for carrying out his promise.

A couple of hours later I went back to the Harder Hall Hotel, where we were staying, and fell into a hot bath. I was so fed up answering the phone that when it rang, I just stayed there. In fact the only call put through at that stage was one from Betty, who had spent the evening at home at Dorking chain-smoking with a few friends. Keith Challen of the *News of the World* had kept the party informed of the progress of the race as it came over the news agency tapes. The last report they had before the finish was that, with three laps to go, I was still out in front and going well. They were as staggered as I had been when the result came over.

It was later that I worked out what had happened. Bruce had finished with nearly four gallons in his fuel tanks. The fact that he had slip-streamed me for most of the way would only account, at the outside, for a saving of a couple of gallons. There must have been a leak somewhere—but where? It was then that my mind went back to just after the start, when the engine had started to run on three cylinders. It must have lost a lot of fuel out of the overflow and the breather tube had been spilling the fuel down past the carburettor and making it run rich. Once the fuel had gone down a bit it started to run properly.

I wasn't very keen on the public side of being a World Champion—I suppose it was the only thing I had against it, that you were expected to make speeches and so on. It was my first experience of this sort of life, going to functions where you have to get up and say a few words. But I did realise then that it was possible to make money apart from driving. We didn't make much in 1959, but at least it was good experience for 1960; when I won again, we knew how to capitalise on the title. It hadn't dawned on me before, and as I hadn't seriously considered the possibility of being World Champion it didn't worry me. It was only after winning the British Grand Prix that I thought I might just stand a chance.

CHAPTER IX

Improvement

After Sebring I came back to London for a brief visit to pick up a couple of awards for being Driver of the Year or something, but I couldn't stay for long because the family were expecting me in Sydney for Christmas. By dashing off to Australia and New Zealand so quickly, after what was a very late decision for the Championship, I must have lost out on quite a number of awards and dinners and so on that the World Champion usually has to take in his stride. At the time I was quite glad, but looking back I can see it was something of a mistake.

However, Coopers were sending two cars out for the New Zealand Grand Prix for myself and Bruce, and Stirling was also to be there in a Yeoman Credit Cooper, so I could hardly stay away. The race became a dice between Stirling and myself, with Bruce waiting just far enough behind to pounce if necessary. I was leading Stirling and we were setting a cracking pace, when his transmission failed. He walked back to the pits feeling pretty disgruntled because his goggles were broken and his face had been cut by stones thrown up by my wheels.

After Stirling dropped out, Bruce came up to try and pass me, and we had a wonderful battle. I finished only six-tenths of a second ahead of him. Bruce then announced his engagement to Pat Broad, whom he had met the year before at Timaru in South Island. Another little item of interest at this meeting was the appearance of Denis Hulme and George Lawton in 1960 cc Coopers; they were so promising they shared the 'Driver to Europe' award and both came to England at the beginning of 1960.

Improvement

1960 was a good year for Coopers and for myself as a driver. It was much more satisfying than the previous year because we won more races and the car was much improved. We had been quite pleased with ourselves at winning the Constructors' and Drivers' Championships, but not winning the American Grand Prix and having to push the car home rather took the shine off it. And then there were a lot of people who thought it was a rather flukey win, because I had only *won* two races, the same as Moss and Brooks. But I had gained a fair number of other placings and, in fact, under today's system, I would have finished the season as Champion with 35 points against Brooks's 28 and Moss's 24.

However, at the time we wanted to do better in 1960. That year's Cooper was, in my opinion, the first really good Grand Prix car they produced. It wasn't all that different basically—it still looked like a Cooper though lower and more aerodynamic—but for the first time it had double wishbones all round. It also had coil springs at the back instead of a transverse leaf, and it was quite a good body shape for top speed. Although the Lotus was smaller and lighter, the Cooper was always quicker in a straight line, much to Colin's amazement and disappointment.

The first big Formula 1 event of 1960 was the Argentine Grand Prix, which was a particularly hot race, weatherwise. The cars were late getting there because the boat from England was late, and there was a big problem with the Customs people. The organisers were left to sort this out, which took some time. We were hoping to get the cars running prior to practice but this plan never came off because they only arrived the night before official practice began.

I remember we were all standing around the pits waiting to get word from the organisers as to when the cars were due to arrive. We had heard that they had left the boat and were being transported to the circuit. We waited around all day at the track for them to arrive and we were getting really frustrated.

In the pits was an old-fashioned telephone with a handle you wind; John Cooper, in desperation, decided he would ring the Automobile Club to see what he could find out.

When the Flag Drops

He eventually got through, but of course they couldn't speak English properly, so John just wasn't getting anywhere. It was hot and it was sticky, and there were no cars, and the Automobile Club people couldn't speak English. All this was too much for John. After several attempts, in great desperation he wrenched the whole telephone from the wall and threw it on the ground. There were springs, bells, and all kinds of bits and pieces flying out of this thing, and they spread all over the floor. That really fixed the telephone up in a big way.

I think we missed the first day's practice but the rest was all right and I finished up on the third row of the grid, on the inside. The people in the Argentine were certainly a lot different from the people we were used to racing amongst, and they were so enthusiastic that it is a wonder more of them didn't get written off. It was very difficult to control the crowd and keep them off the circuit. Taking pictures of racing cars was evidently more important to the photographers than their own lives.

On the first lap I was first into the first corner though I must have been tenth or twelfth off the line. I was going down the inside of everybody and was preparing myself to get in there first and nudge everybody else out of the way when a photographer rushed out to take a photograph of the field coming down to the corner. He just stood there, about three or four feet out from the edge of the road, looking up the track through his viewfinder. I had to jam on the brakes and nobody gave me room to move out, naturally. By the time I had sorted it out I had missed running over his feet by inches. He just stood there – didn't move. It was a miracle that I was able to miss him altogether; in fact, I must have just brushed his trousers, and I came out of the corner about tenth. I should have been first.

On the next lap round on the back part of the course, where there is a righthand/lefthand sort of loop, there was a photographer right where the cars go off the edge of the road. Obviously he knew the spot to go for the action photos! He just lay there on his stomach, with the camera actually on the edge of the circuit, taking photographs of the cars

David Phipps

Gavin Youl at the wheel of our first Formula Junior MRD – we changed the initials
later because of their unfortunate French meaning!

Driving the Honda-engined Formula 2 Brabham in 1966.

David Phipps

The Repco Brabham B[?] at Monaco, 1966 – I retired with gearbox trouble.

David Phipps

Me, driving Alan Brow[n's?] Ford Mustang, leading Jimmy Clark's Ford Cortina, Snetterton 196[?]

David Phipps

coming towards him. It was really unnerving to see some-body lying there in such a stupid place. He was there for a couple of laps until he got the message that he shouldn't be. You couldn't afford to risk losing it because you would have gone over his head.

I managed to get back in the lead, but the gearbox packed up on my car. The reduction gears on the gearbox broke through a bit of faulty heat treatment and Bruce went on to win. Whilst I was in the pits I was able to witness a couple of fights in the stands; it was amazing to see fifty or sixty people fighting furiously. I had no idea what started it, but everybody was watching the fight instead of the race for quite some time—it was far more exciting and people were getting thrown down on the top of the seats. There was a terrific brawl going on.

Then we went off and raced in two other places—there was a Formula Libre race at Cordoba which was unbelievably hot as well. We had to fly up from Buenos Aires to Cordoba and we all went out to the aeroplane and they started it up. The outer engine on the port side was running as rough as anything so they decided they would try to fix it. They took all the cowling off the engine and worked on it for quite some time and eventually we got out of the aeroplane and went back into the terminal where we stood watch-ing. After they had spent about half an hour appearing to work on this engine they just looked at one another, shrugged their shoulders, put all the cowls back on and away we went—with the engine sounding as rough as ever. I knew a bit about flying by that time, and I was very un-happy all the way to Cordoba. In the race, when the tem-perature was even higher than in Buenos Aires, I led until I had to retire because of problems with the fuel pump overheating. Trintignant won that race in the Rob Walker Cooper with Dan Gurney second in a BRM.

I can't remember the exact itinerary of events that spring, but I know that I was in Tasmania where I won the Longford race and then back in Australia to win the Philip Island race; I then dashed off to Syracuse for the Formula 2 event, where I retired with electrical problems—magneto, I think. The

Grand Prix of Brussels was a Formula 2 race also, in which I had a big carve up with Moss. He won the first heat, but I won the second and won overall. It was pouring with rain in the second heat, and Stirling was driving a Porsche that year in these Formula 2 events. He spun at a vital moment in the race and Trintignant snatched his second place, though he remained second overall.

These Formula 2 races were becoming as important as Grands Prix, and it was now that Jim Clark began to show his potential in a Lotus. But on the whole, Formula 2 was still very much a Cooper benefit. We won again at Pau a bit later.

The 1960 Formula 1 Cooper had its first outing at Silverstone for the International Trophy Race, but unlike the previous year it did not win first time out. It was damp and grey at Silverstone, and the track was wet during practice, which caused some accidents. First of all Stirling collected one of the new Aston Martins just as he was passing the pits, completely tearing off its front suspension. That made two wrecked cars before the meeting was really under way. Then, at lunchtime, just as the chequered flag was about to go out and everyone was making for shelter, Harry Schell crashed his Yeoman Credit Cooper at Abbey, was thrown out and killed. All this happened so unexpectedly and when Harry was just about alone on the track too, that it took a long time for people to believe the news. Harry had been a friend of mine for a long time, and was very popular, very amusing, and got a tremendous kick out of life. We had shared quite a few hilarious episodes.

Anyway, the Cooper was very new and didn't handle at all well, so on race day I was beaten fair and square by the Lotus, driven by Innes Ireland. Innes was on the crest of a wave at the time, and made all the headlines in the newspapers as being a rival to Stirling Moss. He finished two seconds ahead of me, and Graham Hill's BRM—it was his first year with them—was third. Denny Hulme won the Formula 2 section in a Cooper. We very quickly went to work to improve the Cooper's handling after that.

The time arrived for the European Grand Prix season to begin and we went off to Monaco. It was one of those Monte

146

Improvement

Carlo races where almost everyone drops out—the total number of runners got down to four, and some of the retired or damaged cars came wobbling out again to go round for a place. I know; I was one of them—I had been disqualified for a push start after spinning in the rain. It was wet after about thirty laps and Moss was ahead of me. He was now driving Rob Walker's dark blue Lotus and was very smooth and fast, but when it started to rain he came up against the difficulty of never having driven a Lotus in the rain before, and I passed him. Then I spun going up the hill from Ste Devote and Moss nipped past me while I was hitting the wall. In trying to clear the track, the marshals pushed and pulled at the car, and so I was disqualified. Anyway, the roll bar fell off and got twisted under the car so I would have had to get back to the pits. Stirling kept the Walker Lotus on the road in these bad conditions, and was besieged by admirers as he took the chequered flag.

We repaired the car in time for Zandvoort and I was quite happy to be in the middle of the front row for the race, with Moss on pole and Innes Ireland on the other side of me. I made a good start, it was sunny and dry, and I really had no problems. Moss was following me closely at first, and round the esses just prior to the finishing straight, I touched one of the kerb stones at the side of the track and hooked it out right into Moss's path. It flattened his front tyre for him and might easily have knocked his wheel off—he seemed to think I'd done it on purpose. So he had to have a pit stop to change wheels and I went on to win the Dutch Grand Prix.

Then, of course, we had that disastrous race at Spa. We got off to a bad start when Stirling had his worst accident up to that time. It was the second day of practice, a hot Saturday afternoon, when Stirling crashed at Burnenville after the rear wheel came off his Lotus. He was thrown out while the car went on spinning wildly, and when I came round he was lying at the side of the road. We were frightened to move him because we didn't know what was broken and we had to wait ages for an ambulance to come and take him away to hospital. He was out of action for some time, with both his legs broken and a lot of cuts on his face. St Thomas's

147

patched him up incredibly quickly, and I remember Stirling being very cheerful when visitors called. He had immense stamina and was always very fit which probably helped.

While we were dealing with Stirling, Michael Taylor in another Lotus had his steering break, which must have been terrifying. To have your steering fail on a fast circuit like Spa is virtually certain to end in a bad accident. Mike went off through the trees at a heavily wooded part of the circuit which wiped all the wheels off. It was amazing that he wasn't killed. Colin Chapman went out after practice to see where these two accidents happened and he couldn't have been too happy about it all. Unfortunately, worse was to come.

The race was all right for me; I led from start to finish. But young Chris Bristow lost control of his Yeoman Credit Cooper and hit the side of a house plus a couple of concrete posts and a fence. The accident looked terrible when I passed, and it was. Chris was killed instantly. Then Alan Stacey, who was driving a works Lotus, was apparently hit in the face by a bird, lost control of the car which hit a bank and caught fire, Alan being thrown out and killed, and the car careering on across a field on fire.

So this took the shine off my winning and really brought home the fact that racing at Spa was a bit stupid because of the speeds. If you went off the road it was almost inevitable that you would hit a house or a tree or a telegraph post, or go into a great big drop. I can remember winning the race well enough, but feeling pretty bad about there having been so many accidents throughout those two days.

At Reims I had a big dice with a Ferrari driven by Phil Hill. We were both off the line very quickly—it was a Toto Roche start and a big shambles—and Phil and I slipstreamed one another for a long time. I can remember having one very narrow squeak. I had passed Phil on the straight and was on the lefthand side of the circuit in the braking area, and just before turning right across the track to take the righthander I fortunately looked in my rear-view mirror. I could hardly believe me eyes. There was the Ferrari coming down the inside with all four wheels locked and not a hope of stopping. If I hadn't seen him I am sure he would have run straight over the top of me. Having seen him coming I managed to keep the car straight before turning, and Phil went past me. I guarantee he was going 50-60 mph faster than I was. He went straight on up the escape road as though he were going right into Reims. So I won the French Grand Prix.

The other thing that made that meeting worthwhile was winning all the bottles of champagne. In practice I think we were quickest two days on the trot, and we collected 100 bottles each day. Of course, we had a lot of problems getting the 200 bottles back to England. We sent the transporter out to the champagne chateau to pick them up, and we later arrived back in England with these 200 bottles, which created a big problem at Customs and cost us quite a few quid. But it was well worth it, because we wanted to give most of it away to the people who had helped us win the race, accessory firms and so on. We used to have some pretty good parties at Reims; some of the best ever.

The British made it four wins in a row for the Cooper and myself. The Grand Prix was at Silverstone that year and I had a really big dice with Graham, who was by now on top form and a challenge to the rest of the Formula 1 drivers. It was two years before he was to take the Championship in the BRM, but he so nearly won this 1960 British Grand Prix that one could only be sorry for him. He got by me somewhere and was pulling out a bit of a lead. This was incredible driving, as he had stalled his engine at the start while in the middle of the front row. He had been 24th at the end of the first lap, and had carved his way through the field at a fantastic rate — it must count as one of his greatest races ever. He passed me on the 55th lap of the 77-lap race, and I think it suddenly dawned on him that here he was, *leading* the British Grand Prix. We were coming near the end of the race, and John Cooper was waving at me madly, signalling that time was running out. So I started pressing on and I was gradually picking Graham back. It got to the stage where I reckoned I would be within striking distance by the last lap and, of course, it saved me a lot of trouble when Graham went off the road backwards at Copse! I had really been chasing him hard, I was 1.6 seconds behind him so he could see me in his mirrors and I suppose it put him off a bit!

For the Portuguese we went back to Oporto, and this was the year I had my big incident on the second lap. After the long straight there is a lefthand corner which goes uphill and along the tramlines, then you have to turn left; but the tramlines go straight on, while you are supposed to turn left. I was just behind Moss — I think I was third at the time — somebody else was in the lead, Gurney, if.I remember rightly. I came up and moved inside to take Moss and intended to outbrake him at the next corner. But I got myself into the tramlines, going straight on like a tram, and it was obvious that I wouldn't be able to stop. I moved from the inside to the outside between two cars, and I had to forget about turning the corner altogether. By the time I had got out of the tramlines we were already in the braking area, so I went straight on, stopped, turned around and came back to try to catch them up. I was eighth by then, and I had to drive hard to catch up with the leaders.

I was pretty relieved when I got to the front again. Eventually I took the flag as the last few laps were reasonably comfortable, except that the engine was running pretty hot. This gave us a run of five Grand Prix victories in a row, which virtually assured me of the World Championship before we finished the season.

All the British teams boycotted the Italian race because the organisers insisted on using the banking. They still held the race, but there were people driving in it I'd never even heard of. That was quite a big fight we had over the banking — and I am glad to say that we haven't raced on it since. It was broken up so badly that we reckoned the Grand Prix cars weren't strong enough to stand up to that kind of hammering, and we weren't prepared to make new cars for just one race.

So the last event of 1960 counting toward the World Championship was the United States Grand Prix held that year at Riverside. That was quite a dramatic race, too. After running out of petrol at Sebring in the US Grand Prix the previous year, John Cooper made sure we weren't going to do the same thing again! He filled the car as full as possible, right to the brim. The weather was very warm, and with the car standing on the start line the fuel tanks began to warm up so that there was petrol already dripping out of the overflow. As the flag dropped I got off into the lead and was pulling away within a few laps of the start. But fuel was coming out of the breather back across the engine, and it must have caught fire on the exhaust pipe. Anyway, the whole car burst into flames going down the straight; there were flames in the cockpit and all round me, so I sat up and crouched forward against the wheel while I tried to get the car stopped. By the time I halted the fire had gone out of the cockpit and was only in the engine compartment, but I had to bring the car into the pits. It had burnt all the wires on top of the engine and made quite a mess.

We shifted the breather and fiddled with a few wires and John sent me out again. But the car didn't run properly any more; we kept having electrical problems and I was never in the picture again, though I finished fourth. Stirling won, Innes Ireland was second and Bruce third. I think it was a race we could probably have won easily if John hadn't been so conscious of the fuel. There was no way I could be beaten for the Championship, however, and I finished the year with 43 points, with Bruce McLaren second to me with 34. I think that was Bruce's best year, and it was certainly Cooper's. It had proved to be the most successful car of that particular formula—unfortunately, Riverside was the last race for the $2\frac{1}{2}$-litre cars, and I couldn't see us being competitive the following year. I was already turning over in my mind the prospect of building a car of my own . . .

This time I really enjoyed being World Champion. I felt that five victories in a row wasn't a bad record, and we tied with Porsche for the Formula 2 Championship, so it was a good season all round.

CHAPTER X

Green Cars in Gasoline Alley

We first went to Indianapolis in October 1960 with the conventional 2½-litre Cooper we had been using in Formula 1 all season. We were only there two days, and caused a minor sensation in the world of USAC racing. I got myself into trouble the very first day I took the Cooper on the track, because all the new rookie drivers have to have a driver's test, and you are supposed to do your first ten laps at a certain speed—I think it was 125 mph then. I had no way of judging what 125 mph was, and I went out just stroking it around and virtually only warming it up. And my first lap was 135 mph.

They went berserk. Harlan Fengler rushed out into the middle of the track and practically lay down in front of me. They all acted as if the world had come to an end, and they called me in and gave me a hell of a rocket. I just looked at him and didn't understand what he was talking about anyway. So after that I had to judge my speed by the revs, and I was able to cope with it; but going around at 125 mph was just unbelievably slow. Eventually my fastest lap was 144.8 mph, which would have been enough to qualify for the third row of the 1960 '500', so John and I were fairly pleased with this result and impressed with the friendly welcome we had received. We thought we had better do the thing properly, build a 'Special' Cooper for Indy, and go back for the next '500'. I felt that if I'd had a couple more days out there that October I could have gone faster—and third row times weren't bad considering the Cooper put out 230 horsepower against the Offenhauser's 400.

Green Cars in Gasoline Alley

The car we built for our first attempt at Indianapolis was only slightly different from our Formula 1 car. The frame and the suspension were stiffened in order to stand up to the banking and the race distance — 500 miles. Coventry Climax, after long consultations, agreed to build a special version of their FPF engine with a capacity of 2750 cc.

A roll-over bar had to be fitted, and I had to wear safety harness for the first time since the midget days on the speedway. The oil tank would have to be sealed for the race, because you are not allowed to take on oil during the '500', and every part on the car had to be crack tested. The engine was converted to run on methanol fuel.

The big drama was the question of tyres, because in those days we were racing solely on Dunlop, and they had no experience at Indianapolis. They began making a special tyre for us, which worked reasonably well, but tyre wear was very marginal. It was quite a tricky situation. It was doubtful whether, in spite of the new hard compound from Dunlops, I could get through the race without three pit stops, when it would obviously be preferable to have only two. In the end it was left to me to keep an eye on the tyres and decide when to come in. On the first pit stop I think I only just stopped in time, because the tyres were beginning to wear and the inner layers of cord were beginning to show. But at least I knew what to look for during the rest of the race, what the tyre looks like when it is getting near its end. They would start to show a white line round the centre of the tyre which I was able to see in the rear-view mirror.

Our car, when it was finished, was nothing like any other car they had had at Indy before. It was small, lightweight, rear-engined and — for the Americans the worst thing of all — it was painted British racing *green*. The old superstitions are now beginning to break down a little, but there were three things that struck terror into the hearts of the die-hard Indy people — the appearance of women in the pits or in Gasoline Alley, where all the cars are garaged; the colour green; and eating peanuts! Women, in fact, were completely forbidden to be anywhere near the cars until 1971; I broke the 'green' barrier in 1961; and I suppose you still can't eat peanuts.

153

When the Flag Drops

It certainly shocked a lot of people when we first turned up with the car. It acquired the nickname of 'the funny car', and everybody was coming round to our garage to look at it. Some were disapproving, some were sceptical, some were impressed.

One of the things I remember most about that first visit was the fact that Eddie Sachs, a leading Indianapolis driver, really enjoyed our being there. He was a great character and very popular with the crowds, with everyone. We got on well together and he was very helpful to us in many ways. He came round to our garage one day and started to talk about how to drive on the oval circuit, what to watch out for, and all his varied experiences. The more he was telling me, the more people were gathering around listening, and at the finish we must have had about thirty people round the car. I was sitting in it at the time. I only wish I'd had a tape recorder, because there is just no way you can reproduce or repeat a thing like that conversation—it was really fantastic. It impressed me very much, and I liked the guy for himself, because he had a great sense of humour and used to take a delight in playing up to the crowds. When a wheel came off his car in the 1963 race, he simply climbed out, captured the wheel, and rolled it back to the pits like a hoop, laughing and waving at the people in the stands, who cheered as if he'd just won the race. It was a great pity to see him killed in the '500' three years later.

Rodger Ward was another chap who was encouraging. In fact we let him drive the Formula 1 car when we were there the previous autumn. It certainly shook him, and he was impressed to the point at which he was going round telling all the other drivers that the rear-engined cars were on the way. He was absolutely right, and it has been proved by the fact that Indy cars are all rear-engined today. But at the time it was very difficult for most of them to accept this revolutionary change. By the time Lotus and Jimmy Clark got there in 1963 they were getting the message loud and clear that all the machinery they had was obsolete—and it is pretty hard to believe that when you have millions of dollars wrapped up in the stuff around your ears.

Green Cars in Gasoline Alley

At that first attempt in 1961 I was allowed to go out first on the qualifying runs because of getting back to Europe for Monaco—the only time they were to co-operate on that problem. After two laps you were supposed to raise your hand to signify that you were ready to start the qualifying runs. Unfortunately, the starter missed my hand coming up out of the little, low-built Cooper, and I was flagged off the track. But I qualified later at 145.144 mph, which put me on the fifth row.

The car was going well during the race, but it was a bit overpowering having all those front-engined monsters surrounding me on all sides, and I felt very boxed in for a time. Later on I began overtaking cars in and coming out of the turns, but I had less power on the straight, of course.

We had two tyre changes as planned, and I think I was running sixth when I convinced myself that I could see the dreaded white line on the tyres again. There were only about fifteen laps to go, and I signalled the pit that I was coming in. The wheel was changed very quickly, but unfortunately the chap who was fitting the right rear tyre put the wing nut on cross-threaded. Not only cross-threaded but banged on hard with a hammer. This delayed us considerably in the pit, and put me back a few places. But the car was running very reliably, and the engine gave us no trouble whatsoever in all the 500 miles. I finished ninth, which surprised everyone and we were delighted to be up that far.

The big thing we learned from that race was that, if we could get more power, the small rear-mounted engine in that sort of chassis was ideal for Indianapolis. We were miles slower than the other cars on the straight, but our cornering speed was by far the quickest. But in the race this didn't seem to have much advantage at first, because it isn't only difficult to pass in the corners at Indy when everyone is looking for the lowest part of the banked turns, but a lot of other cars were lapping at the same speed as myself. As the race went on and I began to get the hang of the whole thing, I was able to overtake just after the apex, because the Cooper did not have to use the line used by all the big, front-engined cars.

155

When the Flag Drops

I was at one of the meetings they had where discussions took place about a 3-litre Formula to match up with the coming European Formula 1 for 1966. They eventually decided they would change to 3 litres in 1967. The people who had a lot of money invested in engines decided that this was a ridiculous way to go, and they couldn't afford to throw all this money away, so they referred the matter back to the committee. Of course, the engines they had been using were obsolete by then anyway, so they would still have to throw away all their existing machinery. I think it was very disappointing that Indianapolis didn't go through with the 3-litre Formula, because I am sure it would have made even better and safer racing than they have today. I'm sure, too, that the cars would be going more quickly than the 4.2-litre cars were going then. The organisers were reluctant to change because they thought the racing would be slower, and if you have slow racing you don't have crowd appeal. I think this would not have been the case.

Indianapolis used to have a bit of a reputation for dirty driving and double-crossing behind the scenes. This sort of thing is a bit of a myth, really. The whole problem was the machinery they were driving. It was difficult to sit up in the stands and watch those old-fashioned cars racing and *not* get the impression that there was a lot of cut and thrust going on. But I am sure the drivers didn't have the control of their cars that they have today. Now they all have rear-engined, good handling cars this sort of reputation has died down, but I don't think the drivers or their attitude to racing has changed. People like Mario Andretti and Bobby and Al Unser just don't believe that that sort of reputation even existed.

Qualifying at Indy became a bit of a drama for me on two occasions. There I would be on the qualifying line, knowing I had to get the qualifying done that day and get back to Europe to race at Monaco. Twice I just managed to get in by twenty or thirty seconds before the bell went at six o'clock, and I think that is the most tense and worrying moment one has at Indy. It is so frustrating knowing that you have this one chance and there is nothing in the world you can do about it. At six o'clock it is finished, and they couldn't care if you came from China or England or Greenland, you name it. Rules are rules and, boy, they stick to them.

I also missed out in 1964, I think. I had to do the double trip to get back to Zandvoort and back to Indy again just because I missed getting out to qualify by *one* car. That really stuck in my throat. In fact it is the only thing I hate about Indy—that they are unable to bend their rules by one single bit. You would think that being so close to qualifying, and knowing the problems involved in the tie-up with Grand Prix racing, they might have relaxed a bit. All the people over there knew what the situation was—my having to fly all the way to Europe and back again in the minimum time possible just didn't alter the situation one bit. The rules are not to be bent by anybody. I suppose they are right in a way, because if you start bending them for one driver it becomes the thin end of the wedge. But it was unfortunate for us that we could never spend the whole month of May there like the others do.

The year we could have won was 1964. We built and drove the car for John Zink, and it was basically an extremely good car. We went there full of confidence that this was the car that would beat everybody, but unfortunately John Zink led us completely astray by insisting that the car be set up on Formula 1 springs. He was absolutely convinced that light springing was the way to win Indianapolis. Of course we arrived there with a range of springs that were nowhere near strong enough, and there was nothing we could do about it because no one else's springs fitted the car. We couldn't get them made in time, either. It was such a pity, because this was the car in which Andretti proceeded to win everything in sight later on. After the '500' was over, they put heavy springs on it and then it was far superior to anything else about.

That year is one I shall not forget for another reason. It became obvious during practice that the Mickey Thompson cars were difficult to control and Dave MacDonald, a promising young 'rookie', was driving one. He had qualified fourteenth, but on the first lap he lost control and that terrible accident happened. I was right behind it all and it was really terrifying. You couldn't believe such a thing was happening in front of you. MacDonald's car burst into flames immediately; Eddie Sachs was unable to avoid the wreck and ploughed into it; and five other cars became involved. On the first lap everyone is bunched together and it happened in Turn Four, just as the cars come onto the pit straight in front of the grandstands. MacDonald and Sachs were killed, but the other five managed to survive, though their cars were obviously out of the race.

I got through all right. It was probably one of the luckiest things that ever happened to me. MacDonald's car hit the inside wall, the tanks burst, the thing went up in flames, skidded across towards the outside wall at a fairly acute angle, and there was just a wall of flame right across the track. When I saw it all happening, I did my best to stop, but when I put the brakes on the car seemed to go faster—at least it wasn't slowing down as quickly as I wanted it to, for sure. So I was going down this tunnel, with a wall of flame on one side and the retaining wall on the other, and as I ran into this vee I decided the best thing to do was to turn and go through the fire at right angles to reduce the amount of time I spent going through it. I got the car sufficiently slowed down to turn left and drive through at a reasonable right angle, which was just unbelievably lucky, because if I hadn't I would have run into the wreckage of Eddie Sachs's car which was up against the wall. I couldn't see him in the middle of the fire and I must have missed his car by inches. I ran over a lot of debris from the wreckage while I was going through the fire, anyway, and this damaged the fuel tanks on my car. After the restart of the race it wasn't long before the tanks bent out of shape, vibrated through and split. We had to retire the car.

But that was about the most terrifying experience I've ever had. It was an absolute inferno; the flames rose probably fifty feet into the air, and to feel yourself going virtually blindfold through the middle of that and knowing there is nothing you can do about it is terrible. It was just an unbelievably good sight to come out on the other side and see the track again. I didn't go back for a long time after 1964.

Green Cars in Gasoline Alley

Indianapolis has a certain fascination, but a month there nearly drives you up the wall. It's the most frustrating place I have ever been to. You can be there for a month, and you get so little actual running it is maddening. There always seems to be an excuse as to why you can't be allowed to run. It either rains, or you just get out there and there has been an accident and you have to stop for ages; they close the circuit for an hour while they clean off the mess and sweep the track.

After the 1964 race the rules and regulations were changed. The cars were to run on methanol instead of petrol, the tanks had to be made of metal with rubber bladders inside, and the tanks were not to be in front of the driver. Tyres improved enormously, too, and became wider, and one way and another Indianapolis has been a lot safer the last two years I have driven there. But I still feel that the Formula is all wrong. These turbo-charged engines—well, I think the whole idea is ridiculous because of the potential horsepower. I am sure that getting on for 1,000 horsepower is possible and driving round a circuit like that with, say, 800 horsepower is just beyond sanity.

If I had not retired from motor racing when I did, I would have liked to have had a go at the TransAm series. I have never been particularly interested in CanAm because the cars, with the exception of the McLarens and a couple of others, never seemed to be designed or prepared to the standard I am used to. I would never have driven in a CanAm race unless we—Ron and I—had decided to build a suitable car and do the thing properly. One thing I hate doing and have never approved of, is jumping in and out of anyone else's cars. I would never undertake a drive just for the sake of it; I always wanted to know that the car had a good reputation and was expertly prepared. I had faith in the Cooper up till 1961, and I had faith in the Brabham, but, with a few exceptions, I was never very keen on driving sports cars. Although I had fun racing saloon cars at one time, especially against Jimmy Clark, I concentrated on Formula 1 and Formula 2 racing almost exclusively.

Apart from going to Indianapolis in 1961, it was rather a

thin year for Coopers. We just weren't in the picture at all. The Formula had changed from $2\frac{1}{2}$ to $1\frac{1}{2}$ litres at the beginning of the year, and Ferraris had been running a Formula 2 car, 1500 cc, during 1960. From the beginning it looked like being the biggest contender in the new Formula and it did, in fact, run all over us and captured the Championship. Their engines were all ready to go before the season started and gave more power than the four-cylinder Coventry Climax units. We still had to use these until the new V8 Climax was ready. The Ferraris were now rear-engined and were easily identifiable, not only by their colour, but by the swept back nostril-type radiator air intakes.

The Ferrari drivers for the year were the Americans Phil Hill and Ritchie Ginther, and the German Wolfgang von Trips: a strange trio for the Italian team, but a very strong combination, as it turned out. 'Taffy' von Trips, who was extremely popular and very talented, was well in the lead for the Championship when he was killed so tragically at Monza in the Italian Grand Prix, and Phil Hill went on to take the title by winning that same race.

Although Stirling won a memorable first race of the season at Monaco, in the Rob Walker Lotus, von Trips won the Dutch easily. I finished sixth, one of my two miserable placings for that year, but I remember best the battle between Jimmy Clark in his works Lotus and Phil Hill in his Ferrari. They were passing and repassing with tremendous speed and skill on the Tarzan bend and at the Hunze Rug, and Jimmy showed us what he was capable of doing in no uncertain terms.

At Spa Olivier Gendebien joined the Ferrari team, and the Italian cars finished first, second, third and fourth. Porsche had now joined the Formula 1 struggle, with Dan Gurney and Jo Bonnier as their drivers. These two drivers had had an unsuccessful year with BRM in 1960, but the silver Porsches seemed to their taste. Dan apparently had the race sewn up for him at Reims in the French Grand Prix when an almost unknown young Italian driver, Gian Carlo Baghetti, overtook him on the long straight on the last lap. Baghetti won by a car's length, his first and last Grand Prix victory. I didn't

David Phipps

The BT19 at Zandvoort, 1966 – 'I went out to the car with the beard, leaning heavily on the jack handle. I just had to win after that.'

The 1966 Repco engine.

David Phipps

The French Grand Prix, Reims 1966 – 'I was the first driver ever to win a Grand Prix in a car bearing his own name.'

David Phipps

One-two in the British Grand Prix, 1966 – Hughie Absolom signals that I am leading from Denny Hulme (also Brabham) by 14 seconds with five laps to go.

David Phipps

even finish, yet again. The engine was unreliable, to put it mildly.

Ferraris were one-two-three again at the British Grand Prix at Aintree, in appallingly wet weather. I was fourth. The new 1500 cc Coventry Climax V8 engine was installed in the Cooper by the time we went to the Nurburgring, and we thought it showed some promise when I put up second fastest lap. I was first away in the race, ahead of Moss, but this was one of the occasions when I came a cropper at the 'Ring.

Dunlops brought out a rain tyre for Nurburgring and just before the race it was obviously about to rain. Then I found out that Moss had the rain tyres on. I had to fairly rush round to get some and so we only had time to change two tyres. I went out with two rain tyres on the front and two ordinary tyres on the back. On the first lap round we came across a wet patch. It wasn't actually raining but it was a wet patch underneath the trees. The front wheels went round, but the back ones didn't, so I lost the back and by the time I got it straight I'd gone through a hedge and was driving down behind it. I stayed there and watched the race from behind the hedge. The car wasn't too badly damaged. In fact I could have driven it back to the pits, but I couldn't get it out because there was a ditch behind the hedge; it just wasn't physically possible for me to get the car out.

It was a fairly slowish corner on a quick section of the circuit and I *almost* got it straight before I hit the hedge. But once the wheels got in the vegetation, it pulled the car further in, and I proceeded through the hedge and down the other side. A few of the boys came along later and said: 'That looked real good, quite a sight.' Apparently, I was still rubbing along the hedge on the other side and the whole thing was quivering. I didn't know at first whether I was going to pop out of the hedge again and onto the track or not; unfortunately, there was this big ditch which prevented me from doing anything or I would have had a go.

Then we had the disastrous race at Monza on the road circuit, when the Lotus of Jimmy Clark and the Ferrari of von Trips touched; Taffy shot off the track out of control and was

161

killed, along with fourteen spectators. Phil Hill won the race and became a rather sad Champion. As in all accidents at Monza, the police moved in and wanted to arrest somebody, in this case Jimmy. He was forced to hide in his hotel, and was later rushed onto a commercial flight before things could get difficult. The following year there was the possibility of his being stopped from leaving the country. I flew him out of Italy in my private plane because there was talk of his being arrested again.

As for the accident itself, I think it was just one of those unfortunate things that can happen at any time at all on a slipstreaming circuit. I am staggered that we haven't had more of this type of accident, particularly at Monza, because when you get a pack of cars switching and swopping places in the first few laps, you have a potentially dangerous situation. I have always tried not to get mixed up in those early battles and tend to sit back and watch rather than get involved, because it is all so pointless. I don't think either Jimmy or Taffy were carving each other up, as was suggested at the time. I'm not even sure that theirs were the only two cars involved — it could have been a third one, which touched one of the other two and caused the Lotus to veer enough to touch the Ferrari. At that speed, early in the race on a slipstreaming circuit, this kind of thing is a constant possibility. Jimmy was always a driver you could really drive hard against and be quite confident that he wasn't going to do something stupid.

The only time I was really mixed up with Jimmy in a serious situation was at Rouen in a Formula 2 race. There were four of us having a big dice for the lead, changing places, slipstreaming and what have you and each time Jimmy went past his right rear tyre was obviously going flat and we could see more and more of the rim each lap. I think all three drivers had noticed that this was about to happen and we all desperately wanted to give Jimmy the message that his tyre was doing down. As we went past the pits I was right on Jimmy's tail, and I reckoned for sure he wouldn't make it to the bottom of the hill because his tyre had got so bad he just had to have an accident if he kept going.

Green Cars in Gasoline Alley

I tried to get past Jimmy coming down from the previous corner so that I could get alongside him to tell him about his tyre. But when I missed out on that attempt it was time to stay well back. When I knocked off the power and sank behind, Jochen came barrelling by and went down very close to Jimmy. On the second left-hander Jimmy lost it. He went straight off and hit the barrier, missed Jochen because he was so close to him, then bounced out again into the middle of the track in front of me. I took the whole front of his car off, hooked a back wheel off my car, went spinning off down the middle of the road leaving bits and pieces of car everywhere, and came to a shuddering stop. I then had to rush back and give Jimmy a hand to get his car off the road. He didn't know what had happened. When he got out of the car he was completely mystified and just didn't understand how he came to have his accident. But by then his rear tyre was absolutely flat. It seems odd that such a sensitive driver didn't feel the tyre going down, but I think the problem was the difference between the various makes of tyre. For instance, our tyres always ran at a very much higher inflation pressure, so you would notice a big difference from when a tyre was hard to when it was soft. But with the tyres Jimmy was using then it was probably very difficult to get the message early enough; when the pressure was down so low it didn't have to go down all that much before the tyre was almost flat.

Drivers are frequently asked how they feel when they are driving and there is an accident involving one or more of their colleagues. Well, obviously we are affected, particularly when we are not sure who has gone off the circuit. Sometimes you don't recognise the car, or it has gone off behind a safety barrier and you can't see it. Even when you do see a very serious accident on the track you are never able to assess the result as far as the driver is concerned, so you always press on hoping that whoever it was in the car is going to survive.

Sometimes, when you look at these accidents, it seems rather doubtful whether the driver *could* survive; one of the worst recent ones from that point of view, where we really knew the chances of survival for the driver were pretty well nil, was Piers Courage's accident at Zandvoort. I knew there was no chance of his getting out of that, because I was the next car round. The ground lit up in front of me just around the corner, and the whole bank caught alight just as it was coming into view. Although I didn't actually see the car leave the road, I saw the results of the accident almost immediately after it happened. I only knew it was Piers because as I went by his crash helmet was rolling down the edge of the track just like a hoop. It was absolutely parallel with the edge of the road and it must have gone down 200 yards past the accident. I drove past it whilst it was rolling, and it was then that I recognised the helmet. It wouldn't have mattered very much if there had been a lot of marshals around at the time or not, because the fire was so fierce and took such a hold immediately that nobody in the world could have survived it.

The accident involving Jo Schlesser at Rouen in 1968 we didn't know anything about at all until we went past the pits and on down the hill. Somebody waved the yellow flag and as we went across the top of the hill we could see the smoke in the distance, so there had obviously been an accident at the bottom of the hill. I really feel that Schlesser's accident was probably an unnecessary one. For a start I don't think Schlesser had the experience to be driving a Grand Prix car that wasn't properly sorted out and John Surtees said he wouldn't drive it because he felt it was not sorted out. It was an unfortunate decision, particularly in view of the circumstances under which Jo was driving: for a start, he was a Frenchman in France, with the whole French Press and Television watching him. The pressure around him probably outweighed his sense of judgement; probably he felt that he had to make a showing with it. That was one race in which I started with an edgy feeling, and I knew before the race that that driver should not be in that car. But it is very difficult to turn round and tell somebody that a driver shouldn't be in a race.

Most accidents seem unnecessary and foreseeable when you look back on them, but that is only hindsight. Most things are happening for the first time and cannot be foreseen.

164

Green Cars in Gasoline Alley

There is always human error and there is always mechanical failure to contend with. We all try to restrict both, but the unexpected can always turn a normal occurrence into a disaster, and sometimes the rest of us have to witness the results while we are driving.

It is pretty hard to explain the feeling that you get—it probably makes you concentrate on your driving more than you do normally, because it is helping you to take your mind off the accident, anyway, and you have to stay with it and press on.

CHAPTER XI

Brabham and Tauranac

From the time I first made contact with Ron Tauranac in the very early hill-climbing days, we kept in touch by letter or by meeting up each year when I went back to Australia for the season's racing. We talked about European racing, and the subject of building motor cars came up for discussion on many occasions. I often suggested to Ron that he should come to England, but it took a couple of years for this to sink in. As a matter of fact, Ron had a very good job as works engineer at Quality Castings Pty. Ltd. and had no need to move out of Australia, financially or otherwise. But his natural inclinations, his experience with the single-seaters he built for hill-climbs, and his co-operation on all kinds of bits and pieces for the Cooper cars between 1958 and 1960 eventually made the idea of building European road racing cars irresistible. For me, writing letters is almost as much of a misery as giving a speech, but Ron has quite a little collection of letters from me, enclosing rough sketches of modifications or new ideas on suspension.

And when I say rough, I mean it. Ron was always the draughtsman, the boffin, the chap behind the drawing board. Our cars were always a combination of ideas from track results — driving and testing plus collaboration between Ron and myself. The idea people were apt to get from the Press, that Jack Brabham built a Grand Prix car all by himself in his back garden, is a bit far from the truth. Certainly, as a trained mechanic who could design and make parts for a motor car, I knew what I wanted designed and made. As a driver with many years' experience I knew how I wanted my

166

own car to handle. I was the instigator of the project, and already well known as having twice won the World Championship. It was reasonable to call the new cars Brabhams. But the type numbers have always been preceded by the letters BT – B for Brabham and T for Tauranac.

Ron eventually came over to England in 1960. By that time I was already running a garage and filling station at Chessington, and had formed a company called Jack Brabham Motors. Betty and I moved into a house in Surbiton, quite near the Cooper factory. Through the garage business and previous contacts in Australia I already had a good relationship with Repco, the Australian firm which specialises in replacement parts, and this was to become very useful indeed as our project grew.

I had always wanted to build and drive my own car. I built the first rear-engined Cooper Bristol at Coopers, but I had this restless desire to create a car from the ground upwards, as it were. It wasn't until I was able to get Ron to come over that this was possible.

Ron started building the first car, a Formula Junior, in a lock-up garage that wasn't far from Coopers, and it was all a bit secret. Ron was working for me on the conversion side, putting Climax engines into Triumph Heralds in the daytime, and he had a drawing-board in his bedroom so he could work on the design of the car at night. We formed another company called Motor Racing Developments, and initially called the car an MRD. We moved to larger premises in Surbiton which were run by Repco, and eventually bought our own premises in Byfleet near Weybridge, but all this took time.

In the meantime I continued driving for Coopers in 1961, which was the year of the change to the new 1500 cc Formula. During that year Coopers used the new 4-cylinder Climax engine to start with, but towards the end of the year the Coventry Climax V8 appeared for the first time. However, after two Championship years, Coopers had been left behind a bit, and it was obviously too early to hope to get a Brabham made and ready to race in Formula 1.

I did some initial testing in the Formula Junior MRD with

the 1100 cc Holbay engine and it seemed to be on the right lines. An Australian driver, Gavin Youl, who was having a season in Europe, bought the car and took it out for its first official appearance at Goodwood in August 1961. He managed to get onto pole position, and subsequently finished third. Later he took it around the Continent for Formula Junior races, with enough success for us to consider carrying on with the manufacture of similar cars.

It was time now to tell Charles and John Cooper that I would have to stop driving for them at the end of the 1961 season, and although John knew how I felt about making my own car, and sympathised, I don't think old Charlie ever quite forgave me. To him it seemed like gross ingratitude for me to desert them. They still had Bruce McLaren, who now became Number One for the team, and Bruce who, like me, had his own ideas as to how a car should be designed and made, had the same dramas until he left to make McLarens in 1964/5.

As our Formula 1 car didn't stand a chance of being ready till quite late in 1962, I had to keep my hand in at Formula 1 racing driving something else. I bought a Lotus 24 — that was the one before the first really good Formula 1 Lotus, the 25, which took Jim Clark to the World Championship in 1963. Our Formula Junior cars, meanwhile, were being made and sold as fast as we could keep up with the orders. Frank Gardner, whom I had known at the Speedway in Sydney when he was racing motor cycles, had many successes as our works driver, and Jo Schlesser became the 1962 French Formula Junior Champion in one of our cars. We now had different companies handling different parts of our organisation — there was Jack Brabham Conversions, which installed single-cam Climax engines in ordinary saloon cars, and Brabham Racing Developments, which now handled all the racing car manufacture. The change to the initials BRD came about largely because the French pronunciation of MRD has an unfortunate meaning to the French!

Actually, building racing cars was more difficult than we had thought when we began. Fortunately, Ron is of a very similar disposition to myself in that he doesn't like to be beaten or to give up, so we pressed on. The business went from strength to strength, as a matter of fact, and by 1964 we were well-established. But in the latter part of 1962 it all looked pretty marginal.

By July 1962 our Formula 1 car was finished. I still think it was probably one of the best looking Brabhams made. We used a Coventry Climax V8 engine mounted at the rear in a multi-tubular chassis suspended on double wishbones and coil springs. We stuck to the tubular chassis for many years—right up to the end of 1969, when we were building the BT33—because we felt that from the customers' point of view (and our own) a tube chassis is a lot easier to repair after a shunt! And as we always seemed to make our chassis work as well as any of the monocoques, there didn't seem any reason to change them. It wasn't until the regulations came along about fitting bag tanks that we decided we had to make a monocoque.

Ron and I believed in a stiff chassis, relatively high roll centres, low spring rates and minimum frontal area. We have always thought that every part of a motor car should be strong enough for the job it has to do, and maybe even stronger than strictly necessary. If I had to drive the cars I was going to make sure they weren't going to fall to pieces! On the first Brabham we doubled up the chassis members around the top of the cockpit to reduce injury to the driver in case of an accident, and we made a very strong bulkhead. We did not use chassis tubes to carry water between radiator and engine as most constructors did at the time, but had separate water pipes running outside the bodywork for much of their length to reduce temperatures. I remembered only too well what it was like to be cooked in the Cooper in the days before we solved most of those cooling problems.

My whole aim was to make the car a finisher. If it won races, all to the good, but in order to win you must finish. We thought we had considered every detail, but in engineering projects of this kind—the production of a very 'highly strung' vehicle intended for the prestige Formula of motor racing—there had to be things we didn't know till we had run the car; in fact, our teething troubles were mostly in the engine department, and we had remarkably few changes to make on the chassis. This was made of 1-inch and some 0.750-inch, 18 gauge mild steel tube. The front suspension loads were taken out over a wide base by leading top wishbones and trailing bottom wishbones, which provided extremely positive location of the modified Standard Triumph uprights on which the 13-inch front wheels were mounted. There were double, wide-based wishbones at the rear too, with the upper one providing stiffness against toe-in loads. The rear wheels were 15-inch and were fitted with 6.50 tyres on 7-inch rims to cope with the power of the Coventry Climax engine.

The coil spring/damper units were mounted in the airstream in both cases, as was the upright for the front anti-roll bar. We tried using a rear anti-roll bar, but I found the handling best with just a 0.5-inch front bar. We also put 1 degree of negative camber on the front wheels to counteract any camber change due to body roll.

The Coventry Climax engine was exactly the same as everyone else's, except that the twin tail pipes for the exhaust were made in Australia by my friend Len Lukey and called 'Lukey Mufflers'. The power output was about 174 bhp at 8,300 rpm, and the transmission was by a 7.250-inch, diaphragm-spring-type, twin plate clutch and Colotti 6-speed gear-box/final drive unit, type 34. We used splined drive-shafts, but there was very little spline movement.

The disc brakes, which were mounted outboard all round, originally had 9.750-inch discs at both front and rear, but the pad area at the front proved inadequate, so we substituted 10.25-inch discs with large calipers.

I am a fairly large person and I hate to be cramped in a cockpit; so, as the gear lever was on the left, we scooped out the left side fuel tank to allow space for me to move my elbow. And, as I also hate to be too hot in a racing car, we covered the fuel tanks with leather wherever they might touch me (or me touch them) and we spaced the pedals far enough apart to cope with large feet.

We fitted the fuel tanks behind the reclining seat and on both sides of it. The two side tanks were joined underneath my legs, and there was also a small tank over my knees. I would not like to have this arrangement nowadays, but it was good in that particular car. The oil tank was mounted just behind the combined oil and water radiators, and was shaped to duct the warm air from the radiators out through the sides of the body. The battery was mounted to the right of the seat and the spark box above my left shoulder. The Stewart-Warner electric fuel pump was at the rear of the car, alongside the gearbox.

The whole car was slim and low. We chose the Brabham colour — turquoise — for our first ever Formula 1 car, and went back to it at the beginning of 1970 with the BT33. This car, the BT3 (the BT2 was the 1962 Formula Junior car, of which we built eleven), was a true prototype and we went racing with it to iron out any problems before we committed ourselves to making successors.

We took the BT3 to the Nurburgring for its first race, and I must admit it had an inauspicious debut. We were plagued by engine troubles throughout practice, and then the throttle cable linkage broke during the race. In the Oulton Park Gold Cup race we finished third, without brakes. We thought it best to miss Monza and get the car right for the United States Grand Prix at Watkins Glen, which was a good idea, as it turned out. We were fourth fastest in practice and I finished fourth in the race — scoring my first Championship points in a Brabham; a very satisfactory feeling. In Mexico I was second to Jim Clark, and we really felt that we had started off quite well with an entirely new marque.

BRD also made three Intercontinental chassis for non-Championship events using a $2\frac{1}{2}$-litre Climax engine. I also raced one of these in the Australian Grand Prix. We started the meeting with a 2.75-litre Climax engine, which blew up in practice. I borrowed a 2.5-litre sports car engine from Bruce McLaren, and was right behind him during the race when we came up against a slower car we were lapping and — it seems the story of my life, when I look back — the tail ender moved over for Bruce and put me off the road!

For 1963 we really had some ambitious plans. The BT5 was a sports car using the 1600 cc Lotus-Ford 4-cylinder engine. Ian Walker ran the first of these cars with Frank Gardner driving, and a second one was made for Pete Ryan to drive for the same team. Unfortunately, Ryan was killed before he could drive the car, the order was rescinded, and the car ended up in the hands of a private owner.

The 1963 Formula Junior car was a big seller. We made twenty BT6 chassis, some with Holbay engines and some with Cosworths. Each time we made a new car the design progressed, sometimes in minor details, sometimes in more important ways. Our aim was to win the World Championship, of course, and we worked steadily towards our goal. But to make two Formula 1 cars each year was an expensive business, and this is where the commercial success of the Formula Junior cars helped so much. The BT7, which was the type number for both Formula 1 and Formula Intercontinental cars, was very similar to the BT3, but we redesigned the rear suspension and used 13-inch wheels instead of the 15-inch on the preceding model. We adapted the rear of the chassis to take a new gearbox, designed and constructed 'communally' by Hewland, Knight and Brabham. The fuel tanks formed part of the bodywork on each side of the car.

I had a new driver to work with, the first time I had taken on a 'name' driver to join me in Formula 1. Dan Gurney had been driving for Porsche and had not had a very successful time with them. Dan was a driver I admired a lot — so much so, in fact, that I almost decided to retire from the driving side and leave Dan to carry on, with myself directing operations from the pits. During 1963, however, the great things we expected from our efforts did not quite materialise. Twice Dan retired when he was holding a certain second place in a Championship race. He finished second in two other races, and I achieved one second place. It was Jim Clark's year, and Lotus won their first World Championships, both Drivers' and Constructors'.

During that year we created the Brabham Racing Organisation, which was to look after Formula 1 racing and my own personal racing affairs, with offices in Guildford.

For 1964 Formula Junior became Formula 3, and we also

had Formula 2 and Formula 1, Formula Intercontinental—
and Indianapolis. We also built a new 2-litre sports car, the
BT8; in fact we built nine of these in 1964, two in 1965, and
the last one in 1966. For the latter we used a Coventry Climax
4-cylinder, 2-litre engine. This car was very successful, and
our ever-hopeful driver/mechanic, Denny Hulme, won the
Tourist Trophy in a BT8.

Denny's place in our team came about mainly through Phil
Kerr, who was my manager. Obviously, Phil had been watching Denis closely, being a fellow New Zealander, and by the
time Phil had finished telling me how great Denny was, I
let him drive a Formula Junior car to see how things went.
He drove very well, and when the suggestion came up that
he should join the team we decided to give him a couple of
drives in the Formula 1 car in 1964, with Dan as Number One
and myself as a kind of backer-up when I felt like letting
someone else drive.

Denny always did a good job for us. He drove well and
sensibly—quite a safe driver. He wasn't a car shunter, and
the only problem we had early on was that he didn't seem to
be able to sort his car out as well as we had hoped. We eventually learned that we had to work on the car to convince him
that it was all right and pointing the right way, and then he
could go as fast as anybody!

Dan was a fine driver, and someone who was easy to get
along with. In 1964 he won the French Grand Prix at Rouen,
and the Mexican Grand Prix at the end of the season. I was
third in the Belgian and the French and fourth at Brands
Hatch. We felt that our Formula 1 car was just on the verge
of really good things. The Formula 2 car, with the Cosworth
engine, was already showing the way things might go by a
series of victories throughout the second half of the 1964
season, when Denny and I drove works cars, and Alan Rees,
Jo Schlesser, Silvio Moser, Jo Bonnier, Jochen Rindt and
Frank Gardner were also doing well with Brabham Formula 2
cars. We made seventeen of these BT10s, thirteen Formula 3
BT9s and five Formula 1 cars, our highest total ever, I think.
That was also the year I drove a Ford Galaxie in saloon car
races against Jack Sears, Dan Gurney and others in similar

cars, with the Lotus Cortinas always breathing down our necks. We had some good races, real door handle to door handle stuff, especially around Brands Hatch, Silverstone and Snetterton.

The 3-litre Formula was coming in 1966, and we started 1965 with a problem on our hands. Coventry Climax were getting to the stage where they had too many engines racing, and too many to service and keep running. It was obvious that we were going to have to look for another engine for 1966 anyway, and during 1965 I made contact with both Honda, for Formula 2, and Repco for Formula 1. We could see that there was no way everybody was going to be sorted out with a good engine early on, and during 1965 the engines we had just didn't seem to be any good; Coventry Climax weren't able to do anything about it because of the lack of time between races.

So I contacted Repco early in 1965 with a view to persuading them to make a 3-litre Formula 1 engine. I had the idea that perhaps we could start by making something around the aluminium Oldsmobile block to get us going quickly, as there obviously wasn't time to make a complete engine. Luckily for us, Repco thought this was a good idea. They sent Phil Irving over to England to work with me on designing an engine, and I spent most of my spare time with Phil on the design of cylinder heads and a sump unit based on the Oldsmobile. Although we would have liked to start with a complete engine, cylinder block and all, we decided we would have to make that the second stage. Phil went back to Australia towards the end of the season and the engine was built ready for us to use in South Africa at the beginning of 1966.

We picked Repco for several reasons; we had always had a good relationship, because I had been using their replacement parts and bits and pieces for years. They were Australian—a fact which, owing to the distance from Europe, later became a disadvantage. And we thought the unit would be a good reliable one. It might not have a lot of horsepower, but it would be a good torquey engine. We tried to do the same thing which had proved so successful in 1959/60, when we had the 4-cylinder Climax engine. It was far from the quickest in those days, but it was reliable and had torque and flexibility; we hoped the same thing would happen with the Repco. We wanted to be the first in with a reliable engine.

So during 1965 I spent a lot of time sitting on the pit counter with a stop watch letting Dan and Denny get on with the driving. I wanted to drive all the time, but Phil Irving and I were staying up until two and three in the morning working on this project. That was the first year I thought at all seriously about retiring. (I remember letting Denny drive at Clermont Ferrand instead of myself, and he came fourth. I still can't understand why I did that.) As a matter of fact, we collected quite a lot of Championship points between us when I come to look back on it. Dan was second at Watkins Glen and Mexico, third at Zandvoort, the Nurburgring and Monza, and sixth at Silverstone. Denny was fourth at Clermont and fifth at Zandvoort. I was third at Watkins Glen, fourth at Spa, and fifth at the Nurburgring. We came third in the Manufacturers' Championship, but it wasn't exactly what we had in mind!

In Formula 2 the Brabham.Cosworth was doing remarkably well, especially as Jochen Rindt and Alan Rees were running in the Winkelmann Team. Towards the end of the year I ran the Brabham Honda, but it was obvious that the engine needed development, which we gave it during the winter.

Back in Australia, Phil Irving was working hard on the cylinder heads, the timing cases, the sump, the oil pumps and other items. Two factors basically dictated the choice of a single camshaft and vertical valves for each bank, rather than two shafts and inclined valves. One was that the engine should be capable of installation in existing Brabham chassis. The other was a desire to keep down frontal area to existing limits with the Climax engine, so we could keep the excellent penetration of the 1965 cars.

We also aimed at making the Repco engine a mechanic's dream from the point of view of accessibility, with easy maintenance and replacement of parts. When we received the engine it was all we hoped it would be. It was giving over 300 horsepower to start with, it was very flexible, and it had very good torque. It was an ideal engine to drive. To be able to use the Oldsmobile block we had to stiffen it with steel plates, which was quite a worry in the first year, but it saw us through in fine style.

Repco *lent* us the engines, for three years. If we sold any, the money went to Repco, and any that were unused or obsolete went back to them. In fact, all the engines we had in 1968 went back to them, and they still have them. Frank Hallam of Repco took charge of the project towards the end of 1966 and we started work to improve the engine for 1967, but where the whole thing came unstuck was when we realised we would need a new engine for 1968 or the Cosworth-Ford would run all over us. Repco wanted to make a new engine, but it was far too late, although they did their best. Being 12,000 miles apart and still trying to work closely together became impossible. Frank Hallam, Norm Wilson and John Judd all worked hard on the project, but eventually, at the end of 1968, Repco decided the cost was too great and they wouldn't go on with racing engines. It was a bit late for us to do much about it for the 1969 season. We were faced with going to Ford and buying Cosworth engines, which was a pretty expensive proposition, but we raked up enough finance to get going with one car, and Ickx was able to bring us some extra help Ford-wise which enabled us to run a second car.

Repco were not particularly upset by the arrangement. They realised that at that distance they couldn't possibly hope to keep up with the Ford-Cosworth developments, and it was going to cost them so much money it just wasn't feasible. We parted good friends and are still in very close contact. It was a wonderful project, an excellent relationship, and one that we shall always be proud of sharing.

CHAPTER XII

New Life Begins at Forty

'That's the end,' they all said. 'Turned forty! Dear, oh dear.' I got a bit fed up with all the stuff in the papers — why are they always so obsessed with a person's age? On April 2nd, 1966, I didn't feel any different from the way I felt on April 1.

But for four years the Brabham Formula 1 car had been in the doldrums, and I wanted to change all that. We had our new engine, the V8 Repco 3-litre for the new Formula 1 regulations installed in the previous year's car, the BT19. We had a wonderful tie-up with Honda who made us a Formula 2 engine to use in our BT18. These were both proven chassis, though the two new deals with Repco and Honda had yet to show their value. We started the New Year with a lot of confidence that we had the right combination, at the right time, for both Formulae.

The team consisted of Denis Hulme and myself, and our opposition came from the following cars and drivers. BRM had its own V8 engine and Graham Hill and Jackie Stewart driving for them. Lotus were using BRM engines, too, after trying to carry on with a 2-litre Coventry Climax, which was underpowered for a 3-litre Formula. The much-heralded BRM H16 eventually made its appearance, but though it was a beautiful piece of engineering it was always giving trouble. Some people think they should have persevered with it. Jim Clark and Mike Spence were Lotus drivers.

Ferrari started the season with a V6 engine in a rather heavy car, and later a four-camshaft V12. John Surtees was still their number one driver, with Lorenzo Bandini, Mike Parkes and Ludovico Scarfiotti to back him up. But John left the team in mid-season and drove a Cooper-Maserati for the rest of the year.

The Cooper Car Company was still in racing with the Maserati V12 engine, Roy Salvadori was team manager and Jochen Rindt was their main driver until Surtees came along. Ritchie Ginther drove for them only till the Formula 1 Honda was ready, which wasn't until the Italian Grand Prix. The Honda for the 3-litre Formula was a mass of good ideas and brilliant potential which never quite came off. It was so nearly a world-beater that it was a pity they retired from the sport.

The McLaren was a newcomer, for Bruce had left Coopers at the end of 1965, attracted Robin Herd to his team as designer, and produced a Formula 1 car which made its debut at Monaco. The car itself seemed to be a workmanlike construction, but the choice of engines was poor. Bruce started with a destroked version of the Ford V8 Indianapolis unit, went on to try the V8 Serenissima and made various attempts to make it competitive, but ended the season looking forward to using a V12 BRM engine for 1967.

Then there was Dan Gurney's Eagle, with the Gurney-Weslake V12 engine. Dan set up the headquarters of his All American Racers at Rye, in Sussex, behind Harry Weslake's factory, but he was more taken up with the Indianapolis Eagle-Ford project in the early months than with Formula 1. The first Formula 1 Eagle came out to race at Spa and finished fifth, which was promising.

So there we all were that year, scratching about with various untried chassis/engine combinations; but we felt better prepared than most teams because the Repco engine, although it only delivered just over 300 bhp against the 420 of the BRM H16, for instance, developed very useful torque. This was to prove handy on twisty circuits, and the compactness of the engine allowed more streamlining of the chassis, which was good for a circuit like Reims.

The South African race that year was on January 1st and was a non-Championship event at East London. We made fastest lap and led the race for a time until the injection drive belt broke. At Silverstone for the International Trophy Race the Repco-Brabham won its first race. I beat John Surtees by about seven seconds, and I felt very happy with the car.

But at Monaco, the first of the 1966 World Championship races, I was ill. I was really ill. I don't know if I had eaten something bad or what, but on the morning of the race the last thing I felt like was getting into a racing car. I can remember being very, very glad when the car got stuck in one gear and I had to retire. I felt so ill, I just went across the circuit, jumped the fence and caught a bus back to the hotel. There was no way of getting a car out, the whole place was so packed no one could move. So the easiest way was to walk up to the main road and catch a bus. I went straight to bed. Denny dropped out with a broken drive shaft coupling, so no one took us very seriously at Monaco.

Spa was next, the Belgian Grand Prix. The track was dry at the start and we all had dry tyres on. Actually, I probably had one of the narrowest squeaks ever there, because I was second going over the top of the hill and down to Burnenville. Halfway down the hill we realised we were on a wet road. It wasn't actually raining, but there had been a shower a few minutes beforehand, just enough to wet the road. I can remember going into a terrific slide—it was fantastic. I was sliding sideways, aiming straight for a house. I don't know why, but the car suddenly stopped sliding as it reached the edge of the road, and I missed all the strawbales and concrete posts by inches. I must have passed them doing 120-130 mph at least and never hit a thing. When I had recovered from this we ran into a sudden and very heavy rainstorm. The road was really flooded when we reached the esses in the straight where Jackie Stewart went off. Half the field didn't complete the first lap. I must have given myself a fright, because I remember taking it easy for the rest of the race. That was the day when Jochen Rindt really impressed me—he drove so well in that awful weather. He passed me just prior to the esses and he spun going in, spun round completely about three times, and went round the esses at the same time! He never left the road, which was staggering. Apparently, though I didn't see him, he backed into the side of the road without hitting anything, and I passed him.

179

When the Flag Drops

When he took off to rejoin the race he did it with such a burst that he spun again, but he caught me up a few laps later and went past me very quickly. John Surtees won the race and Jochen was second, which was quite an achievement in that drenching rain. I made a mental note to keep an eye on Rindt—that was when I first realised he was going places. Bandini was third and I was fourth at Spa.

Reims—that was the next Grand Prix and my *big* day. It was a bit lucky. Mine wasn't the quickest car there, but I managed to get a good start and hang on to one of the Ferraris on the straights. We got into a slipstreaming/towing situation, and the Ferrari actually towed me away from the rest of the field. It was Bandini in front. Eventually Bandini's throttle cable broke and he left me in the lead. He would probably have won it if he'd kept going—I could stay with him but not pass him. That was a great day. I was the first driver ever to win a Grand Prix in a car bearing his own name, so all the journalists wrote over and over again. We won a lot more champagne, too.

After that we went off to Brands Hatch for the British, and we won at Brands fairly comfortably if I remember rightly. Denny was about ten seconds behind me. Yes, we were first and second for the first time. Denny had been third in the French, his first outing with the Repco engine—we felt that wasn't bad, first and third and then first and second. I had a real burst of confidence around that time, and at Zandvoort for the Dutch Grand Prix I decided to have a bit of a go at the Press for labelling me the old man of motor racing. They were giving me a hard time.

Betty went off shopping and bought me a false beard and I got hold of a jack handle; just prior to the start of the race I went out to the car with the beard, leaning heavily on the jack handle. I just had to win after that. The race developed into a duel with Jimmy Clark, but the Lotus had a tiny hole in its water pump casing, and was steadily pumping all its water away. He had two pit stops to take on more water which left me well out in front and able to ease off. Graham was second, a lap behind, and Jimmy still made third place two laps behind. It was a ninety-lap race, in which I led for forty-one laps and Jimmy for the other forty-nine. Denny went out with ignition trouble.

The German Grand Prix was extremely wet. It was a shocking race, actually, and a very dangerous one; I guarantee we drove every lap under a different set of circumstances, because of rain showers on different parts of the circuit. One lap you would come round and the track was dry, and the next lap it would all be wet. And then you would come across rivers running across the road. There were quite a few times when the conditions were really dangerous — we were sliding all over the road in mud and water.

I got a lot of satisfaction out of winning that race, because it was the first Grand Prix I had won at the 'Ring. I look back on that as more satisfying for me personally than perhaps any other race. John Surtees was second and Jochen third, both in Cooper Maseratis. Denny had worked up to fifth place before he retired with ignition trouble again.

By then I had 39 points in the Championship table, Graham was second with 17 and Jochen Rindt and John Surtees tied third with 15 points each. The Italian Grand Prix hardly changed the picture, because I didn't finish, neither did Hill nor Surtees, and Jochen was fourth, gaining three points to put him up to second in the table. I had a plug fall out of the engine early on in the race. I led for four laps, then I lost oil and had to stop at the pits and retire. Denny finished third, and Scarfiotti unexpectedly won the race, which delighted the Italians.

The United States Grand Prix at Watkins Glen was a bad race for us. We were using Alfa Romeo camfolds at the time and we ordered some new ones. Somehow or other a cast iron one had got into the batch, and it was put into my engine. Of course, it broke. That was a complete mystery. We had bought the camfolds in Switzerland, actually, and there were, in fact, *two* cast iron ones in amongst them, because we found another one later that hadn't been used. It was maddening, because I led for most of the race, alternating with Bandini until he dropped out with some kind of engine trouble. Then Jimmy Clark was running second to me in the Lotus-BRM H16. I retired just after half distance, and Jimmy went on to win. Jochen was second and Surtees third, but the gap between us on points was still enough for me to be quite happy about the Championship.

The last Grand Prix of the 1966 season was the Mexican, and John Surtees won this in a Cooper-Maserati. I was on his tail for most of the race, and I think the gap was never more than about two seconds. I eased off a bit towards the end and settled for second place. Denny was third, and we came over the line nose to tail, but he was a lap behind.

So we finished the year as Champion Constructors and I'd taken my third World Championship for Drivers. Obviously, I was more pleased with these two things coming together than I had been in the Cooper days — or maybe more satisfied would be a better way of putting it. When you are older you definitely appreciate things more, and I felt that Ron Tauranac, Repco, Esso, Goodyear, the accessory firms and all my mechanics were as much involved and as much to be praised as the driver. I feel that the Manufacturers' or Constructors' Championship is just as important as the Drivers'. It meant a lot to a firm like Repco to be able to say it had produced the engine that powered the Brabham to this world-beating status, and I feel that the driver always overshadows the publicity which ought really to go to the people who make the cars and provide backing for them in one way or another.

It was the same for Honda with our Formula 2 activities. I made several visits to Honda in Japan for at least two years before we started anything at all between us. We first used their engine in our Formula 2 car during 1965, but we had quite a few problems with it, so I went back to Japan at the end of the season. We went over all the difficulties that we'd encountered and they decided they would build a new engine for us for the 1966 season. This was early November when I talked to them, and they designed the engine, made the patents, the castings and machined the new engine and tested it, and had it back in our factory by March, which was a fantastic effort. Quite amazing. Nothing in that engine was retained from a previous engine. They really impressed me with the way they had done that job. I didn't believe them when they said they'd have it ready by March, but sure enough, in March it was back at the factory.

We had a marvellous year—a Brabham won every start in Formula 2 except one. Jochen was using the Cosworth engine in his Brabham, and he was really the only opposition Denny and I encountered. Out of fourteen races we started, I won ten and was second once, while Denny won two and was second in six, third in two. I retired from the race at Rouen when the crankshaft seized, but Denny won anyway. In the last race of the season at Brands, I had my big dust up with Jochen, and just in the last few laps I was leading and Jochen was right on my tail. We came through Clearways and we had to lap Chris Lambert. He signalled me to go round the lefthand side as we approached the corner, which I started to do; but as soon as he got round the apex he just drifted out to the outside and I ended up on the grass at Clearways. Of course, by the time I had recovered from that and got back onto the circuit, Jochen had pulled out quite a lead. Although it didn't take me very long to catch him it wasn't possible for me to pass him again before the end of the race.

That Honda engine showed fantastic reliability, and we had a Japanese crew working with us at the factory all year. They were a really dedicated crowd of mechanics—they knew how to work hard. It must have been an expensive effort for Honda, because they were flying engines and people backwards and forwards from Japan. Actually, at the end of the year we were considering using their Formula 1 engine, and we thought we'd go and discuss the problems and tell them what we wanted and how we wanted it made to suit the chassis. But for some reason they wanted to make this engine all on their own, and at Monza the engine turned up in a chassis that was their own—they had built their own car. When we first saw it at Monza we felt the engine was too big and heavy, and we decided there was no point in going on with Honda to do a Formula 1 effort.

We were still working on the Repco engine, which was just as well anyway because we won the Championship again. We would probably not have done so with Honda. It was a pity our association with Honda finished right there and then, because if we could have worked with them their whole effort in Formula 1 might have been a lot better than it turned out to be. They tried to do it all on their own, and they found that building their own motor car was more difficult than making the engine. It was just one of those pities—the whole venture collapsed. But ours was a very successful partnership while it lasted.

I was awarded the OBE at the end of that year and, of course, I had to go to the Palace to collect it. That almost changed my mind, because I found out that you had to go in a top hat and tails, and there was just no way it was going to happen to *me*. I had never been in top hat and tails, and I wasn't about to start then. But after a week or so I got used to the idea and I thought perhaps Moss Bros was the answer—I'd never been there before and it was about time—everybody has to have a first. So I went to Moss Bros and I hired this ridiculous get-up and when the big day came to go to Buckingham Palace, we had a long list of instructions—where you had to be at every split second. I decided it would be safer if I had somebody else to drive the car for me, so I got a friend of mine to come along and drive and I sat up there like a lord being driven for once. We drove in at the Palace gates at the precise time, parked in the forecourt and went in. I was very impressed by the whole thing. It was quite a big event really.

After the ceremony was over I went downstairs and got into the car, and the blasted thing wouldn't start. The starter had jammed solid. It was an automatic car so there was nothing we could do about pushing it to free the starter or anything. It was just jammed and that was it. So then I had to jump out of the car run round and lift up the bonnet. The starter was so far down at the bottom of the works it looked impossible to reach. I looked round quickly but most of the cars were just disappearing out of the gates. I had a quick check round the starter to see if I could do anything with it but I couldn't without spanners. I rushed to look into the boot but there were no spanners—no tool kit at all.

By this time there were only one or two cars left and one

of them was an old Triumph sports car. The driver had started the car and was about to drive off. I ran over and asked him if he had any spanners; he pulled some pretty ghastly ones out of his car, but they were better than nothing. I went back and finished up with two legs stuck out of the top of the car and the only thing I took off was my top hat. Anyway, after I had been down to the bottom and freed the starter, I started to back out of the front of the engine compartment, and almost stood on a great big policeman's toes. He just stood there and looked at me and said: 'Do you think you are going to be very long?' When I stood up and looked around ours was the only car left. I promptly slammed the bonnet and prayed it was going to start; it did, and off we went! I had grease all over me from head to foot and my hands were in a shocking state. The next day I took the suit back up to Moss Bros. . . . I think it took a lot of cleaning.

The episode got into the newspapers the next day — I don't know how — and a few months later I was invited to have dinner with the Queen and Prince Philip. It was a very big affair. I arrived in the forecourt in a different motor car for fear the same thing would happen again and I went in to have a few drinks before dinner. The Queen must have read her newspapers because she came over to me and made quite a big joke about my being upside down inside an engine in her forecourt and asked me to make sure I didn't get stuck out there again!

During 1966 it had become obvious that Denny Hulme could be classed among the really top-line drivers, and he proved this fact in 1967 by winning the World Championship for Drivers and giving the Repco-Brabham its second consecutive Constructors' Championship. In fact, once Jimmy Clark had virtually dropped out of the running with a lot of teething troubles on the Lotus 49, it became a straight fight then between Denny and myself, which Denny won with 51 points against my 46. Jimmy was third with 41. I won the French and the Canadian Grands Prix and came second four times, while Denny won in Monaco and Germany and picked up points at almost all the other races. It was a close-fought battle, but a well-deserved result for Denny.

CHAPTER XIII

The Changing Face of Grand Prix Racing

At the end of 1967 it would appear to outsiders that we were sitting pretty with two World Championship awards as Constructors and two World Champions in the same team. But things were not so good under the surface. For one thing, Denny had not agreed to drive for us again the following year. We asked him half a dozen times during the autumn of 1967 and the answer we got was that he hadn't decided yet, and we were not in a position to screw his arm over it. It looked as though, if we were to run a two-car team, I would have to be one of the drivers simply from the economical point of view. I wanted to go on driving anyway, although a lot of people were suggesting I should give it up. I read it so many times in the papers and magazines that I was beginning to think: 'Crikey—perhaps I *should* retire!' I personally think that age has nothing to do with whether a person should stop driving a racing car or not. It is a matter of the physical and mental outlook of the person involved, and that varies. Some people of thirty shouldn't be in a racing car, while Fangio was winning World Championships at forty-seven.

Anyway, I decided to go on, and when Denny let us know he was going to join Bruce in the McLaren team we brought in Jochen Rindt as the second driver for Brabhams. We had been keeping an eye on Jochen for some time, actually. He had been driving Brabham Formula 2 cars for the Winkelmann team for some time, and had won almost every race in that formula. So we had had an interest in what Jochen was

186

doing all along. I had always been impressed by the way he drove—he was forceful and certainly showed that he had the quality I thought necessary to win. In the past Esso had always negotiated our drivers for us and, suddenly, with the withdrawal of the fuel companies from racing, we were back to negotiating the drivers ourselves. Unfortunately we had committed ourselves to a hell of a lot more expense for 1968, so we were beginning to look round for other sponsorship—but it never came off.

People used to think we were financed entirely by Repco, but this was not so. There was no *direct* financial backing from Repco at all, but their help had come in a different way. We had done well with Repco engines for two years and we weren't in a position to change to Ford at that time. Repco had put a fantastic amount of money into developing a four-cam V8 engine for the coming year, and we were also having a 4.2-litre engine built for our Indianapolis car for Jochen to drive in 1968.

We had been toying with the idea of making a sports car for about three years, but our Grand Prix and Formula 2 racing was more than we could handle anyway. With our financial backing looking as though it would be a lot less in 1968, we were obviously going to have to cut down on our activities, and the thing that would have to go by the board was Formula 2. In our organisation it had become impossible to handle both; Formula 2 had become as big a job as going Grand Prix racing. We thought we would rather tackle Indianapolis, which is only one race and over early in the year, than spend a full season in Formula 2.

Looking around at the prospects for 1968 before the season began, we felt that Lotus had to be our number one rival, and Ferrari a very serious contender. Gurney would be there too, with his AAR Eagle. Then there would be Tyrrell with Jackie Stewart in a Matra-Ford—that sounded like an ideal set-up for going racing. We felt they might upset quite a lot of their rivals' plans. In fact, 1968 looked like being a very competitive season with a lot of good cars, and we felt we would be in with a good chance with the new four-cam Repco.

When the Flag Drops

Unfortunately, 1968 became a disastrous year for us. The Ford Cosworth V8 engine virtually swept the board, and our hopefully awaited Repco 860 engine, which had been intended to compete strongly with the Ford DFV, was not reliable. When the engine was performing properly, the car went very well; Jochen put in some tremendously fast practice times. But we had unexpected mechanical problems which followed one another in a very discouraging way.

Jochen drove Denny Hulme's 1967 car in South Africa and finished a good third to Jimmy Clark and Graham Hill, who were both with Team Lotus. Tragically, this was the last most of us saw of Jimmy, for he was killed at Hockenheim on April 7th. He was billed to drive a saloon car at Brands Hatch that day, but for tax reasons he had to stay out of the country till the following weekend, so he went to the Formula 2 event at Hockenheim instead. The loss of Jimmy shook the motor racing world considerably, because he was undoubtedly the best driver around at the time. It was a great shock to Lotus and to Colin Chapman, who missed the Spanish Grand Prix because of his distress. This was the first time I could remember a Grand Prix without Colin for years, but the morale of the team was much strengthened by the victory of Graham Hill at Jarama.

We had the new 1968 car at Jarama, but I only managed a few practice laps before my engine blew up. Jochen sorted his car out all right, although it still had overheating and oil breathing problems. He managed to get on to the fourth row of the grid, but when my replacement engine blew up during the last practice session I had to face the fact that I would be watching the race from the pits! After only nine laps of the Grand Prix Jochen's engine decided to quit as well.

There is really no point in going through 1968 race by race in any detail. It was a wet year; it was the year that wings began to be used and reached great heights by the end of the season. And the list of my races runs like this. South Africa: retired, broken valve spring, 17 laps. Spain: did not start. Monaco: retired, broken radius arm mounting, lap 8. Belgium: retired, throttle slide, lap 7. Holland: retired, spun off

188

in the rain at the Tarzan hairpin and could not restart. France: retired, fuel pump failure, lap 16, after three pit stops. Britain: retired, exhaust camshaft, lap 1. Germany: I finished, I really did. I finished a race! I gained two points for fifth place, after I'd been plagued with a sticking throttle all through the race. Italy: retired, no oil pressure, lap 57, when I was lying sixth. Canada: retired—a very unusual thing for our cars—a suspension failure, as far as I can remember; I had a front wishbone mounting break and my exhaust pipe fell off—apart from that, a good time was had by all! United States: retired, broken cam-follower, lap 77. Mexico: retired, engine ran out of oil a few laps from the end when I was lying third.

And that was my year in Grand Prix racing. I only finished one race out of eleven starts, and I was all ready to retire. Jochen had done a little better and had finished up with eight points by coming third in South Africa and again in Germany. But he had endless troubles, mostly with the engine. He never made a fuss about it. I am sure that no other driver would have gone through the year like Jochen did, with the frustrations we had that season, without getting bitchy. At the end of the year when Repco announced their retirement from motor racing, and we had the opportunity of getting the Ford engine, we hoped Jochen would drive for us the following year. But I certainly couldn't blame him for not doing so after we had given him such a bad year. He went to Lotus. It was a great pity to lose him really, and I'm sure if we'd had the right engine in 1968 he would have stayed with us, because he liked driving the car. However, he desperately wanted to win, and winning is really what it is all about for someone as ambitious as Jochen.

As a driver I thought Jochen was the sort of person who tended to drive at ten-tenths most of the time. Not that I was worried about him from the point of view of flying off the road. But something could happen to the car or to someone else's car which might affect him, and he was always driving that near the edge that something was liable to happen to him through no real fault of his own. As for what happened at Monza in 1970, had he been driving at nine-tenths or ten-

189

tenths, I am certain that he would have got out of the situation had something not been wrong with the car. In my opinion, it was obvious from the angle at which the car hit the guardrail that it wasn't driver error. At that particular part of the circuit, the worst he could have done if he had missed his braking point was to have gone on into the bank after the end of the guardrail, as Fittipaldi had done the day before.

Anyway, at the end of 1968 we had to find another driver. One we had been watching closely was a young driver who, we thought, had plenty of time to mature into a champion—and that was Jacky Ickx. I think Ickx's driving in 1969 in the Brabham was the time he proved himself to be a driver who was going to reach the top very quickly. He was pleasant to work with, though we had a small problem in the language barrier. We find with foreign drivers, although they speak English very well, it is still very difficult to convey messages about motor cars and what is wrong with them. Also, Jacky is a driver who prefers to be number one in a team and performs best when he *is* number one. After I had broken my ankle at Silverstone, he tended to drive faster. In fact, in the next three Grands Prix, he finished third (at Clermont Ferrand), second (at Silverstone) and first (at the Nurburgring). I think Silverstone was his first really shining drive. Then he scored another victory in Canada (where I was second) and by the end of the year he had certainly proved himself as someone who was going places.

Unfortunately for us, he had decided by the end of the Monza meeting to go back to Ferrari. I had already decided to retire at the end of that year, and had told Betty and a few friends. But when we learnt—between Monza and Canada—that Jacky was leaving us, I hesitated to carry out my decision. In any case, we had to find another driver whether I carried on or not, and we started to talk to Jochen. By the time we got to the Canadian Grand Prix Jochen had agreed in principle that he would drive for us. There was just the matter of sorting out the Goodyear contract and a few minor details to get fixed. Then he told Chapman he was thinking of driving for us and the scene changed. Unfortunately, money and the chance of a Formula 2 team swayed the balance; in the end we couldn't match the Lotus offer.

After we got the news that Jochen was remaining with the Lotus camp, I thought about the monocoque car which was coming along back home and which I felt was going to be a competitive car in 1970, and I took the plunge. I rang Betty from Canada and talked her into the fact that I should drive for one more year. It was a long phone call and went over like a lead balloon!

At first we thought we would only be able to run one car. In fact it was quite a long time after the Canadian Grand Prix that the idea of taking on the young German driver, Rolf Stommelen, was put to us. He was a good, steady driver, wanting to make haste slowly, and he brought some sponsorship with him; he had the backing of Ford of Germany, Eifelland Caravans, and the magazine, *Auto Motor und Sport*.

This question of sponsorship is one I have always felt fairly strong about ever since the rumpus with the Australian organising bodies back in 1954. Formula 1 racing has changed considerably in recent years and it has certainly become more professional. When I first came to England in 1955 it was still pretty amateurish, and I suppose it wasn't until 1958/9 that it became a serious business, for me at any rate. The whole thing became more competitive around that time, cars, drivers, engines, everything. Perhaps one could say that Stirling Moss first put motor racing on a proper professional level — and we all ought to be grateful for it.

The big difference between 1959 and today is that there are a lot more closely competitive cars, a lot more keenly matched drivers, and a lot more people involved in the business side of the sport. Of course, running a Formula 1 team is a hell of a lot more expensive, and in many ways it is a lot more difficult to achieve success. It is more difficult to win because of the number of good drivers and the wealth of good machinery, but it is also more difficult to keep on top financially. It has been quite a struggle for Brabhams, anyway. With the tyre companies cutting back and the fuel companies not in it as they used to be, the sport in the future is going to be relying more on outside sponsorship.

When the Flag Drops

When I first came over here the fuel companies were in strongly. They were really the only people we could look to for help. Dunlop put a lot into getting everybody fitted out with tyres, but moneywise it wasn't worth anything to us. Coopers used to rely on selling motor cars each year and this kept them going, apart from Esso. The Esso money was really the only money of any consequence that came into the team as far as outside sponsorship was concerned. The rest of it was mostly a matter of selling cars and making the business prosperous, which we did for a few years. In 1962, when we began building and selling Brabhams, the fact that we sold cars was quite a help to us. It would have been much more difficult to build Formula 1 cars if we had not built Formula Junior, Formula 3 and Formula 2 cars for sale.

The main thing that saved the sport some years ago was the arrival of the American tyre companies, Firestone and Goodyear. Goodyear's entry in 1965 came at a stage when motor racing was beginning to look pretty thin and, after they had joined the circus, Firestone came into it, too; this was probably the best thing that had happened to the sport in a long time. Without the competition between the tyre companies some teams would not have been able to carry on. It was quite a blow when they decided to cut back in 1971. Somehow or other motor racing in the future has got to get its finance elsewhere. Of course, the one team that always comes up smelling like a rose is Lotus—they took up with Players and became Gold Leaf Team Lotus at a time when everyone thought sponsorship was going dead. Then we had Yardley coming in with their backing for BRM; Elf, the French petroleum firm, arrived with the Matras in 1968, good old Shell and Esso revived their interest, and Gulf joined the big sponsors. Then we had Brooke Bond Oxo supporting Rob Walker, who in turn is now backing Surtees; America's STP Corporation financed the March operation; and suddenly all the old national colours were gone, except the red of Italy's Ferraris.

Our other main sources of support came from accessory firms such as Girling, Champion, Lockheed, Ferodo, Lucas, Armstrong and Autolite. At most Grands Prix nowadays

Victory at the Nurburgring in the German Grand Prix of 1966 – on the rostrum with
John Surtees (left) and Jochen Rindt

'The 1966 German Grand Prix was extremely wet' – me heading for victory.

First outing for the BT24 –
final adjustments before
practice at the Dutch Prix,
1967.

David Phipps

Ron Tauranac and I at the
Mexican Grand Prix, 1969.

David Phipps

you can hardly see the cars for decals, once so fiercely frowned on in both England and Australia, although accepted in the United States for many years. Most of the drivers' overalls are in themselves an advertisement, while the various badges just about cover their chests — even their backs, too, in some cases. And this is the sort of thing that the sport needs.

The cigarette companies may be the ones to look to in the future because they are finding it more and more difficult to advertise, since the ban on television commercials for cigarettes, both here and in the States. I see that more and more races are sponsored by tobacco companies, and I was pleased to see the Woolmark people — the International Wool Secretariat — sponsoring the British Grand Prix this year.

Any manufacturer who decides to make motor racing one of his advertising shop windows obviously has to have a product which is sold worldwide, because motor racing is a billboard which travels all round the world. That is why it is difficult to find a purely British company to sponsor a team, because it is possibly not interested in selling abroad.

One sponsor that I haven't mentioned yet has been about as big an asset to motor racing over the last few years as one could hope for, and that is Ford. In fact, I don't know where the sport would be today if Ford hadn't sponsored the Cosworth engine. It is a great pity that more motor manufacturers have not shown interest in the same way. Ford have done a terrific job in promoting the sport and they seem to be the only people who are prepared to do a good and thorough job in that direction; and it must have paid them back by improving their image with the public. They certainly deserve a lot of credit for the whole-hearted way they went about supporting motor racing.

The other thing that has changed enormously since I first drove a road racing car is safety. On the speedway in the midget days at least it was compulsory to wear safety belts, and we did have crash bars at the back. We also had things called nerthing rails which stopped the interlocking of wheels on the track. Fuel wasn't so much a problem because the races were very short and the maximum amount of fuel we carried was about five gallons. Then I moved into road racing, where the idea in those days was not to wear safety belts, which in eight out of ten accidents was probably an advantage. The way the cars were made in those days you nearly fell out before you started anyway, and it was comparatively safe to be thrown out on impact because there was nothing to impede your progress as you came out of the cockpit.

But as we progressed to rear-engined cars, and we began to sit lower and lie back a bit so that we were very much part of the car, it became necessary to have safety belts. The trouble was, it took quite a few years to get around to making them compulsory. I didn't need any encouragement to start using them because I knew the advantages from the speedway days. I didn't have them in the Cooper era—nobody did—though I used them in the sports car because I felt it was a car you couldn't fall out of easily, and I thought it was better to be strapped in.

The thing that started off the use of safety belts in single-seater racing cars was going to Indianapolis. Over there it was compulsory to use belts when we first went in 1961, and it still is. A lot of the Indianapolis safety rules should be adopted in motor racing over here, as a matter of fact, but it is taking a long time for people to come round to the idea.

I am very much in favour of everybody using safety belts in ordinary saloon cars. Driving about the place these days, I reckon, is more tiring and more dangerous than Formula 1. Probably it should be made compulsory and people should be fined if they are not wearing them. I think a lot of people who drive genuinely need help; they don't understand the problems, so they should be *told* to wear belts. They have tried to make them compulsory in Australia, and the only catch was that they were unable to make it 100 per cent. Belts were only fitted to cars made after a certain date, so the only law they could bring in was that if a car *were* fitted with belts, then the occupants had to wear them. If you were pulled up you would be fined if you weren't wearing one.

Fitting belts on the older cars will come, but there are a lot of rough cars around, in England and Australia, and it will take a long time. In Australia they are very safety conscious at the moment. They have put me on the Common-wealth Special Safety Group—actually, the correct title is the Expert Advisory Group to the Minister of Transport; in other words the expert group is supposed to advise the Minister of Transport on what he should do about road safety on a long-term basis.

Going back to racing cars, it is obvious that as the cars have improved the speeds have gone up, and one by one safety features have had to be incorporated. We are not nearly far enough ahead with this, and not quick enough to get new regulations off the ground. It usually takes a fairly bad accident or a series of accidents to get the governing bodies to see the necessity of making rules on safety at all.

However, we are progressing. One of the very good things that has been done recently is the fitting of on-board fire extinguishers. I have been very grateful for them in two accidents I have had. I am not sure that I could have been saved by them in either case, but I can assure you it is a nice comforting feeling to know you at least had a chance of defending yourself against fire.

I have mixed feelings about rubber fuel tanks—probably from a general safety point of view it may be better to have rubber tanks; it is easier to come up with some regulations and specifications on them, but they can be more dangerous than the metal ones if they are not made properly. We raced for many years with aluminium tanks and we had very little trouble with them. We have certainly had more fuel leaks and allied problems with the bags than we ever had with the tanks.

I think that filling the bag or tank with foam rubber is going to make the biggest contribution to safety in this field. It is much safer from the explosion point of view—the fuel tank full of foam virtually cannot explode. And if the tank splits the fuel is not going to gush out quickly but will take quite a time to trickle through the foam, which could make a lot of difference in an accident.

There isn't much to be done about the combustible side of the fuel itself, so the best thing to do is cut down the capacity of the cars. I think cutting down the race distance so that less fuel is required to be carried at one time is a good move. This is the one thing that makes Indianapolis very dangerous—the fact that you are really racing a fuel tanker. They carry 75 US gallons, which is a fantastic amount. Fortunately there are moves afoot in the States at the moment to make four pit stops compulsory at Indy, which is at least a step in the right direction. In the old days there was no way anybody could go the full 500 miles anyway, because of the tyres. There was nothing around that could go anywhere near that distance, but when the tyre people suddenly came up with improved tyres which could last the race, then the Indy people were trying to get as far as they could on the fuel. In my opinion they should not only make regulations about the minimum number of pit stops, but they should limit the capacity of the fuel tanks down to 50 US gallons. The use of methanol means that you have to use double the amount of fuel to go the same distance as you would with petrol, but with today's Indy engines it is not feasible to use petrol. I don't like methanol because you can't see it burning, but you can certainly feel it, as Denny Hulme discovered when his car caught fire in practice at Indy in 1970.

Where safety is still sadly lacking is on the circuits. There are a lot of circuits still used which are just not suitable for motor racing—not the sort of motor racing we are involved in today. The old Nurburgring and Spa were obvious examples, and I don't blame the Grand Prix Drivers' Association for not agreeing to race at Spa. Hockenheim is basically the kind of circuit we should be racing on. It is not the ideal shape by any means, but it is on the right lines. Personally, I'm not mad about slipstreaming circuits, but it is a matter of driver ability which makes it dangerous or otherwise. Monza, I think, is a reasonably safe circuit, but that doesn't mean I like driving there. The first 75 per cent of the race seems pointless. It doesn't matter whether you are first or tenth as long as you are in the leading bunch. Who leads round on each lap doesn't necessarily mean a thing until the very last part of the last lap.

I would very much like to see properly-dressed and trained fire marshals at every potentially bad point on every circuit.

The Changing Face of Grand Prix Racing

They have to be able to get in amongst the flames and get a driver out within a very few seconds, but most circuits still seem to rely on people just dressed in short-sleeved shirts and other ordinary clothes. Maybe some of them have an extinguisher or two, but it isn't nearly good enough.

One of the worst problems we have had at various circuits is the question of using the Grand Prix Medical Unit. In my opinion the Medical Unit is a very good thing and something that has been needed a lot more on the Continent than in England. But this is where the project has fallen down. The organisers at the Continental meetings tend not to want the Medical Unit as they feel their own medical arrangements are good enough. Well, on many circuits I am sure they are not, and if you have a fully equipped Medical Unit, with resuscitation equipment and an operating theatre and so on right on the spot, it just has to be a terrific advantage. The thing that is needed now is a bit of liaison between the medical people at each circuit and those in charge of the Medical Unit vehicle. It might just be lack of understanding on the part of the local people because of the language barriers. Most of the problems that have cropped up could be ironed out with a certain amount of good will and understanding on both sides, but nobody ever seems to have the time.

I think, in general, tyres have been pretty safe – they are a lot safer today then the skinny things we used to race on. In fact, quite big strides have been made in this area. We have had a few problems, but usually you couldn't blame the tyre itself. Anybody can get a puncture, you can't make a tyre that doesn't. Normally, the tyres we are using today don't go down quickly. The one that put me off the road at Zandvoort had a cut in it half an inch long, a sort of semi-circular cut. You couldn't make a tyre to prevent that sort of thing happening. In my crash at Silverstone the situation was a little different, because we were experimenting with various new types of tyre, and the ones I was using at the time of my accident had never gone into production. I decided that that wasn't the tyre to continue with!

We are making improvements all the time, such as putting

bolts in the wheels to prevent tyres coming off the rim, which would have saved Graham Hill from his Watkins Glen accident, for instance. We have always been a little on the conservative side as far as rim width was concerned which has helped us safety-wise. Progress in tyre construction has led to much wider rims and lower profile tyres, so it has become necessary to try and keep the tyre on the rim if it goes down —in fact, having bolts in the wheels would have saved my accident at Zandvoort. That really taught us a lesson. We have never raced since without them.

Many, many things ought to have been foreseen in this sphere. Unfortunately, it takes an accident to highlight them.

CHAPTER XIV

The Dangerous Side of the Game

There aren't too many things that put the wind up me. The only time I get a bit scared is when something happens to me over which I have no control. Providing I *have* reasonable control over a situation I can feel calm and confident; my only real exception to that would be flying on a commercial jet plane. As a pilot myself I can appreciate only too well the many things that can go wrong, and if the weather were really bad and I had no confidence in the aeroplane or the pilot, I would be thoroughly panic-stricken! But there really isn't a lot of risk in flying a big commercial jet today and once aboard there is nothing *I* can do about it, so I am resigned and relaxed.

But when I come up against a very dodgy moment on the race track, that is when I want to be very much in charge. Of course, the whole business of motor racing, when you come down to brass tacks, is concerned with conquering the forces of nature and the effects of these forces on the machine and the driver. It is a challenge. I like to pit myself against the elements—it is something I can't resist. That is why I am hoping to take up gliding and power-boat racing in Australia, in an attempt to fill the gap left by giving up motor racing.

It wasn't until I began to write this book that I realised just how extraordinarily lucky I have been throughout my racing career—*and* before. Remembering all the hair-raising things I did as a boy, and the near escapes from disaster I had as early as my tricycling days, I can only marvel at the kindness of fate. I never thought I was in the least fatalistic, but reviewing your own life is a salutary experience. You realise you are not as much in charge of your actions and their consequences as you thought you were.

Accidents in motor racing can only really come in two categories, however; mechanical failure on the car, or driver error. There have been some odd exceptions, some fatal, such as the time a bird flew into Alan Stacey's face at Spa in 1960 and caused him to go off the road and crash. There is always the stray dog situation, which has often cropped up, causing damage to cars and near-accidents. Rabbits, hares and even deer have been known to turn up on the track in the path of cars — while in Mexico you have to contend with stray people!

But taken over all, year by year, case by case, motor racing accidents are mostly caused by some kind of failure on the car or by the driver making a mistake. Sometimes it is difficult afterwards to tell exactly which was to blame, especially when the driver is dead or, like Stirling Moss, cannot recall the moments leading up to impact. I go into my personal feelings on accidents and safety elsewhere in this book, but I want to recall my own three dramas on the track — at least the only ones which might have been serious. Three out of twenty-three years of motor racing isn't a bad score. I know I have been very lucky.

In 1959 we went to Lisbon for the Grand Prix of Portugal, which was held in very beautiful surroundings, the track taking in parts of Monsanto Park, which is wooded and overlooks Lisbon harbour. It is a little like Barcelona, but the track surface had about three variations — something we were used to in those days, and to which the Cooper which I was driving was well suited.

The days that led up to the Grand Prix were rather unusual for me. I was persuaded to relax and take some time off! The first night we were in Lisbon we went to a bullfight, and four of us piled into a taxi. I was left to pay the driver when we arrived and I remember getting out my wallet and extracting a note — and that was the last I saw of my wallet. I don't know what happened to it — a pickpocket at the arena maybe; but I lost £50, my driving licence, a lot of personal papers and what have you. *And* I didn't like bullfighting.

The Dangerous Side of the Game

Then the next day we went along to Estoril Beach which is one of the nicest places in Europe, and as I always enjoy 'messing about in boats', I took out a little canoe. Everything was fine until I came to beach it. A big wave took over, had me out of the canoe, and the keel ran over my big toe, scraping the nail right off. Very nasty.

Well, they bandaged me up and John Cooper said he didn't think my driving would suffer, but *I* was beginning to think that all this relaxation they kept telling me about was not what it was cracked up to be.

The front row of the grid turned out to be Stirling, in Rob Walker's Cooper, Masten Gregory and myself in the works Coopers, and at the back of the grid were the two Lotus cars of Graham Hill and Innes Ireland plus a Centro-Sud Cooper Maserati driven by a Portuguese youngster.

It was a sixty-two-lap race and I led away from the start, but Stirling soon overtook me. There didn't seem to be any reason why he should't run away with the race, the car and Stirling were so good. By lap twenty-four he was forty seconds ahead of me, and Masten eight seconds behind me with Bruce McLaren, our other team-mate, fifteen seconds behind him. One rarely gets these sort of gaps nowadays.

At this stage the first six of us had lapped the field twice, and Stirling had just lapped the backmarker for the third time. We had noticed in practice that he was inexperienced and a bit erratic, and I was keeping my eye on him. As I had passed him on two previous occasions I thought he must have got the message that I wasn't far away, even if he hadn't looked in his mirrors.

We were approaching a righthand corner, and he was actually on the right of the road where I thought he was going to stay. I anticipated wrongly. Just at the wrong moment he turned to the left to get over onto the lefthand side of the road – to take a righthand corner. Now I thought he knew I was coming and he wasn't going fast enough to warrant his taking the lefthand side of the road. The net result was that he came out and cut me off when I was doing at least twice his speed, and he just ran me into the strawbales; I think I hit the back of his car, too.

When the Flag Drops

I can remember vividly going up over those strawbales. The circuit was quite heavily wooded there and I can recall looking at the trees and thinking: 'There's no way I am going to miss hitting some of those.' The car hit a telegraph post with the righthand front wheel – and this simply sent the car back into the middle of the road and rolled it. As the car was rolling down the road I was holding myself tense expecting to hit trees; I couldn't imagine the car rolling so far without hitting something else. I didn't know I was on the track! I thought I was on the other side of the strawbales.

Eventually I came out of the car and went on rolling all by myself, and it wasn't until I'd stopped rolling that I realised where I was. I sat up in the middle of the track – and found myself looking straight into the radiator of Masten Gregory's car! He came belting out of the corner straight for me and this made me wake up. I can assure you I was off that circuit pretty damn quick.

Masten went whistling by at a great rate of knots, and a few people at the side of the track came and grabbed hold of me and sat me on a strawbale. I realised I wasn't badly hurt, only winded and dazed. It must have taken me a minute or so to get my senses back and come to the conclusion that I was still in one piece. I remember wondering if I could get back into the car and into the race – I *must* have been dazed. The car was totally undriveable, just a nasty looking piece of scrambled metal.

After that I wasn't too worried about myself or what was going to happen next, because as far as I was concerned the race was finished. I was a bit indignant when ambulance men arrived on the scene and started pushing and poking at bits of me, and asking whether this hurt or whether it didn't. I wanted to get back to the pits and let them know I was all right. I knew Betty would be in a nervous jelly. But before I realised what was happening they had shoved me into the back of an ambulance and I had the most frightening ride I've ever had in my life. The driver was obviously short of business and going to prove he was the all-time great among ambulance drivers. The siren was going full blast, and this chap was driving as fast as he could into Lisbon as if I were going to die the next minute. There was nothing I could do about it except hold on tight and hope that we were going to arrive at a hospital very soon. I was more frightened then than at the moment when I sat up in the road and looked down Masten's radiator!

Of course, as soon as we arrived at the hospital I wanted to leave, but they took me in, and put me on a bed and fussed around, and X-rayed me in various spots. I had some skin off here and there, but apart from that I was OK. I was more worried about what was going on back at the track. Of course, the team eventually found out what had happened; John Cooper brought Betty down to the hospital with Bruce McLaren and his mother and father, and I persuaded the doctors to let me go back to the hotel with them. I was extremely stiff and sore for a few days, and I hoped it would be my last accident—I didn't like the feeling of helplessness as I saw all those trees just waiting for me—and hobbled off to England with the others next day.

I experienced a number of 'incidents' in the following years, some of which *could* have been fatal or seriously injurious, but miraculously were not. It was not until 1969, ten years later, that I got myself into real trouble, and that was during a testing session at Silverstone in June. We had just come back from Zandvoort, and I missed all the other Grands Prix until Monza that year, which was a bit frustrating.

It was something that happened very quickly, and I didn't get time even to attempt to do anything about it. If that particular situation had occurred at any other corner at Silverstone I would probably not have been hurt. But it was at Club Corner, and we go through there at 115 mph, and drive within six inches of a dirt bank on every lap. I went into the corner perfectly under control, braking at the right moment and so on, and had the power back on when I was three-quarters round. Suddenly the car took up a violent understeer when I was no more than fifteen feet from the bank. A tyre had lost air and those fifteen feet just disappeared in a flash. I didn't have a chance to do anything about it. The car was under control right up to that point, and then it went straight into the bank like a dart. If that bank had not been there, I probably wouldn't have needed much more time to have reacted sufficiently to get the thing back under control. But this was one of those times when you can't do a thing because of insufficient room.

The rim went into that bank like a shovel — you can imagine how a wheel with a flat tyre on it, travelling at 115 mph would dig into an earth bank. The stopping force was quite something. The rim came around and pushed the side of the car on top of my legs. The car went up on top of the bank and it was only a miracle that it didn't go over. If it had, things would have been a lot worse. It went along the top of the bank for ten or fifteen yards before it eventually stopped; it was twisted round with its two front wheels hanging over the bank and the two rear wheels on the track. The whole car was bent and twisted and had my legs caught up in front with the wreckage. The pain was just unbelievable. It was as though somebody were trying to break my leg and hadn't quite got there. It was bent beyond what you could stand by about five miles!

There was nothing I could do but get my breath and my senses back. I wasn't knocked unconscious or anything, but it takes a couple of seconds to realise what sort of situation you are in. I desperately wanted to do something about it. Luckily I was able to twist myself in the car, and lift myself up a little. I undid my belt first, and then I twisted myself further and tried to work on my foot which was jammed high up in the lefthand corner. As I gradually worked it down it suddenly came free, and you have no idea how good that was! It hurt like hell, but it was not trapped any more. Once my leg was free I turned all the switches off because the engine was still running from when I first hit the bank. Actually, I couldn't get at the ignition to start with because the whole side of the body was pushed in over the switch, and I just couldn't get my hand in to turn it off. Fortunately, I was able to sit up and look down into the mass of tangled bodywork and, by putting my hand up underneath and feeling about with my fingers, I was able to find the switch and turn it off. If I hadn't I'm sure the car would have caught fire within seconds. The tank was split and petrol was beginning to run out; if you can imagine petrol running down the back of a car with the engine still flat out—well, it could have been on fire in a flash. I could smell petrol and when I looked out I could see this patch of fuel getting bigger and bigger—and I was in the middle of it. So I pushed the fire extinguisher and shot it off while I was sitting there, thinking that, if it did catch fire, the extinguisher could not have coped with it. It would just have gone *Woof!* and the fire extinguisher would have been a joke.

My next effort was to try to get out of the car in some way, which was impossible because the bottom of the car was bent as well, and was pushing up under my legs. As I tried to draw my legs back, the undershield, which was torn away and folded up inside, kept catching on my ankles and wouldn't let them out. My left ankle was completely numb. I couldn't move it and I couldn't twist it. It was obvious I couldn't get out by myself, although I broke off the wheel and twisted the bodywork of the car and really tore at everything. I was just pinned there.

Eventually a chap came round the track in a saloon car. He had done a complete lap of the circuit before he had come upon me, as I had just been coming up behind him when I went off. He was the first person on the scene and he tried to help me out. I explained that it was impossible and that we had to have something to cut the car with. He went off to the pits to get our people, but by that time the mechanics had already left the pits on the way round looking for me, and they arrived without any tool kits or cutting gear. So off they had to go back to the pits, get all the tools, drive round the circuit again and start cutting me out.

I must have been in the car for at least half an hour before I was eventually freed and taken to hospital. The most worrying thing about that incident was whether I would go up in flames or not.

At the hospital they X-rayed my foot and found that the ankle itself was broken at the joint. It had broken off the inside part of the left ankle bone, about the last three-quarters of an inch, and there was no way they could put it in a splint or put it back in the right place. The foot was badly bruised and swollen by that time and they couldn't do anything about it anyway. They reckoned they couldn't attempt to attach it for a couple of days, so I got a lift and went home.

We then got in touch with a doctor at St Thomas's and showed him the X-rays. He decided there was nothing to be done until the swelling went down. The skin wasn't actually damaged but it came out in a rash due to lack of circulation in the area. They have learned over the years that they must never work on any part of the body that is in a deteriorating condition—once it has turned the tide and started to improve and the swelling is going down, then you can operate on it. So they operated on it about five days after the accident. They put a screw into the bone from the bottom, purely to hold it together whilst the bones knitted. It could be taken out if I wanted it done, but they didn't recommend it because there is no reason why the screw shouldn't stay there. So it stays.

I still have a bit of a problem with the tendons at the top of the foot when I don't use it. The one thing it doesn't like is resting.

My last and perhaps most potentially dangerous mishap was again in a test session, this time at Zandvoort in June 1970. We went over to Holland early with Goodyear, and the tyre test had shown up a particular tyre as being the best for the circuit. We fitted these to Rolf Stommelen's car—he was our second driver in 1970—and he was due out there to do some testing but hadn't arrived. We only had half an hour to go before the circuit was closed, and Ron Tauranac wanted me to run Stommelen's car. We had new brake pads, new tyres, and the gear ratios had been changed from the ones I had been using. We thought we had changed to the right ones, but when I started off from the pits I found that there were two gears with the same ratio. In other words, I had two second gears and no third; with two second gears, whether I went from second to fourth or third to fourth there was still the same gap. I spent a few laps scrubbing the tyres and then started to speed up. I came to the righthand corner, after you go over the brow of the hill round the far side of the circuit, which is a third gear corner. So I took it easy round there in fourth gear. If the right gear had been available and I had taken the corner quickly I would probably have noticed at that stage that the left rear tyre was going down, because it must have been already on its way down.

Of course, from there the track speeds up considerably, and then I was in fourth gear and going quite fast into the left-hander, lying heavily on the good tyre, so I didn't notice anything wrong with the car even then. But as soon as I started to steer back to the right I realised that something was wrong with the back of the car. I tried to do all the corrections, but the tyre was down sufficiently to come off the rim, and when the rim hit the ground it was just like taking both wheels off the car. I had absolutely no control over it from that second on. It went into the sand sideways, the wheel rim dug in and the car flipped over. I hadn't actually hit anything. It rolled a couple of times and went on rolling up the bank and into the wire fencing. And as it rolled across the fence, it just wrapped the wire round the car until I was trussed up inside it like a turkey ready for the oven.

It all seemed to happen fairly slowly. The car didn't even roll violently. I wasn't as worried about it as I might have been if I had flipped it into some trees or something. But the fuel situation soon began to worry me. The car came to rest upside down straddling a ditch, and there were then about twenty gallons of petrol in the tanks. I was hanging by my safety belt and my head was just about moveable, but very slightly. And it dawned on me, while I was suspended there, that the first thing I ought to do was get all the switches turned off. It was a bit funny looking for them upside down. It is surprising how confused you can get when you're trying to do something in a hurry, but I managed to get them turned off.

Then I began to think of ways of getting out of this situation. There seemed to be no one about at all—the last few moments of a tyre resting session at Zandvoort on a rather grey and chilly afternoon. So I started moving myself about to see how I could get out, but everywhere I pushed my hands there was wire fencing. There was just no way out. I needed a large pair of wire cutters—the wire was absolutely taut on the car.

It was pretty terrifying, I must admit; the thought of fire was very much in my mind and I looked for the extinguisher button. I didn't fire it off, as I did at Silverstone, but just sat there with my finger on the button looking about for problems. The petrol was all starting to run out of the filler caps, and going down between my legs onto the sand. That wasn't too bad because at least the sand soaked it up.

When people did arrive, I was getting used to hanging upside down and the blood running to my head. Somebody started to pull the wire away and unravel the car and I thought: 'Now is the time there is likely to be a fire and the best thing I can do is be ready to get out.' So I unfastened my safety belt—forgetting I was still hanging upside down in it. Naturally, I fell on my head! I was lying with my head twisted in the sand and my whole weight resting on my neck. That was the silliest thing I did and I suffered from a very stiff neck afterwards.

Anyway, the people who were helping me were spectators who had been up on a sand dune some distance away, and by the time the mechanics arrived from the pits I was already released from the car. I'll always be grateful to those Dutch spectators, but it was an experience I would not like to have again. It was one of the few times when I had something happen to me over which I had no control. And that is something I hate.

...ading for a wet victory on
... in the International Trophy
...at Silverstone, 1969.

...hipps

...rabham family – Betty and I
...ur three sons: David (left),
...ey (standing) and Gary (right)

Britain

Betty and I on the balcony for our farewell meeting at Brands Hatch, November 1970.

David Phipps

My last Grand Prix, Mexico 1 – my engine failed when I was my way to a third place!

David Phipps

CHAPTER XV

The Twenty-Third Year

My very last year of Grand Prix driving, 1970, started well and was then followed by a series of events which piled disappointment upon disappointment. One of my reasons for wanting to go on driving for another year, after 'promising' to give up at the end of 1969, was that we had the new monocoque car, the BT33, coming along and I was pretty confident that it would be good. I have to admit that I probably couldn't face up to the fact that I wouldn't be driving it!

I started the year with more confidence than I have had for quite some time—certainly since 1966. The first race was the South African Grand Prix, and we went to Riverside to do our testing: initial sorting out of the car combined with some tyre testing. We had one or two problems, like vibration where one of the brake pipes ran, and which we had to move, but very little else. The sorting out went extremely well. Then I went to Australia for my usual escape from the English February, and turned up in South Africa prior to the race reasonably full of confidence that we were going to do well.

I have said previously that although we, Brabhams, hoped to start the season off well, the car to watch was the Ferrari. The shaping up of the Italian car at the end of the previous year made it clear that the Ferrari would be the car to beat eventually. We hoped we could collect sufficient points early in the season before the Ferrari overtook us. We weren't too worried about Lotus at that time, because we expected that their new 72 would take quite a lot of sorting out and it would be a long time before it became competitive. Actually, we were wrong about this, because the 72 got going before we thought it would.

When the Flag Drops

At Kyalami it looked as though we were going to be on pole position, but unfortunately, when we put our race engine in on the last day of practice, it didn't go as expected. The timing gears had gone adrift, and the engine not only wouldn't go, but it started to rattle. So we had to change the engine and put in one that had been used previously rather than take the risk of using a fresh one. This proved to be OK.

On race day itself, everybody had got back onto the tyres they intended to use — tactics in this field are to use a fast compound for practice and a more lasting one for the race — we found ourselves in a reasonably competitive position, which nearly expired on the first corner! Too many people arrived there at the same time and there just wasn't room for everybody. Amon, it appears from film of the race, pulled across the road — causing Jochen to touch wheels with me and his car actually climbed over the top of mine.

I was absolutely staggered after this had happened to find that I still had my front wheel with me, because two tyres revolving in opposite directions to one another can cause quite a dangerous situation with the type of cars we are racing today. Luckily the direction of my wheel was in my favour, while Jochen's was against him.

At the time I didn't really know what had happened except that in the confusion I got tangled with Jochen, and I actually had two wheels on the dirt, trying to get over as far as possible and still get round the corner. It certainly took the shine off me for the first few laps, because I was unable to accept the fact that the car was still in one piece. So I took the first two or three laps very carefully, watching the front end and the wheels and steering and what have you and convincing myself that there were things wrong with it all the time. It is pretty easy to do this when you are worried about something, but after three laps I decided there was nothing wrong with the car, that it wasn't damaged and hadn't got to the point where it could be dangerous. Then I had to take off after the field, because I was in sixth place and my main contenders had had a break. I managed to catch up with the leader, Stewart, after a while and pass him, and from there on I never had a problem. It was quite easy to stay in front.

The Twenty-Third Year

When I was trying to overtake Stewart he went off the edge of the road a bit and his wheels threw up a stone which welted me in the face. The cut is visible on all the photos taken after the race and is now an established battle scar. Naturally, after winning at Kyalami, we came away on the crest of a wave, knowing that the car was good, and that we had a head start over the other teams. All we had to do was try to keep it up.

The next race was Spain, and we arrived at Jarama with the first of our 1970 Cosworth-Ford engines, which gave us added confidence. But it is always a bit of a lottery at race meetings, picking which engine you're going to use. If you have a choice it always seems as though you pick the wrong one. We felt that the new engine, having all new parts, must be the better bet. In fact, it didn't give a lot of power—it was probably one of our poorest engines, powerwise. But we ran it for 200 miles before the race, and as I had tested it such a lot we felt the difference between winning and losing would not lie with the engine on that particular circuit. Anyway, we decided to use it.

I made a rather poor start, but I wasn't too worried about this until the big shunt occurred. Jackie Oliver's BRM had a stub axle failure, went straight on at the hairpin, and smashed into the side of Jacky Ickx's Ferrari. Both cars burst into flame, and Oliver was lucky enough to get out unscathed, but poor Ickx, who hadn't had time to realise what was about to happen, took longer to get out of his burning car, and then slipped on the fuel and sat in the flames. It was a very unpleasant accident, and it took Ickx a couple of months to recover from his burns sufficiently to drive competitively again.

Naturally, having such a thing happen on the very first lap made things a bit difficult for the rest of us. Although, initially, it wasn't a great problem going through the area where the fire was, it soon became very, very slippery from oil and fire extinguisher fluid plus the cement and water that they were putting on the track. Denny, who was running second at that time, was just ahead of me, and I was closing on him hoping to get by on the next lap. But we arrived at this wet area and Denny entered it first. He got all crossed up and I was under the impression he was about to spin. So just before the wet patch I got myself all crossed up too, thinking that I couldn't afford to go straight into him. However, he straightened up, and I didn't, because I was committed to my position by then. I spun, and this put me quite a long way back. I got going again all right, but because of all the ground I had lost, I just plain tried too hard to catch up and spun again. Coming out of the wet patch, I put my foot down a bit too early and a bit too much, and round I went again!

Then I had a little problem with Beltoise who had got by me —and the Matra is a very wide car. At Jarama, a track which is particularly narrow and twisty, it is pretty disheartening to look at a Matra from behind, especially if it is quicker down the straight, which it was. I was beginning to wonder if I'd ever get by this thing, and all the time Stewart was pulling out a big lead at the front. Denny had dropped out by then, so I only had the Matra to contend with before I could go after Jackie. Then I began to feel a bit more hopeful because the Matra started to smell hot. I could actually smell it, and it was obvious that something was about to go wrong with it. Sure enough, it was not long before the engine expired in a big smouldering heap!

After that I worked really hard to get after Stewart, and after a few laps I caught up 14 or 15 seconds on him. Then I drove even harder to get right on his tail, and we went round the circuit with me breathing Stewart's exhaust. We were really tied together through one or two of the corners, and I was trying to weigh up the chances of getting by him, and choosing the right part of the track to do it, because he obviously wasn't going to make it easy for me.

Eventually I had convinced myself that the only possible hope was to outbrake him at the bottom of the straight. While I was working myself up to the right pitch to do this, my engine expired with a broken crankshaft. This put a finish to it—all that race did for us was to prove we had chosen the wrong engine. If only I could have scratched by Stewart I'm pretty sure I could have pulled away from him quite comfortably. Certainly I was able to get round most of the twisty bits more quickly than he could, but his car was faster on the straight, and I had to get into an ideal slipstreaming situation to be able to do anything about it.

So that was one that got away. The third Grand Prix of the year was Monaco. Do I *have* to talk about that? It was one of the worst things that ever happened to me, going into the strawbales on the last lap when I was in the lead. . . .

The meeting started off with a few problems in practice which stopped us from getting a good grid position. The brakes were playing up rather badly, and I finished up only fourth fastest, on the second row of the grid behind Hulme, Amon and Stewart. I was situated on the two-by-two grid immediately behind Amon and I had to sit behind him, while Stewart dashed away into the lead. As you probably know, it is very difficult to get by anybody at Monte Carlo. It is a terrible situation to be sitting behind someone knowing that the leader is drawing away and there is nothing you can do about it.

Eventually I was able to scratch by on the brakes on the promenade, and take Amon. Six laps later Stewart's engine failed and I found myself with a reasonable lead within a few laps. I didn't really feel I had any problems after that. My mistake, when I get into a situation like that, is a tendency to make sure I get to the finishing line, and perhaps take it a little easier than I should. I had, at half distance, a lead of about three seconds over Amon and about fifteen over Jochen Rindt. I thought that was just about right. But it all backfired on me towards the end of the race when Jochen was catching me up. I didn't worry because I had worked out that at the rate he was catching me there was no way he could get by me in the time. Chris dropped out with broken suspension, so it was a straight fight between myself and the Lotus, and I was confident I could win.

Unfortunately, with about five laps to go, I had the most shocking run of slow cars that I have ever encountered. On one lap alone I must have lost 7 or 8 seconds. When I arrived at the top of the hill after Ste Devote I found Siffert sitting in the middle of the road — he'd run out of petrol and was swinging his car from side to side trying to get the fuel to pick up. I almost ran straight into the back of him, and then I had to wait until he saw me. The flag marshals were going mad – I had to go up on the footpath to get past him, actually. I practically had a standing start on that lap. I'd been doing 1 minute 24 seconds and suddenly I'd chalked up a 1 minute 29·3 seconds! That was when Jochen really caught me. It is just unbelievable that you can arrive on somebody and they just haven't any idea you are there, or don't care, or something. On the second to last lap I struck somebody in the tunnel; I don't know who. All the slow dogs were struggling round to the end. But even starting the last lap I still had plenty in hand and no real problem as far as Jochen was concerned. I had told myself that I mustn't get excited and overdo it just because Colin Chapman was hopping up and down on the pit counter and making 'come on' signs that he knew I could see, long before Jochen came round the Tobacconist's.

I kept everything well under control until I came to the chicane, where I found three slow cars like Brown's cows all ambling along towards the Tobacconist's. I arrived on the scene in the middle of them. I had virtually to stop and just crawl round on to the harbour straight towards the Gasworks. It was then I realised I had a problem on my hands, because I knew Jochen was coming, and that he would not have my difficulties because I was, in effect, clearing the track for him. I had to start along the promenade very slowly, and when I got to the braking area I found Piers Courage apparently coasting with a dead engine, right in the middle of the road. It is always a problem to know which line someone is going to take in a situation like that, and whether one should overtake on the inside or outside. While I was trying to decide how to cope with this, I passed my braking point by just a few yards. In addition, a lot of sand had been deposited during the race on the inside approaching the Gasworks hairpin, which simply served to help me into the strawbales!

The television caught this incident, and even if I didn't win the race I made a name for myself! I found myself in the position where I had actually shunted into just about everybody's living room in England and America. When I went to

214

America, everyone I spoke to had seen it on television – but unfortunately they'd missed the best bit.

I had nudged into the barrier and stalled the engine at the same time. You don't want any outside assistance, or you get disqualified, and there were a couple of flag marshals standing right behind the barrier where I ran into it. Of course, they got excited and one of them jumped over to give me a push, which I didn't want. When I saw the bloke coming I fumbled with everything and got the engine all fired up and shoved it into reverse. When he arrived it was an absolute dead-heat – I went backwards as he leant over the car to push. He lost his balance and fell flat on the car; absolutely sprawled right across it. Then I had to shove it into low gear and went to move off with this marshal still struggling on top of the car. 'Well, I can't go down the road with this bloke sitting on the bonnet', I thought – so I jammed on the brake and stopped again. With that he slid down and was in a heap on the ground. By this time he was completely flustered and he couldn't get up – the more he tried the worse his position became. His hands were grabbing hold of nothing, and he was struggling to get to his feet. I had to sit there and wait for this bloke to pick himself up and move off the track before I could go on down the road, and I damn near lost second place over it!

Honestly, most of the damage done to the car was by this bloke falling on it. I damaged one wing on the left-hand side. But if he had pushed me, things would have been much worse. Second place gave me another six points in the Championship table, giving me a total of fifteen to Stewart's thirteen.

One thing must be said for Jochen Rindt after all my misfortunes. His last two lap times were 1 minute 23·3 seconds and 1 minute 23·2 seconds – and that was simply fabulous driving on that track under any circumstances.

At the Belgian Grand Prix at Spa, Stewart put up a good practice time on the first day – a 3 minutes 31·8 seconds. Well, people will tell you all sorts of tales about me, but one true one is that I tend to wait until I know exactly what way to drive on every section of the course, then go out right at the end of a practice session and string together all the things I have learnt. So I managed to drop in a 1 minute 31·5 seconds.

But after that we seemed to be down on top speed for some reason, and I never got that time again. The problem was completely mystifying to us, and the whole way through practice we tried to do things such as knocking off the wings and seeing what minimum wing we could get away with, but it didn't seem to make any difference. We were down on top speed compared with the other cars. So we didn't have much hope for the race. We had a hard tussle deciding which tyres to use, because we had a choice of two and hadn't fairly tried either of them. I chose the smaller diameter tyre. Then there was some confusion prior to the start because the original instructions we received stated that the race was due to start at 2 pm, but it was afterwards put forward to 1 pm. Anyway, everybody was wandering about, refuelling the cars and it suddenly dawned on us that the race was due to start in 15 minutes. There was a terrific flap then, getting the car out onto the circuit. Then the thing wouldn't start! But eventually it fired up and we rushed out just in time to start the race. It wasn't an ideal situation — to get yourself all steamed up — and for the first few laps I found it quite difficult to pass anybody. I was able to slipstream and hold people, but I couldn't overtake. I was sixth, and then fifth, fourth, and finally third behind Rodriguez in his BRM and Amon in his March. I was about 15 seconds behind, so I settled for third place — but suddenly the car got a tremendous vibration in it — I wasn't sure whether a drive-shaft was going to come out or what, so I slowed up and looked in my rear-view mirrors to see if the drive-shafts were out of line, or if the suspension was falling off. It looked all right except that the mirrors were vibrating so much I could hardly see. Then I took it out of gear and let the revs die down, and of course the vibration died down with the engine. That made me realise the chassis was not at fault, only the engine, so I drove slowly round to the pits and pulled in. Actually, what had happened was that the clutch had come apart and great big pieces of clutch had come out and put the whole flywheel assembly so far out of balance that it just wasn't feasible to go on. Beltoise took over my third place.

Pedro won — in fact the BRM was extremely fast at Spa, and Chris Amon did very well to keep so close to him in his March.

Zandvoort was one of those meetings when it would have been better to stay at home altogether! For a start we decided we would do the Dutch Grand Prix properly and went there early to do some testing. That was the test session which ended up with me upside down in Rolf Stommelen's car! During practice we found that we weren't really competitive; we were having a traction problem getting in and out of corners and we weren't all that quick down the straight. We couldn't pin down the trouble, and I ended up on the fifth row of the grid. When I started the race I was really battling to try to hang on to the people I was with. As the track got a bit more oily and sandy the car seemed to get less competitive and I just couldn't get going with it. It was truly disheartening to see Jochen come round and lap me, which he did a couple of times; I also had two pit stops for punctured tyres. This was the race in which Piers Courage's de Tomaso went off the road, hit a bank and caught fire; Piers died, and that accident didn't help anyone's morale, especially after losing Bruce McLaren a few weeks earlier.

The Lotus 72 was clearly superior by that time, and Jochen would just take off up the hill and accelerate round the hairpin leaving me standing there with wheels spinning, getting nowhere. We came home from the meeting really worried, because we then realised that the 72 had a lot of advantages which were coming home to roost. It looked as though they'd really got the thing going after all.

The next race was the French Grand Prix at Clermont-Ferrand, and this was a circuit I had visited but never raced on. I went there in 1965 when I was in one of my spasms about giving up motor racing, and I gave Denny a drive in the car instead of myself.

I went there a couple of weeks before the Grand Prix in 1970 and walked round the circuit helping the organisers decide where the barriers should be, which is something I shouldn't have taken on. To walk round a circuit and see all the sheer drops over the side and the places where you could write yourself off without much trouble, is bad for confidence. It took me two days of practice to get myself into the groove to be up there at all. I finished fifth fastest, doing a 2 minute 59·67 seconds on the last lap in the last few minutes, which put me on the third row with Rindt.

I made a terrible start. We weren't too sure whether the clutch slipped or the differential gave trouble, but for some reason or other the thing just didn't go off the line and I had to have a second start. By the time I'd sorted out this second stab at getting away, Pescarolo and Beltoise and all the others were round my ears and passed me even before I got to the first corner.

It is always difficult passing people at Clermont, and passing those wide Matras on a circuit like that is almost impossible. It took me a long time to take Pescarolo, but after that I was able to get cracking. Denny and I seemed to be involved together and had a big thrash trying to get up with the leaders. But they got too much of a break on me—I felt disheartened. I wasn't in the right sort of mood to catch Ickx, Beltoise and Rindt, but I got away from Denny for a little while. I put up the fastest lap I think—3 minutes 00·75 seconds—but near the end I thought I was running out of petrol and Denny closed right up on me again.

I finished third to Rindt and Amon, but I felt if I'd had a good start I'd have been having a dice with Rindt at the front. As it was, everything went wrong within the first 100 yards. However, we were resigned to the fact that third was better than nothing.

After the French Grand Prix came Brands Hatch. I wish I could skip that! Of all the disappointments in my racing career, maybe that one hurt more than most. Jochen had now won three Grands Prix and had 27 points, while I had won the South African, been second at Monaco and third in France, which gave me a total of 19 points. I *needed* to win at Brands. But the whole meeting was a fiasco from beginning to end.

There was all that fuss about the hundred bottles of champagne, to start with, which was unnecessary and a bit childish. Jochen made fastest time on Thursday at 1 minute 24·8 seconds. I equalled that time on Friday morning towards the end of practice, and as it has always been the custom for the fastest driver of the Friday morning session *only* to win the champagne we thought we'd go down and collect it. But the announcement had gone out over the Public Address that Jochen had won it, even before my 1 minute 24·8 seconds had been recorded. It was all a silly muddle on the part of the organisers, but Colin and Jochen were already—with some surprise—being presented with the champagne. So what could we do? I wandered down to the presentation and had a glass with Lotus, then had to let Dean Delamont sort it out. Eventually, we received thirty-six of the hundred bottles, which we gave away to the accessory and tyre people who worked with us. This wasn't the fault of Lotus, it was just a muddle, but it started the meeting on a sour note—and it ended on a worse one.

Then, of course, the Ferrari was beginning to show its real form, and we realised it was going to be a big threat. At the start of the race, Ickx's Ferrari roared off into the lead, I was following it and Jochen was behind me, and that was the pattern of the race in the first few laps. The Ferrari was going very quickly, actually, and if anything was drawing away from us, and there wasn't much either Jochen or I could do about it.

But after about seven laps the Ferrari's transmission failed. I slowed, not knowing quite whether Ickx was going to make it as far as the corner, because it would have been a dead heat between Ickx, arriving at the corner running slowly, and myself. I slowed a fraction too much, and the next moment Jochen was beside me when we arrived at the corner, and we went round there, at Paddock, side by side—I was on the outside. When we straightened up Jochen had the inside running, kept it at Druids, and left me in a position where I could do nothing about it. I had to be satisfied with following Jochen for the next sixty laps! His car was quicker than mine on the straight, although I could hold him anywhere else on the circuit. I pressed as much as I could, sitting right on his tail for a long time looking into his rear view mirror, hoping he'd make a mistake somewhere along the line. It took a long time to happen, but eventually he missed a gear coming out of Bottom Bend and with this I was able to get close enough to him to do a little bit of slipstreaming as well, and I outbraked him at the bottom of the straight.

By making that outbraking manoeuvre I took the wrong line on the corner and slowed up quite a bit—luckily it had put Jochen off-line as well, or else he would have been able to sweep past me between that corner and the next. We both staggered through there quite slowly, because the corner had been messed up with me getting underneath him. From there on I was able to draw away from him, and after a few laps it was obvious that Jochen had had enough anyway. He slowed up and resigned himself to the fact that he was going to be second.

Then came the last lap. I was 13 seconds ahead as I went past the pits for the last time, and my team was beginning to allow itself to think I was all set to take the flag. It was a bit shattering for everybody, but especially me, when I came to Stirling's Bend and the engine died and never ever fired another shot. There was nothing at all to worry about—except that there was no petrol left.

We never really established why that happened. Ron reckoned there was some fuel left and it just wasn't getting through. Certainly, there should have been two gallons left. I remember it was topped up on the line. It is one of those things we shall never find out.

Actually, that episode made me feel like giving up there and then. Really. I had felt that everything was going for us that day, and we deserved to win. After I passed him Jochen seemed to give up trying, or his tyres were wearing out and making him slower—something. Anyway, he'd already re-signed himself to second place and I don't think he was very happy at winning that way.

Anyway, we were packing up to leave, when somebody came down the Paddock and told us Jochen had been dis-qualified; something to do with the rear aerofoil being of an illegal height. The scrutineers said it had been bent deliber-ately during the victory ride on the tractor, and when they asked the Chief Mechanic to straighten it, he refused to do it without Colin's permission. This upset the scrutineers, and they disqualified the car and sent word to Colin, who was having a celebration in the Firestone tent.

Well, I didn't take it seriously, because I didn't think for one minute that there was any way *anybody* could talk Chapman out of those 9 points! While Chapman was in there fighting I just resigned myself to the fact that nobody else stood a chance! Not at any stage did I think there was even a possibility of my being made the winner, plus the fact that I wouldn't have liked to see Jochen disqualified anyway. Running out of fuel on the last lap is one of motor racing's little hazards, and it wasn't my first experience by any means. It was a good race, and we didn't win, and that's it.

However, it more or less put paid to any ideas I had about going out of motor racing in a blaze of glory. Jochen was now 11 points ahead of me and from that day on everything seemed to go wrong.

The German Grand Prix was held at Hockenheim, a circuit which I like very much, surprisingly, as I don't normally care for slipstreaming circuits; but this place, with its vast grandstands around the stadium area, and its Indianapolis-type atmosphere was quite exciting. But it was a really bad race for us. In practice the car seemed to be going reasonably quickly and reasonably well, but suddenly everything went bad on the last day of practice when the thing wouldn't stay in gear and the chassis didn't seem to be handling all that well. We started changing things, but there wasn't time during practice to do anything about the gearbox.

We finished the end of the practice period going back to the transporter to look at the gearbox. We had the back off it, but it all looked perfect. We couldn't see how there could be anything wrong with it. Eventually somebody discovered that one of the studs that held the engine to the chassis was broken, and the engine was coming away from the chassis, pulling the thing out of gear. There were only three bolts holding the engine to the car, and it would have been quite embarrassing if another had gone. It was a bit lucky we found that, actually, as it was one of those things that would have been easy to miss. This immediately solved our chassis and gearbox problems all in one go.

We were then faced with an engine change in pretty unfavourable conditions at the circuit. The next day prior to the start we had the car all going and the mechanic got into it to move it around. The clutch wouldn't work properly! There was a big panic trying to adjust it but of course that is a very, very difficult job—to adjust the free travel on the clutch when the engine is hot and all in the chassis; a long and tedious job.

It went out to the line obviously still not right by quite a long way. We went round on the warming up lap and came to the line, but I knew I had a clutch problem and I deliberately left my move up to the grid-proper as late as I could, hoping I could arrive there just as they dropped the flag. But I had to come to a halt before the flag dropped, or I would have been penalised, and as I stopped the clutch started to drag badly. I was trying to stop the car from rolling with the brake, and the clutch was dragging like mad, so the flag dropped about two seconds too late for me—two seconds earlier and I would have got away. The engine stalled just as the flag fell, and left me standing there—everyone disappeared in smoke. I complained to the other drivers afterwards that no one had bothered to wait for me! We couldn't start the car and I still had to get it in gear somehow and dash after them.

I completed just one lap. Then the screw came loose on one of the oil pipes bolted to the engine. I looked in my rear view mirror and couldn't see anything because of this cloud of smoke everywhere. It was obvious that it was coming from my car, and equally obvious that there was no point in my going on. I pulled into the pits. It took some time to find out where the oil was coming from, and then it was in an impossible position to do anything about it. Two laps flashed by, and it was pointless to go on. We retired in disgust, packed up and went straight home. It was some measure of consolation that my second driver, Rolf Stommelen, finished fifth after a good race. Jochen Rindt won his fifth Grand Prix of the year.

That really finished any chances we had left of the Championship. Pressure had been mounting, inside the family, for me to give up driving ever since Zandvoort. They knew it was my last year and they couldn't see the sense of my flogging on to the bitter end when the effort was virtually wasted. But dropping out with a season unfinished is something very few drivers have been known to do. I still enjoyed driving, and Ron wanted to go on, naturally. Then there are all the people who rely upon you to keep going all year: the tyre company—in my case, Goodyear, who have supported me faithfully; the fuel people—Esso, to whom I have remained faithful since 1955; and all the accessory firms. We rely on all these for sponsorship and they rely on us for publicity and good public relations.

However, all the Austrian race did was confirm that we might as well have knocked off the season then and there. Apart from the Ferraris—they now had three drivers, Ickx, Regazzoni and Giunti, who were really flying—we were reasonably competitive. I got onto the fourth row of the two-by-two grid. But the first lap was one of the worst experiences I have had in motor racing for a long time, which didn't help. I didn't get the best start, and was passed by two or three cars down the straight, including the March of François Cevert. Coming back towards the pits on the rear straight, just prior to getting into the first really tight right-hander, I was moving up to slipstream him. I was right on his tail when his engine blew up, which not only covered the track and my car with oil but absolutely blanked me out vision-wise. I couldn't even see where I was going, so I had quite a problem on my hands, really, with the car sliding all over the track in the oil and the braking area coming up when it would be time to start slowing down. With one hand I was trying to steer and with the other I was attempting to get my visor off. The top sheet of it came off all right, just as I was about to go off the road, and I managed to get the car all sorted out and back on the right line. But this blessed visor had only come off one side and blew back over my face again, right when I was in the middle of the braking area and sliding. I had a second stab at getting this damned thing off and succeeded, but by then the leading pack had had quite a break, and I had to take off to try to overhaul them. I was catching them reasonably well — Jochen blew up then — and I caught up with the Ferrari of Giunti which was running fourth. But he was much too quick for me on the straight. I was finding it very difficult to get by him. Eventually we went up past the pits and the Ferrari got both wheels off the edge of the road on the inside, and a rock came up from his wheel and went straight through my radiator!

A great stream of water came out of the air ducts — like a big fountain. All I could do then, because there was no point in going on, was to come into the pits. The radiator had such a big hole in it that there was only one course open to us; we had to change the radiator. If we didn't beat any track records at least we beat the record on how fast a team can change a radiator. I went out again and finished thirteenth, the third disastrous race in a row.

I have never seen such an enthusiastic crowd in all my life as there was in Austria. Every Italian that was anywhere near the border must have crossed into Austria. It was quite impressive, actually, just going round the top of the hill past the pits — there were people waving an enormous red flag and every time a Ferrari went up the hill, there they were jumping up and down and waving this big red flag. Of course, when Ickx won, I have never seen such a storm of people coming down the hill waving flags and throwing hats in the air and God knows what. I was sure 90 per cent of them must have been Italians. It was a big day for Ferrari because it was their first win since Rouen in 1968.

At that time we really were convinced that luck wasn't with us, so we might as well pack it in there and then. But we all went home and in the morning when we woke up I suppose things looked better, because we decided we'd go to Monza.

The Italian Grand Prix was a pretty frustrating race as far as I was concerned, and Jochen's death during practice was a great shock to everyone and tended to overshadow other considerations on the last day of practice.

As for our own team, we had problems of a minor sort — we weren't all that quick on the straight for some reason, possibly because we were carrying too much wing, so we tried less

224

wing, and ended up starting the race with even less wing than we had tried in practice. I found myself in a pack of cars and it was obvious that it was all getting pretty dangerous — slipstreaming, passing, repassing, all the way round the track. It doesn't get anyone anywhere. It doesn't matter if you are first or tenth on the first few laps at Monza, because as long as you keep up with the leading bunch, you can change places as many as four or five times a lap. The race is almost always decided in the last few minutes.

I noticed the water temperature was virtually off the clock, so I tried keeping out of the slipstream as much as I could without losing the bunch. Then the engine started to miss badly under acceleration away from the Lesmos, mainly, and also the Parabolica. Coming out there in front of the pits the thing would falter, and when this started it wasn't long before I lost the tow completely. I found myself motoring round on my own with nobody to race with, but at least now the car was out of the slipstream the water temperature had dropped back about 10 degrees, and the engine had almost stopped missing. So I tried like mad to catch up with the others.

Eventually I caught the leading bunch which consisted of Stewart, Oliver, Regazzoni, Hulme, Stommelen and Cevert, in a different order on almost every lap. When I got in their slipstream again, I found I'd run on them quickly and felt as if I could motor past everybody and keep going; but I was only in the pack for a couple of laps when the water temperature was back off the top of the clock — and the engine was misfiring again! The car had set up a pattern in which it would go through the first quarter of the turn missing quite badly, and then would run cleanly, and keep going for the rest of the corner.

I was relying on this, and trying to keep up with the bunch as well, quite anxious to get back on the throttle and stay with them, when the engine quit altogether just when I needed it most, on the exit from the Parabolica. I was all crossed up on the outside of the circuit — everybody was using the outside at the time because somebody had dropped a lot of oil on the inside. The next thing I knew I was half sideways, but

225

I got it all straight again just in time to slide into the guard-rail. That finished Monza for us then and there.

Regazzoni, the Italian-Swiss, won the Italian Grand Prix in his Ferrari, and I think it was a good thing he did. If Stewart had beaten him by half a wheel as he had Jochen the year before I believe the crowd would have lynched Jackie! Actually, I think that was Regazzoni's finest drive, up to the time of writing, certainly the best he had done till then. A terrific drive. He pulled away from the pack at exactly the right moment and increased his advantage yard by yard until he was 5.73 seconds ahead of Stewart—an immense distance at Monza.

The European season was now finished, and we all went across the Atlantic for the last three Grands Prix of 1970—the Canadian, the United States, and the Mexican. The second half of the year was just one disaster after another, and Canada was no exception. We weren't at all competitive. It is almost unbelievable how things could go so right in South Africa and so wrong afterwards.

Ste Jovite was a terribly rough circuit and I was unable to get motoring properly there at all. We had a little incident in practice when someone suggested I try Rolf Stommelen's car, and on the first lap round I went down to the bottom end of the straight when suddenly the steering went stiff. I wasn't going very quickly, luckily. The front wishbone had broken, and broken right on the joint. The bottom pivot pin was the only thing holding the wheel on at the time. I did the best I could to try to stop but I was unable to turn right, and the next corner coming up was a right-hander; the steering was locked and it wasn't possible to turn the wheel. I actually got the car to turn about 5 degrees towards going round the corner, and that was about all. When I reached the edge of the road I kept sliding, nudged the bank with the wheel that was about to drop off, and knocked it right off.

It was bad luck on the mechanics, because it meant a lot of work for them, not only sorting out the handling problem of both cars, but repairing Rolf's. Practice was simply a series of irritating and mysterious maladies in the handling department.

The Twenty-Third Year

I had to start the race from the back of the grid, which is not my favourite position, 4 seconds slower than Stewart, who was on pole, and nearly a second slower than Stommelen. In the race we were not in any way competitive and eventually I retired with a vibration on the car. I was convinced that the rear end was about to drop off, and I'd also just about worn out a front tyre. We changed all four wheels to a different compound tyre, but didn't get anywhere when I went out again, so we gave it up as a bad job. I think Ste Jovite was easily the roughest and worst circuit we raced on that year. I'd lost interest in the car and the reasons for its inefficiency by that time. This was another Ferrari victory — with Ickx at the wheel — and Regazzoni second. The promised Ferrari threat had definitely materialised in a very dominant way. Stewart, however, was showing us the potential of the new Tyrrell-Ford by being on pole position in Canada.

Watkins Glen was just as bad for us, unfortunately. The practice period was fairly uneventful if I remember rightly, but the Glen has never been a Goodyear circuit, perhaps because of the temperatures or something, and we were not competitive once again. We changed the gear ratios several times, and we had a couple of engine changes, but I was landed on the eighth row of the grid.

In the race Stewart shot off and built up a really fantastic lead over the Ferraris. I got completely demoralised because Stewart lapped me — he passed me on the straight going so quickly it was just a joke. He looked out of the car and gave me a little wave, as if to say: 'Come on, get out of fourth gear or whatever it is' — and just disappeared into the blue. He should have won that race easily but his engine started to smoke and finally ran out of oil, leaving the lead to Rodriguez, who had to come in for petrol seven laps from the end, allowing Emerson Fittipaldi to win his first Grand Prix. This ensured that Jochen would certainly be declared World Champion, the first to win the title posthumously in the history of the Championship.

When we reached home we decided it was time to find out exactly why our car was so slow. Even if we used our best

227

engine it didn't seem to make any difference. Eventually we found that after the Brands Hatch meeting, an oil line had been changed from the breathing system of the engine to the oil tank. This had created tremendous back pressure in the engine and it had been getting too much oil in the sump, and wasn't scavenging properly. That was why our car was so slow from the British Grand Prix onwards. It was just one of those stupid things that no one had thought of really checking out till it was all too late.

But at least we went to Mexico in a position to go as quickly as anyone else with a Ford-Cosworth engine, certainly down the straight, and generally more competitive than we'd been for a long, long time. I was fifth fastest on Friday, when I was so livid with everyone — I wasn't able to talk to anyone on that Friday, when my retirement announcement leaked out! On Saturday I was third fastest, and was behind only Regazzoni and Stewart on the grid. This was to be my last Grand Prix, but I felt we were at last competitive again and I began to cheer up.

I did not make the best of starts, dropped back with Rodriguez, Hulme and Beltoise, but managed to pull up to third behind the two Ferraris by lap fifteen. It felt good to be working my way up the field once again. Of course, I wasn't able to match the speed of the Ferraris and was resigned to the fact that third place was going to be the best I could expect. I was reasonably satisfied, because nobody was going to beat the Ferraris unless they broke down.

Then suddenly the engine expired in a matter of a few yards. Apparently a casting inside the engine had broken which had let all the oil pressure go, and the engine seized solid within a few seconds. Thirteen laps from the end — and that was the disappointing end to my career as a racing driver!

CHAPTER XVI

Back to My Grass Roots

We talked about going back to Australia for several years before we really made up our minds. After all, England had been our home for fifteen years, and although we still had plenty of friends and relatives in Australia, our closest associations were naturally with motor racing people in England. I myself had been back 'home' each winter and kept up contacts; but Betty wasn't at all keen on making it permanent until she went back with me for the winter of 68-69. She really enjoyed being out there, and decided that the sooner we made the break with motor racing the better.

So I began to make more permanent plans for retiring, as I have described; we bought a house in a suburb of Sydney, which was convenient for everything we needed. It was four or five years old when we bought it, it is of modern design and practically overhangs the water of Georges River. We have a swimming pool, and the house faces north—which in the southern hemisphere is the desirable direction! Our Ford dealership is in Bankstown, only a twenty-minute drive from home, and there is a six-lane highway which leads almost to it so that I have no great difficulty getting to and from the office. Austin Tauranac, Ron's brother, has been managing the dealership for some years, and does a very good job indeed, which has made my new start in life easy.

Both Gary and David go to a school which is not far from our house, and Geoffrey, who is nineteen, is attending a Technical College. He is doing a mechanical engineering course. He travelled with me quite a lot over the last year of my racing, and got very caught up with it all—he didn't really want me to give up driving, and he wasn't all that keen on going to Australia, but I think he's glad now.

In the few months I have been back in Australia I have had plenty to keep me busy. I had planned it that way for some two or three years, knowing that we would go back. I knew, too, that one day I would have to say goodbye to motor racing, and I got myself involved in other interests so that when motor racing came to an end I'd have something to do immediately. I think it was quite important to do that because, once I'd got over the really difficult weeks, I found it made things a lot easier. Now I can watch a motor race and not want to drive.

But I still have to find some sport or a challenge to get involved in. Once I have sorted out my business problems to the stage where I don't have to worry how I am going to earn a living, I shall look around.

For instance, I have always had a soft spot for gliding—I suppose that is because it is once again a challenge to me from the forces of nature. In motor racing the challenge is to win, and to keep the car on the track. Powerboat racing is something I might have a look at, too. I will investigate it and maybe compete in one or two events just to get the feeling for it and see if that is what I want to do. Austin has done a bit of powerboat racing and I understand it is hard work physically. You get a terribly rough ride, pounding from wave to wave, that takes even more out of you than a racing car—driving a racing car is more of a mental than a physical test. Powerboat racing might be fun—I'll have to look into it.

Of course, my other main interest is in flying. The Bankstown aerodrome is very close to my office at the Ford dealership, and quite a time ago I took a hangar at Bankstown and sent Roy Coburn out there to start up an aircraft maintenance business. He worked for me in England for eighteen months when I had the Queenair. He wanted to go and live in Australia, and he knew I'd be going back one day, so. . . . We have several planes out there now, and we are building up the sales and charter side of the business. The business isn't exactly making a fortune yet, but it is paying its way, and

Back to My Grass Roots

I always have a plane to fly when I want it. I have been flying a bit at weekends, going down to our farm and sometimes down to Melbourne.

This farm is somewhere to take the kids to ride horses and go shooting and fishing and so on. It is in Victoria, over 300 miles from Sydney, and about 350 acres. We raise some cattle on it but it is not big enough to make a serious attempt at farming. The place is called Willow Grove because a river runs through it and there are willows leaning over it. We can catch trout in the river, and we have a horse named Casey, which David and Gary both ride, so there is plenty for them to do when we go down there at weekends. My farm manager, Jim Herne, sees to all the work on the place for me. It is only one hour and fifty minutes by plane — we haven't a landing strip of our own but we can use one down the road, a crop spraying strip. I usually use a Cessna Centurion, because it is often the one left over after the paying customers have had their choice. I take whichever plane is not earning me any money that weekend!

I was busy back in February and March getting the farmhouse straight; it is a little bungalow, and we have gradually been painting it up and remodelling the kitchen, and starting to get all the ground round the house prepared for lawns and an orchard and so on. I can't rely on the place to earn me a living, and I'm thinking of finding something bigger a bit nearer home, but at the moment it is very pleasant to have somewhere like that to take the boys.

When I *am* at home in Sydney, which is not all that much, Gary and David never stop pestering me to go fishing. 'Dad, let's go fishing?' — every time I appear. So we have a pump-up dinghy and a pair of oars and we row out to our boat, which we can moor not far from the house, in the river. It is a glass fibre boat with two diesel motors. We go fishing out through the heads of Botany Bay, and up and down the coast on various reefs and places I am gradually learning about. Austin Tauranac has been showing me the spots. We've never really had anything to do with boats before, so it's all a new thing. We sometimes just go out on Georges River or around Botany Bay for the sheer pleasure of it.

231

When the Flag Drops

Another thing I'd like to have a go at is making a hover-craft. I want to design and build it all myself. If I had a little hobby workshop I could spend hours fiddling around with that idea, just for the challenge it presents, and it would give me satisfaction. When I went into motor racing it was something I desperately wanted to do. I am not sure yet what I desperately want to do in the future, but something will turn up out of all these interests.

I have been to a few race meetings since retiring, but I didn't enjoy them. I suppose I didn't really want to watch and I had no feeling for what was going on. The one notable exception was a USAC race I went to at Phoenix while I was over in the States for the Questor Grand Prix. For the first time since I gave up driving I had a real feeling for what was going on. It was really exciting, and I knew just how the two Unser brothers felt when they were lapping slower cars. I could see how difficult and dangerous it was for them. Bobby and Al were dicing for the lead and were lapping very fast, and there is nothing worse than having a dice with somebody when you are right on top of a slower car out on the circuit. There is no way that you can guarantee just where he is going to be on the circuit when you go by. He has only got to move one or two feet further out than you anticipated and you are in trouble.

That was a really good day. I didn't feel I wanted to get in a car and race; I just enjoyed, for the first time, watching a race. I had a very good spot to stand where I could see the whole of the Phoenix Raceway, and I knew quite a few of the drivers from my Indianapolis days. I had a good time in the pits too — they seemed genuinely glad to see me. I'll be going to a few Formula 1 races from time to time and look forward to that, but the time when I would have given anything to jump into a car again, as I would have at the first Grand Prix at Kyalami, has gone. Actually, the only time it really affected me was watching the start of the British Grand Prix at Silverstone this year. It wasn't a very good start, and I felt the tension of the drivers and was probably more churned up looking at it than if I had been actually in a driving seat; the only seat I had was in the stand. Now I can see what Betty was talking about when she said she used to get all upset watching the start, more than at any other time. I could never understand what it was all about, because where I was sitting it was never a problem.

Grand Prix racing throughout the rest of 1971 should be very interesting. The only Grand Prix I've seen so far is the British and the first thing I noticed when I arrived was that things have not changed very much in the way of engines blown-up, gearboxes broken and the mechanics working very hard throughout the practice periods. At the end of the last season I was pretty convinced in my own mind that Ferrari were going to win most of the races this year. But it looks as though Keith Duckworth has been doing his home-work on the Ford engine and it is pretty obvious now that they are still in front. The Tyrrell has done a terrific job with Jackie Stewart driving—the Tyrrell and the Cosworth engine and Stewart seem to be a pretty unbeatable combination. It looks as though that might continue for the rest of the season. Although the Ferraris go very quickly they just seem to have gone backwards since last year. Last year's car is probably better than this year's car.

The March has obviously been improved and is going very, very quickly and Peterson, their driver, looks like being the star of the new boys coming along. Fittipaldi went very quickly in practice but didn't show up quite so well in the race. I thought he might have done better but there may have been something wrong with the car.

As for the Brabham team. . . . I saw very little of Graham Hill actually—every time I saw him he was walking back to the pits with a blown-up engine—and in the race he never even made the starting line. He got a wheel knocked off before he had even gone a yard by somebody running into the back of him or rather running over the top of him. Tim Schenken, I thought, drove very well and has come on tremendously; I am sure he will keep the Australian flag flying for us. It is yet to be proved that the BT34 is any better than the 33. If I were still driving I would be driving the 34 as it has some good safety features and will be better than the 33 when sorted out. It has a far safer monocoque with the main tub made of heavier gauge aluminium. I would have liked to have driven the 34.

I think John Surtees has a good team but he has a long way to go yet. The car certainly isn't coming up to John's expectations; perhaps it might take a little longer but I am sure he will get there. As for Lotus, I wasn't very impressed with the turbine at all. In fact I don't quite understand why they persevere with it and run it in important events. I wouldn't say the 72 has had its day. It is probably still one of the best cars running, from a design point of view. If you put Jackie Stewart in it the 72 would be going as the Tyrrell is now.

The BRMs seem to be having their usual problems. They show flashes of speed and are nearly there but somehow or other they never quite make it, or if they do, they only do it once. At the moment I can't see anybody beating the Tyrrell combination, but there are drivers who probably need better equipment under them such as Ickx and Regazzoni.

The Matra organisation is good but they just haven't the years of experience behind them that teams like Ferrari have and it is going to take time to catch up. They have a very good car but the engine lacks power. Most of the Grand Prix cars are similar in the main, and it is only in the finer points that they differ. The thing that is going to win races is good preparation, reliability, and a top class driver. Ferrari have a pretty good record for these things, but Tyrrell is showing the way it should be done.

Unfortunately there are not enough people at BRM with the right sort of know-how in control. It needs someone like Colin Chapman to be completely in charge overall. This is the sort of person the sponsors like and the team admire and obey. Politics creep into BRM too much, and politics tend to put a damper on things that could be going forward.

While I'm on the subject of politics, England could do with a firm hand in this department and make unofficial strikes illegal. I thought Grand Prix racing was going to lose its most needed sponsor when that unbelievable strike took place at Ford. I am very disappointed that Ford had to give in to the strikers earlier this year after they had granted more increases than even the government thought reasonable. And then some of them walked straight out again, simply to disrupt the motor industry even further. Won't they ever see that they are destroying their own prosperity? When Sir Donald Stokes gets up at a public dinner, and says: 'Fine, if you want some more money just get some more cars produced and delivered and then we can *all* have some more money,' he's talking the best sense possible. But it just falls on deaf ears.

The point that never seems to get through to the public is the fact that Britain's survival in this world relies on being in a competitive position tradewise, because it can't be self-supporting. It has to rely on imports of food and the export of things like cars and ships and engineering equipment. If other countries are not getting their quota of goods on time they will go elsewhere and stop trading with Britain.

I am not suggesting for one minute that we don't have our problems in Australia. We have strikes as well. But I don't think that Australian people would allow their country to be virtually destroyed by strikes, but people in England don't seem to want to do anything about it.

It was a great pity when Menzies became too old to go on as Prime Minister; if he were still fifty years of age and still in power I am sure that Australia would be a lot better off. And I think that England needs another Churchill. These are the type of leaders we all need at the moment; someone with a strong hand, with confidence in their actions and their own convictions. To have a strong racing team, you need a strong man at the top.

I don't usually go on like this, after being known for so many years as the racing driver who had least to say on any subject. I haven't finished with England, not by any means. I have a small engine development business at Rugby and a motor business near London. I loved living here and enjoyed my fifteen years here; I have an enormous number of friends here. I am just sad to see all the initiative being drained from the country; I would like to see it go back to its old prosperity as soon as possible.

Naturally, I still have a personal interest in Motor Racing Developments and in what the Brabham racing cars are doing, but I have had no financial stake in them for some time. I have great faith in Ron Tauranac and I know he will always build a good, safe car, or what I like to call a 'sanitary' car. I would not like the car that still bears my name to have a reputation for fragility, because a driver needs to have confidence in his car.

People are always asking me what makes a top racing driver. There isn't a short answer to that. First of all, I don't think you can take anybody out of the street and make him a top driver. It is like any other sport really. A racing driver needs what it takes to be a good racing driver in the same way as a good tennis player needs what it takes to be a good tennis player. He has got to be cut out for it in some way. I think a racing driver needs a good sense of feel—a feeling for the car, a sense of balance; it is not just a matter of steering, you balance and guide the car on the road—it is a bit difficult to explain. I haven't tried to before—I just get in and drive. The whole thing revolves around judgement and confidence that you are in complete command of your car. You must have good reactions and you must have good anticipation; foreseeing what the other chap you are racing might do. You have to anticipate where he might make a mistake, and where you might be able to get by him. It doesn't always help to know all about the car either. Often it is a disadvantage to know too much. It has been to me on numerous occasions: I have felt that I should save the car when I shouldn't have worried. I am sure it has cost me races in the past. On the other hand I have often *felt* something going wrong and I have stopped sooner than somebody who didn't have any mechanical knowledge. Jochen, for instance, didn't really want to know. He often used to talk to me about suspension and sometimes he would lock on to something which he thought was going on and ask questions trying to confirm it.

Concentration is one of the important aspects of driving, it is really no different from driving down the street—the first thing that is going to cause an accident is you not concentrating on what you are doing. The whole time you are out there you have to concentrate. Lost concentration is the

Back to My Grass Roots

easiest way to slow down or have an accident. It is probably the most difficult thing we have to do, particularly in a long race. A dangerous thing in motor racing is lapping other people; you have to make a decision and it has to be the right one. You have to try and get some idea whether he knows you are there, and then try to anticipate what he is going to do. If you are just dicing closely with a driver, you are driving *with* him, and you get a feeling for the way his car handles and the way the driver is going about things. But when you suddenly arrive on somebody you are lapping, you are never quite sure if they know you are there, or whether they are going to assist you to get by, or whether they are going to shut the door on you.

You get to know your fellow drivers and this is the thing I like most about Grand Prix racing. There are some people with whom you don't mind driving closely, maybe wheel to wheel, and some for whom you leave more room. Some you could take advantage of, and some you couldn't. I think that when you are having a good ding-dong of a battle (which was the most enjoyable part of racing for me) it is fine if you are with somebody like Jackie Stewart, Graham Hill, Denny Hulme, or John Surtees for instance—there are probably seven or eight people whom you could be sure of, regardless of how desperate the situation became. Somehow or other it would always get sorted out. In other words, you have to have confidence in the chap you are dicing with. You very rarely see any of the top drivers getting into trouble with one another. It is surprising how serious it can all be and still be reasonably safe.

The Le Mans Twenty-Four-Hour race is one event which I feel perpetrates a ridiculous type of racing. I don't go along with it at all. In Europe there are only twenty or thirty really first class drivers who are *capable* of driving really big sports cars at high speeds round a circuit like Le Mans for twenty-four hours. They start about sixty, so at least thirty of those people shouldn't be on the track at all. Unfortunately, in sports car racing you do have quite a few inexperienced people driving with you whether you are at Le Mans or anywhere else. There is less of a problem on small circuits because the

237

speeds are not so high, and if the speed isn't so high you do have more time to judge what other drivers might do. The thing that worries me at Le Mans is the speed difference between cars, a car doing maybe fifty or sixty mph faster than the next one. It is very easy for one of them to do something unexpected and then the best anticipation in the world is not going to get you out of trouble.

I have been very lucky over the years to have got through with so few incidents. But I feel that the main reason for this is that I have stuck to Grand Prix racing or Formula 2 racing, where the major problems I have described are less likely to happen. I am sure, when you look over the records, that a lot more people were killed in sports car races than in Formula 1. So what is the reason for this? I am sure if they only had twenty cars start in all sports car races and you had the same twenty drivers that we have in the Grands Prix, sports car racing would be a lot safer than it is.

The most dodgy situation could be, for instance, at the Nurburgring, where you are racing on a circuit on which there are too many blind spots. You come over the brow of the hill knowing the road turns right and you want to be in a certain part of the road. This would not be the time to find somebody pushing a motor car at the side of the road, because you are committed to a line if you are going round as fast as you should be. When somebody suddenly appears on the road it can put you in serious trouble. I have had it happen at the 'Ring. In fact, the most dangerous thing that has happened to me there was to arrive on the scene of an accident when I hadn't been warned, and there was grass, gravel, bricks and oil, the whole lot spread across the road. You appear on the scene and this is all before you. Luckily I have managed to get out of all these situatins, but I am sure that this is the sort of thing that does catch people out.

There are a lot of things that happen suddenly in motor racing, such as a blown engine putting oil all over the circuit, which I have experienced on dozens of occasions. This is another point. When you get the top drivers, it is surprising how few times you see them go off the road because they suddenly come on some oil. The top drivers arrive on something dramatic and get through it, but somebody following with less experience goes straight off the road. You don't get time to think of anything much. You simply react. It is difficult to react correctly and this is the sort of thing which makes a top driver—anticipation of a situation and being able to sort it out on the spot. You have got to have confidence and, when the car is sliding, you must never give up on the steering wheel regardless of how difficult the situation looks. If you start getting into trouble it is surprising —if you stick with it and keep fighting with it—how it will often come right for you. I have been in dozens of situations where I would only have had to give up slightly and there would have been an accident. Some of the ability to do this comes from instinct, but more from experience. Nothing will teach you these things better than experience. There is just no way you can read it in a book or go to a driving school and be told about it and go out tomorrow and *do* these things —only one thing will teach you, and that is bitter experience. And the experience is often very bitter. I have seen many bad accidents with many drivers killed and wondered what it is all for, what it is all about, whether it is worth racing cars at all. The only answer is that we all race because we love to do so. Although we know it is a risky business, there are plenty of other sports in the world which are also risky. If you are worried about being killed you wouldn't drive an ordinary car around the streets, because 5,000 people a year get killed in England alone. It doesn't stop people driving their motor cars. They just think and hope it is not going to happen to them.

When the young ones start to drive racing cars they find it a very glamorous sport and they are all keen and enthusiastic; the accident part of it doesn't even come into their minds. If it ever begins to, then you should stop driving. I have never at any time felt that I didn't want to drive because I was frightened, because I always drove with the feeling that I had control of myself. I never let my emotions carry me away, and I have just been able to drive within my limits and to recognise how far I could go. I have *had* to be in control of the situation, regardless of how bad it might be.

I have never been afraid of backing off and running second or third, and I have always gone out and done the best I could. And if that wasn't good enough to win, then that was just too bad. I enjoyed the racing and I enjoyed the challenge of it, right up to my last Grand Prix in Mexico. I enjoyed winning — but that wasn't the thing I *had* to do.

I'm sure I'm not unique in this, it applies to a lot of drivers; and the less emotional they are the better they drive. I think this is why Continental people sometimes have a bit of trouble; their emotions tend to carry them away.

I have never thought of motor racing as futile. If I had ever thought of it as a silly way of spending my life I wouldn't have been doing it. This was a thing I enjoyed doing and kept on doing. If I had my time over again I would probably choose to follow the same route; I wouldn't want to change anything. I have been incredibly lucky.